P9-CSS-187

# POLITICS

POLITICS

# ARISTOTLE'S

# Politics

TRANSLATED BY
**BENJAMIN JOWETT**

WITH AN INTRODUCTION BY
**MAX LERNER**
PROFESSOR OF POLITICAL SCIENCE
WILLIAMS COLLEGE

THE
MODERN LIBRARY
NEW YORK

*Random House* IS THE PUBLISHER OF

# THE MODERN LIBRARY

BENNETT A. CERF · DONALD S. KLOPFER · ROBERT K. HAAS

Manufactured in the United States of America

By H. Wolff

# INTRODUCTION

## by Max Lerner

— 1 —

One of the great books embodying the Greek spirit was written by a man who was an outlander among the Greeks. Born in 384 B.C. in Stagira, Aristotle came from one of the frontier outposts of Greek settlement which faced the rising political sun of Macedon and its new "barbarian" energies. Stagira was a small city in a peninsula that had been settled by people from Chalcis. As a colony on the rim of Greek life it was for that reason all the more intensely Greek in feeling, on the same principle that makes the foreign-born in America more slavish in following the stereotypes of our culture than those whose sense of security makes them freer. Unlike Plato, who wore his aristocracy with a sure and quiet grace, Aristotle came of the upper middle class, which may serve partly to account—as it did in Machiavelli's case—for the dryness and realism of his intelligence and its lack of the more inflated and poetic values, but which sheds light also on his persistent emphasis upon the role of the middle class in a healthy equilibrium state. His father was a physician, and from him he may have derived a technical and scientific tradition which made it possible for Aristotle to deal with experience in a more matter-of-fact way than was habitual with the Greek ruling classes. We know very little of

5

his boyhood, except that for a few years before he had reached his teens he lived in Pella, the Macedonian capital, where his father had become court physician to the king. But his parents died while he was still a boy, and he grew up with a guardian—in easy circumstances, possessed of some property.

At eighteen he turned up in Athens, drawn there by the magnetic attraction which cultural capitals have always exerted for young men of talent, whether in the Greek, Roman or American worlds. Unfortunately no Walter Pater has sought to reconstruct imaginatively, after the model set for Rome in *Marius the Epicurean*, what a shining city Athens must have been as it lay before a provincial boy like Aristotle, bent on the conquest of the Greek intellectual world. Plato had built up a brilliant school of philosophy, but he was at the moment absent in Syracuse, where he had gone on one of those missions of turning a ruler into a philosopher, which showed that the Greek thinkers were perennial optimists. The young man must have made something of a sensation at the Academy. He was an unpleasantly sardonic fellow, something of a fop and a dandy, sartorially exquisite, and there are reports that he spoke with a lisp. In part his manner and meticulousness may have been due to the affectation of a provincial, in part to a sense of order which proved to be as much a part of Aristotle's thought as of his dress.

The next twenty years, which Aristotle spent at the Academy, must have been among his happiest. With his craggy mind and his dry, severe logic, he stood out above everyone in the school but its master. He was Plato's disciple, yet without anything slavish in his discipleship. At some point during these two decades of apprentice years he discovered that his intellectual system and his

philosophical salvation were his own to work out. Yet
to insist on re-thinking every article of the Platonic
creed was compatible with a genuine affection and regard for the master. In a very different modern context
one thinks of the parallel attitude of Nehru to Gandhi—
devoted and yet critically independent. During these
years of unflagging study he accumulated the intellectual capital whose rewards he was later to extract in
his writings. Only thus can we understand in secular
terms what would otherwise be the miracle of his im-
mense later productiveness.

When Plato died Aristotle was thirty-seven, better
equipped than anyone else to carry on the work of the
Academy. But that was not Plato's testament; nor could
Aristotle with dignity content himself with a minor role.
He therefore accepted, when it came, an invitation from
Hermias, who was a big landed proprietor in Asia Minor,
a political boss, and a princeling to boot, to visit with
him. Hermias was interested in philosophy, and had
already entertained several members of the Academy
and followed their precepts in establishing a constitutional regime. He liked Aristotle and welcomed the prestige of associating with him. Aristotle lived with Hermias for three or four years, and married his niece. He
had money with which to organize and carry on extensive research, and he built up a school around himself.
But this too came to a close. Hermias seems to have
been playing power politics on a small scale and to have
had an agreement with Philip of Macedon involving
the use of his cities as bridgeheads for an invasion of
the Persian empire. At any rate, the Persian king
thought so, destroyed Hermias's cities, captured him
and—when he refused to reveal the plot of which he
was accused—crucified him. Whether Aristotle was in

any way caught in the tangles of conspiratorial diplomacy is not wholly clear. But here the third stage of his life ended—brief and turbulent, yet not unhappy. At forty-two Aristotle found himself again without home or occupation, a political refugee.

But now an opportunity offered whereby Aristotle could carry on his research and even play a role on the stage of world history. Philip of Macedon invited him to become tutor to his son, Alexander, already at thirteen precocious in ability and ambition. For Philip it meant having the great philosopher of the Greek world to supervise his son's training, and thus associating himself with Greek culture. For Aristotle it meant a chance to influence the most vigorous state of the time, the one that was most creative in the arts of military and political organization. Much might be done to impart a Greek quality to the Macedonian energies, and make certain that if this was to be a conquering state it would conquer with Greek ideas rather than against them. And so he went back to the Macedonian court, where he had spent several years as a boy. He is believed to have remained with Alexander until Philip's death. We know almost nothing of the relations between teacher and pupil, except from what we may infer from the disappointment which Aristotle later betrayed at the course that Alexander's ideas and personality took. It must have been a strange relationship. Everything about Alexander was exuberant and excessive, while the core of Aristotle's thinking was restraint and the mean. Here was Aristotle trying to teach the acceptance of limits to a youth who was drunk on the exploits of the Age of Heroes and who dared aspire to godhead. We must, however, avoid underestimating Aristotle's influence upon Alexander. As General de Gaulle has put it, in his *Army of the Future* (1934), "There has been no illustrious captain who did not possess taste and a feeling for the heritage of the human mind. At the root of Alexander's victories one will always find Aristotle."

When his pupil was ready to assume the duties of kingship and command in the field, Aristotle went back to Athens and to the culminating period of his life work. He was just turning fifty, and was ready to communicate to others the results of his study and reflection. He came back to set up a school of his own, in the Lyceum. The young men clustered about him as he and others had once clustered about Plato; and since he walked about on the school grounds explaining and disputing, the young men asking questions and taking notes, he became known as the "peripatetic" philosopher. There was a vigor in his school which the Academy had lost with Plato's death. For twelve years he lectured and wrote. There was nothing alien to his consuming curiosity, and no items of experience which he did not seek to digest and relate in the form of general propositions. He developed a physics, a metaphysics, a biology, an astronomy, a logic, an analysis of language, an ethics, an economics and politics, an esthetics. For comprehensiveness, order and consistency as a system of thought, the world has not known the like of his system before and since.

Meanwhile, Aristotle's pupil, Alexander, had been driving deeper the rivets of empire over the Greek city-states which his father, Philip, had first established, and he had been expanding that empire over Asia and the whole known world. The reports that came back of his Asiatic exploits were glamorous enough, yet they were also puzzling and vaguely sinister to the Greeks, who felt that, in spreading his empire over Asia, Alexander was not spreading Greek culture but succumbing to the

Asiatic. Their fears were reinforced by the reports of Alexander's drunken excesses, his plurality of concubines, his closeness to Asiatic advisers, and especially by a delusion he seemed to have that he was not only descended of great heroes but was himself one of the gods. Aristotle was as troubled by Alexander's behavior as were the other Greeks. Nevertheless, one of the indirect results of Alexander's conquest was that it endangered Aristotle's position in Athens. For had he not been Alexander's tutor; was not the strange young man's development attributable to him; was he not himself tied in a relationship of too close friendship with Antipater, Alexander's viceroy for Macedonia and the Greek cities?

The political climate of Athens grew unhealthy for Aristotle. His life was dragging to a melancholy close. He had few personal roots left in Greece. He was a sick, bald, thin-legged little man, suffering from acute digestive ailments. He still had his school and his lectures and his writings, but he felt it necessary to abandon them. He could not even go back to his native Stagira, since it had been burned and leveled in the troubled years of Macedonian and Greek war. Remembering what the Athenians had once done to Socrates, and fearing "lest they sin twice against philosophy," he went off into exile in Euboea, and there a year later died at the age of sixty-three.

— 2 —

The *Politics* is a treatise on the science and art of government which, although part of the whole body of Aristotle's work, stands on its own feet. Werner Jaeger, a great German scholar in the Aristotelian field, guesses that the book was written in two stretches: the first (including Books 2, 3, 7, and 8) dealing with the ideal state, using Plato's thought as a jumping-off point, and probably written soon after Plato's death and Aristotle's departure from Athens; the second (including Books 4, 5, and 6) being a comparative analysis of actually existing state forms, their stability, decay and overthrow, and written some time after Aristotle's students in the Lyceum had had a chance to do their research project on the contemporary constitutions. Jaeger's supposition is that these latter books were inserted by Aristotle into the middle of the original draft, and that Book I was written last, as a sort of introduction to the whole political treatise.

At any rate it is clear that Aristotle, no longer content to write on political ideals, meant to focus on political actualities. The Greek world in which he wrote was turbulent enough to throw a political thinker in either direction, depending upon his temperament. Some sought escape from this turbulence in the construction of ideal commonwealths, others were drawn to inquire into the character of shifting state forms and into the conditions of revolution and stability. Aristotle belonged with the latter.

Yet he was not unaffected by the political pessimism which his times bred. The Greeks had never discovered the principle of unification, and the price they were to pay for this failure was political suicide. Their sense of the city-state or *polis*—what would correspond to our sense of nationalism today—was so tenacious that it made them incapable of thinking in terms of a Greek order—what would correspond to a world order today. Because their economic systems were twisted at the very start by their institution of slavery, their contempt for labor and their exclusion of the economic virtues from the pantheon of civic virtues, they did not undergo the industrial expansion which might have compelled them, as it seems to be compelling us, to fashion the image of a world order. Nor was any of them sufficiently strong in itself to establish an imperium. Sparta, with its pride of arms, seemed the logical city for the role. Yet Athens, whose position made it the center of a commercial empire and whose cultural prestige dominated the peak centuries of Greek life, would not accept Spartan hegemony. The result was a mortal clash which left both sides too exhausted and bitter to organize the Greek world, and left that world a ready victim to an external imperium.

It was in this political context that Aristotle wrote his treatise—a context in many respects parallel to that in which Machiavelli wrote the *Prince*. Yet, unlike Machiavelli, there is little nationalistic feeling in Aristotle, little of the realistic exploration of power, little receptivity to the larger political constructions that were emerging. He clung, as a Greek, to the exclusive sense that the Greeks had a monopoly on culture. Not that he was attached to any particular city-state; his links with Athens were cultural rather than political. Yet he never got far enough to see the possibility of a Greek political order. While not hostile to the Macedonian attempts to forge it, he could never wholly champion them. His intellectual break with his pupil, Alexander, was probably due to this difference between them. He had instilled into Alexander a pride in the Greek tradition, but the Greek era Alexander cared about was that of the early heroes; there was in him a daemonic urge to excel them by using Macedonian power to spread Greek culture throughout the world. But Alexander was far more of a political realist than Aristotle. He may have understood—although Wilcken disputes this in his biography of Alexander—the value of the divinity-myth in holding an empire together. Even more important, he broke with Aristotle on the question of the treatment of the conquered Asiatic provinces. Aristotle, with his sense of Greek superiority, felt that there could be no political health in Asiatics; they were the lowest of the barbarians. Like those who cling to the Vansittart thesis about the post-war treatment of Germany, he wished to crush the conquered enemy. Alexander was convinced that the best way to keep the Asiatics as part of his new empire was to give them a stake in it. Nothing could show more clearly that, as objective an observer as he was in the world of science, Aristotle was still caught in the taboos of the Greek political mind.

This is evident in his attitude toward slavery, which he discusses in Book I. He sees slavery as rooted in biology and psychology as well as in economics: "that some should rule and others be ruled is a thing, not only necessary, but expedient; from the hour of their birth, some are marked out for subjection, others for rule." But having made this sweeping statement, he proceeds to hedge it. "The words slavery and slave are used in two senses. There is a slave or slavery by law as well as by nature." In short, there is a natural basis to the institution, although the institution itself may be in practice unjust. What is vulnerable in this analysis is that there may actually have been no relation in Greek life between the two. Even if one grants Aristotle's *élite* theory—of the right of some men to rule others—it remains true that Greek slavery was a historical institution, growing from the helotage of conquest or the need for artisans in the urban handicraft industries. The theory of a natural aristocracy is thus stretched by Aristotle into an

*apologia* for brutal subjection and coercion. What is
striking is that Aristotle, who as a liberal conservative
was ahead of his age in many respects, was here caught
in it. His treatment of his own slaves was humane and
by his will he manumitted several of them. But, like
Plato and Xenophon and the other intellectuals of the
fourth century B.C., his contempt for the manual occupations which the slaves plied, his pride in Greek culture and his sense of the pettiness of spirit which labor
was thought to induce, all fused into an "imperfect preju-
dice" about slavery.

There is another sense in which Aristotle was Greek.
He had the characteristic Greek sense of limits and worship of form. He broke with Plato on metaphysical
grounds because the Platonic "ideas" seemed to him
too misty. He developed instead a metaphysic of "forms"
which was concerned with matter as the stuff on which
the life processes work, and with the life process itself
as the "actualization of the potential." He saw nature,
essentially, as development. Yet there is still a curiously
static residue in his thinking—an insistence in it upon
restriction, an aversion to formlessness, a fear of what
might happen once the boundaries were broken, a dread
almost of anything vital or passionate. In fact, one may
guess that Aristotle's encyclopedic activity was in itself
something that sprung from the Greek aversion to formlessness. He had to organize the material of the natural, individual and social worlds if he was to achieve any
inner peace of mind. Just as his basic ethical concept
was that of virtue achieved through the mean, so his
basic political concept was that of health achieved
through equilibrium. In comparison with Aristotle,
Plato was unstable—a brooding poetic mystic who, for
all the fact that his *Republic* was meant to rationalize

political reaction, burst the bounds of his own intentions and went beyond the flaming ramparts of the Greek world into untraveled areas where men have sought to follow him ever since. Plato was as much a Dionysian as an Athenian aristocrat could be. Aristotle, despite the fact that he lacked the graces of poetry and myth, was an Apollonian.

But it would be unjust to end here the analysis of Aristotle's relation to the Greek tradition. While Spengler had a truth by the tail in saying that the deep cultural pattern of the Greeks was a sense of form, it is a half-truth that misses much of the meaning of the Greek era. One may trace in world history a rough sequence: from the age of fear to the age of knowledge to the age of conquest to the age of organization. If that is true, it becomes apparent that Aristotle as a quite characteristic Greek, although of transcending intellectual ability, stood as the inheritor of the age of fear and the archetype of the age of knowledge. His function was to explain and rationalize the whole known world and man's relation to it. This he did. His achievement was to sum up the ethos of a whole civilization more completely than anyone since him has been able to do. His achievement was an architectural one.

Yet its architecture was not of the sort that went vaulting into the unknown. God was for Aristotle not the supreme mystery, but the "Unmoved Mover," the center of an orderly universe rotating about him—as Whitehead has said, so orderly as to be dramatic. He was thus, like the other Greeks, still operating in the shadow of fear, for only a people fearful of the irrational in them would thus make a fetish of order. That may have been one reason why the Greeks were so concerned to separate themselves from the "barbarians."

Yet Aristotle was moving away from fear toward knowledge, which is a way of conquering fear. His knowledge was chiefly of the external world, the beginnings of science without which the human being is fear-dominated. It was also knowledge of society and of the process of thought. But while he ransacked all the storehouses of knowledge open to him at the time, the Faustian impulse was not yet in him. That was to come with the age of conquest. Knowledge was for him a way of accommodating oneself to the world rather than a way of conquering it, as it was with the scientists of the seventeenth century. It was a form of adjustment, not a form of action.

— 3 —

No single thinker, not even Plato, has had as much impact as Aristotle on the intellectual and institutional history of later centuries. It is true that Aristotle's doctrine lacks the winged fire which has made men Platonists or Marxians, for that there is a need of a single-minded frenzy which can only be described as possession. Yet, there were whole centuries when the civilized world lived in Aristotle's shadow—and not only the European world, but the Ottoman and African; not only the Christian world but the Jewish and Islamic—centuries when all knowledge was held to be contained in the writings of one man. Sandys, whose *History of Classical Scholarship* contains valuable although scattered material on Aristotle's influence, tells us that in the mid-fourteenth century the instructors at the University of Paris had to swear that they would not be inconsistent with the truth as revealed in Aristotle and his commentator Averroës. Unfortunately, the connected and detailed history of Aristotle's influence still remains to be written; there is nothing comparable to Paul Elmer More's book on Platonism or Lord Acton's chapter on Machiavellianism.

During the dark centuries between the Hellenistic period and the Middle Ages, the flame of Aristotle's teaching was kept alive in Constantinople, then in Arabia, North Africa, Spain, and finally to the European world. There is, in Santayana's *Dialogues in Limbo,* a delightful recapturing of the combination of reverence and sharp critical analysis which the Islamic scholars accorded Aristotle. Nor were the analytical subtleties of Jewish theology wholly unrelated to Aristotle's influence in this period.

In the eleventh and twelfth centuries the Latin translation of Aristotle was made available to European thought, and a school of commentators and glossators attached itself to him. What has been written about the aridity of this school is in the main true: there is in all commentaries an inherent tendency toward the drying up of the original creative impulse. Yet even in the Greek world, as Jaeger has pointed out, the creative possibilities in Aristotle's thought were not explored. The scientific and philosophical elements were mixed together in his work. But the further expansion of his scientific insights was incompatible with the climate of opinion in the Hellenistic world. Farrington has suggested that the Greek ruling *élite* feared science because it might undermine the foundations of their own rule, which were supported by popular superstitions and the "noble lie." For its further expansion science also required a society which gave more dignity to labor and the industrial arts than did the Greek. At any rate, Aristotle became, both for the Hellenistic world and that of the Middle Ages, a formula for elaboration rather than an avenue to wisdom.

The theologians of the Middle Ages, even including so creative a thinker as Thomas Aquinas and so creative a poet as Dante, welcomed the logical articulate structure of Aristotle's thought because it enabled them to pour into it in an orderly fashion the body of their beliefs. It was not so much his science and certainly not his politics and social science which were taken over. It was rather his logic and his metaphysics, particularly the latter. And it was in the *Metaphysics* that Aristotle sought to use the critical instrument of reason to establish and explore the realm that transcended human experience. Although the medieval Church for a time frowned upon Aristotle, his metaphysics offered a common ground to the religious philosophy of Christianity, Judaism and Islamism.

For these religious systems were philosophically uncreative, although morally creative; what they needed was a logical and critical framework, and these Aristotle made available. The thralldom of the Middle Ages to Aristotle can thus best be explained in the search of the Christian world for a logical and metaphysical structure not incompatible with its theology. The medieval world, creative in its institutional practices, had to fall back on antiquity for its intellectual universe.

So completely did the Middle Ages adopt Aristotle that when the modern centuries sought release from the bondage to the medieval tradition, they had to seek release from the symbol of Aristotle. With the rise of science in the sixteenth and seventeenth centuries, there came a sharp reaction against the scholasticism of the medieval world and against the name which stood in men's minds for that scholasticism. Actually, Aristotle as a scientist might have helped the seventeenth century to find itself; yet so intensely was he rejected that what might have been releasing in him was thrown out along with what had proved to be fettering. In one sense, the instinct of the modern man may have been right. Aristotle the scientist was not mathematician but biologist; hence his characteristic method was classification rather than measurement. The seventeenth century moved toward the method of measurement and therefore toward its own characteristic form. The eighteenth century, the rationalism of whose outlook was as complete and as dramatic as Aristotle's own, nevertheless continued to reject him, largely because it mistook his meaning and ignored the parallelisms to its own spirit which were to be found in him. This rejection of Aristotle has continued until our own time. As late as 1848 Sir William Hamilton noted that in discarding Aristotle the English universities had neglected wholly the study and teaching of logic.

Our own times are witnessing a renaissance of Aristotelian studies and interest. There is a social logic worth mentioning here. In the turbulent times in which Aristotle wrote, the Greeks were caught between the assertion of will and the submission to law—or, as Aristotle expresses it in his *Metaphysics,* between matter and form. Hence Aristotle's method is wholly dialectical— the method that is characteristic of any age, like our own, which finds itself caught in so basic a dilemma. Aristotle's rigorous analysis by the method of division and differentiation is increasingly suited to the temper of such an age, which seeks to find amidst the welter of change some firm ground on which it can stand.

There are also universals in Aristotle's thought—in his metaphysics, his ethics, his politics—which make him attractive to any period which seeks to make itself an organic whole. That is to say, a world in danger of fragmentation, and deeply desirous of welding itself into a unity, must somehow find a philosophy which runs in universals. The nineteenth-century systems, such as those of Darwin, Marx, Nietzsche, Dostoyevsky, Mill, have been found inadequate in our own time. Such twentieth-century systems as those of Spengler and Pareto are too polemical and erratic to get common acceptance in a world which rejects their values while it cherishes some of their insights. The thinkers who may some day create a universal system of thought which will sum up the twentieth-century aspirations toward organic unity have not yet arisen. In the interval, the study of a writer who summed up the spirit of a past age is a good preparation for the coming of writers who may in their own terms sum up the inner strivings of our own age.

— 4 —

What are the relevant master ideas that emerge from a reading of the *Politics* in the context of today? My own inclination is to put the answer in the form of a series of propositions.

*First*, that the state has a natural history, and that part of its meaning must be sought in its development. I have said that Aristotle, as a scientist who is mainly absorbed with biology, saw nature as development. He was thus in a sense a forerunner of those who have seen politics as history, and especially those who have seen it as the unfolding of inner impulses within human society. If there is a trace of the doctrine of inevitability in this, it is not so much as to make the whole system rigidly deterministic. The truth that Aristotle saw was that political forms have an inner history of their own— the history of a growth toward maturity and an impulse toward decay. Thus his analysis of the basic forms of monarchy, aristocracy, polity, shows his understanding that they are not simplistic forms, but go through a series of phases. The implication is clear that at each stage there is room for human action and will. The political material contains within itself from the start the potentials to be made into actuality, but that material must none the less be acted on. If maturity can be hastened and helped, then decay can be foreseen and prevented.

*Secondly,* that the state has a natural basis in economics and family structure, and a natural purpose in ethics. I do not think that modern social thought has improved much upon Aristotle in this respect. While he gives us a naturalistic social theory of the organization of the state and its successive transformations, he does not fall into the trap of seeing human society in terms of biological and economic mechanism, for his conception of nature includes the ethical. It is in the nature of human beings living in society that they must work toward goals which have value. There is a far-reaching implication in this for our own age as well as for Aristotle's: that the study of politics, as well as the art, must effect a synthesis between mechanism and ethos, between survival and meaning.

*Third,* that there are basic state forms into which political activity falls, and that the art of politics lies in the choice among these forms and their combinations. Aristotle's itch for classification has often been noted. His most famous classification in this book is that which divides states into monarchy, aristocracy and polity, and which gives the parallel corruptions of each—tyranny, oligarchy and democracy. We need not today accept Aristotle's valuations literally, and we must see that his base of classification is wholly political and excludes the economic. Nevertheless, there is a truth here not to be ignored. Let us say that there are broad forms within which the state may be organized: one-man rule, the rule of an *élite,* the rule of the mass of people within the framework of law. What is more important is that each state form has characteristic methods and each can get out of hand. The state as a going concern must represent the best working synthesis possible. One-man rule allows for unity and decisiveness, and Aristotle's remarks are still applicable to military operations and other administrative situations. The rule of an *élite* allows for the selection of the best abilities in the state —and in this sense even a democracy must embody the *élite* principle. The rule of a polity—that is, of a constitutional democracy—allows for freedom and economic equality, and even dictatorships will not find stability until they have embodied a measure of these values. Here again what Aristotle tries to tell us is that we cannot have a simple choice. His own theory was that mixed government is the best in practice—a theory which may either be interpreted mechanically as a mixture of the basic state mechanisms, or may mean that the aim of politics is to develop a state form and state ethos which, by whatever mechanism, synthesizes the values which the basic forms embody.

*Fourth,* that the art of government is the art of finding a proper equilibrium for the forces in the state. In individual ethics Aristotle saw the good life in the mean; in the ethics of the state, he saw it in an equilibrium between power and liberty, between authority and its checks. In his equilibrium thinking Aristotle was a characteristic Greek—far more so than Plato, whose thinking cheerfully vaulted beyond the equilibrium toward the totalitarian. There are those who project Aristotle's theory of mixed government into the seventeenth and eighteenth centuries, and who attribute the equilibrium politics of Locke, Montesquieu, the social contract theorists and the American founders to Aristotle. There is a measure of truth in this. Despite the seventeenth-century rejection of Aristotle's logic and metaphysics, the political forms that grew out of the eighteenth-century revolutions were not very different from Aristotle's: the idea of government by poise and counter-poise, the idea of limited powers, the fear of governmental encroachment, the use of constitutional limits to set boundaries to the operation of governmental power. Yet it is probably true that the history of equilibrium political thinking in our own world owes more to seventeenth- and eighteenth-century science, and particularly to the concepts of Newtonian physics, than to Aristotle.

Equilibrium thinking is today once more beginning to assert itself. The separation of the various branches of the government, as Locke and Montesquieu and the *Federalist Papers* had it, is being replaced by a new type of "separation-of-powers" thinking. In this new thinking there is an insistence on the separation of social and economic power from political power—the idea being that a people can risk a social and economic tyranny, or can risk a political tyranny, but it cannot risk the joining of the two. Hence the Aristotelian theory of mixed government has been replaced by a theory of the separation of political control from economic functions, and by the exploration of mixed economies. Thus we are wit·

nessing a return to Aristotle on a plane that has more meaning for our own age.

But what Aristotle did not see—nor perhaps his modern followers—is that in history political equilibrium has been achieved only by the ebb and flow of revolutionary movements. This does not, however, prevent Aristotle from being one of the best analysts of revolution in the political tradition. Which brings us to his *fifth* master idea. Aristotle was interested in the rise and fall of political systems, but he did not make the mistake of tracing that rise and fall to autonomous factors within politics. His views on the economic basis of revolutions had to be rediscovered, as Charles Beard has pointed out, by later thinkers—by Harrington, Sir Thomas More, James Madison, Karl Marx.

Yet while Aristotle saw revolutions as arising from the injustices and the blindnesses of ruling classes, he regarded revolutions themselves with distaste. Here again he speaks for the Greek mind. From this fear of revolution one can derive much of his characteristic political theory. That is to say one can approach his political theory logically, from his metaphysics, science and ethics, or one can approach it psychologically, from the Greek mind. In psychological terms Aristotle's distaste for the confusion caused by revolutions leads directly to much of the rest of his political thinking: its fear of democratic rule, its stress upon constitutional polity, upon the limits to be set to the operation of power, upon the distrust of government, upon the rule of law. In this context it is not surprising that sections of his treatise become a guide book for dealing with revolution. They contain many shrewd insights as to how revolution can be prevented, not the least shrewd of which is the insistence that since it follows from economic injustices and from the blindness of ruling classes, it can be prevented only by the removal of their causes.

The *sixth* of Aristotle's master ideas relates to political psychology. Like Plato, Aristotle believed that much in politics depended on the image which was stamped on the young by birth and education—by nature and habit. To this theme he devotes his concluding pages. Yet the modern educator will miss the sense of concern with the individuality of the child. We must remember that personality and individuality, as we understand them, were not Greek concepts. Neither was freedom, which—like equality—did not reach its modern meaning until the Judaeo-Christian tradition, with its ideas of the sanctity of man. Since man (the Christians reasoned) is created in the image of God, it follows that he must not be subjected to indignity or curbing. And since all men are thus created, it follows that they must be equal before the law. We must be careful, despite the fact that Aristotle uses the concepts of both freedom and equality, that we do not read a content into them which is post-Greek, although Christianity itself owed much to Greek individualism and Greek ethics. Neither should we read into Aristotle's term "democracy" the egalitarian implications it has now, or the sense of the dignity of the individual.

It has been customary to think of Aristotle as the philosopher of political rationalism, in contrast with Plato's exploration of the irrational in the political myth. It is true that Aristotle used the method of reason in the analysis of politics, but that is different from saying that he saw in reason a mirror of political behavior. His analysis of revolutions shows that he understood the role of grievance and *ressentiment* in politics, just as his analysis of economic forces showed that he understood the role of class interest. His account of how political forms become corrupted shows that he understood the inner impulses in any state toward the expansion of power.

Above all, Aristotle was interested in what constituted the strength and weakness of the political community. For all his discussion of political forms, he saw that the strength of the state depends not so much upon the machinery of government as upon the moral sense of the community. And in analyzing this moral sense he saw more deeply than did the later individualistic theorists. In his famous statement that "man is by nature a political animal" and that "he who by nature and not by mere accident is without a state, is either above humanity or below it," Aristotle gave the clue to his political psychology. He meant that in their origin and in their impulses, in terms of the end toward which their development tends, men must be part of a whole that is greater than the sum of its parts. Except as he is a member of a collectivity, a man ceases to be a man and becomes either something greater or something less. We who have watched in our time the spectacle of the rise and fall of nations, and who have seen the Americans, the Russians, the Chinese, the British, perform feats of moral strength as nations which they could not have performed outside of the context of their collectivity, have come to glimpse a fresh meaning in the words of Aristotle which have been almost eroded by commentary. We have come to see that the most important element of strength in a community is the sense of greatness that it can generate, and that the most important political emotion in man is the thirst for greatness which, under pressure, stretches him beyond his everyday self so that he reaches the full outlines of his human personality.

It is here that we can best evaluate Aristotle's thought against the imagism of Plato and his stress on the irrational myth. By excusing or glorifying the Noble Lie, Plato became the forerunner of a succession of glorifiers of the irrational and the manipulative who have colored the thinking of our time. As against this tradition, Aristotle stands for the life of reason. But not in a mechanical sense, squeezed dry of intangible values; rather as a framework within which the natural irrational impulses of men—of fear and sadism and lust for power, and above all of a sense of collective greatness—can find expression without bursting the fabric of civilization.

In the light of recent history, who shall say that Aristotle was less profound in his perception than Plato? We have seen the Noble Lie end up in the desperate and cynical manipulations of the Yahoos who call themselves the master race. I, for one, prefer a theorist who taught that, because men are members of a whole, their fullest political meaning lies in helping build a working practicable state which, while it recognizes the naturalistic basis of all living, does not thereby betray the life of reason.

# FOR FURTHER READING

The basic texts of Aristotle are now easily available in English translation in the one-volume edition edited by Richard McKeon (Random House, 1941). For readers of the *Politics* the most relevant other works of Aristotle, which will be found in this volume, are the *Nichomachean Ethics,* the *Rhetoric,* the *Logic,* and the *Metaphysics.* Werner Jaeger, *Aristotle: Fundamentals of the History of his Development* (Eng. trans., 1934) will reward study even by the general reader, despite its difficulty. The third volume of R. A. G. Fuller's *History of Greek Philosophy* is on Aristotle (1931) and contains a good, although at times unduly jazzed-up, exposition of the body of his thought. On the Greek mind I have found Benjamin Farrington, *Science and Politics in the Ancient World* (1940) full of suggestions; and on Greek political institutions Henry Sidgwick's *Development of European Polity* (1903), chs. v-ix, has not to my mind been supplanted by later books. Alfred Zimmern's classic *Greek Commonwealth* (1911; 5th ed. rev., 1931) is however still richly worth reading. The epilogue chapter in J. L. Stocks' *Aristotelianism* (1925) is the best available discussion of the influence of Aristotle's thought. I owe my basic conceptions of seventeenth and eighteenth century science to A. N. Whitehead, *Science and the Modern World* (1925). For my discussion of the master political ideas in Aristotle, I have gone to the *Politics* rather than to the commentators, and the reader of the latter will note that I am often at variance with them. The following are, however, well worth reading: E. Barker, *The Political Theory of Plato and Aristotle* (1906); A. C. Bradley, "Aristotle's Conception of the State," in *Hellenica,* ed. by E. Abbott (1898); G. H. Sabine, *A History of Political Theory* (1937), ch. v-vi.

# CONTENTS

## BOOK I

**CHAPTER**

*Chapters 1, 2. Definition and structure of the State.*

1. The state is the highest form of community and aims at the highest good. How it differs from other communities will appear if we examine the parts of which it is composed.

2. It consists of villages which consist of households. The household is founded upon the two relations of male and female, of master and slave; it exists to satisfy man's daily needs. The village, a wider community, satisfies a wider range of needs. The state aims at satisfying all the needs of men. Men form states to secure a bare subsistence; but the ultimate object of the state is the good life. The naturalness of the state is proved by the faculty of speech in man. In the order of Nature the state precedes the household and the individual. It is founded on a natural impulse, that towards political association.

*Chapters 3-13. Household economy. The Slave. Property. Children and Wives.*

3. Let us discuss the household, since the state is composed of households.

## BOOK V (VIII)

*Cetera desunt.*

# Politics

Translated by Benjamin Jowett

# POLITICS

## BOOK I

**1**  Every state is a community of some kind, and every 1252ᵃ community is established with a view to some good; for mankind always act in order to obtain that which they think good. But, if all communities aim at some good, the state or political community, which is the highest of all, and which embraces all the rest, aims at good in a 5 greater degree than any other, and at the highest good.

Some people think [1] that the qualifications of a statesman, king, householder, and master are the same, and that they differ, not in kind, but only in the number of their subjects. For example, the ruler over a few is called 10 a master; over more, the manager of a household; over a still larger number, a statesman or king, as if there were no difference between a great household and a small state. The distinction which is made between the king and the statesman is as follows: When the government is personal, the ruler is a king; when, according to the 15 rules of the political science, the citizens rule and are ruled in turn, then he is called a statesman.

But all this is a mistake; for governments differ in kind, as will be evident to any one who considers the matter according to the method [2] which has hitherto guided us. As in other departments of science, so in politics, the 20

[1] Cp. Plato, *Politicus*, 258 E–259 D.    [2] Cp. 1256ᵃ2.

compound should always be resolved into the simple elements or least parts of the whole. We must therefore look at the elements of which the state is composed, in order that we may see in what the different kinds of rule differ from one another, and whether any scientific result can be attained about each one of them.

**2** He who thus considers things in their first growth
25 and origin, whether a state or anything else, will obtain the clearest view of them. In the first place there must be a union of those who cannot exist without each other; namely, of male and female, that the race may continue (and this is a union which is formed, not of deliberate purpose, but because, in common with other animals and
30 with plants, mankind have a natural desire to leave behind them an image of themselves), and of natural ruler and subject, that both may be preserved. For that which can foresee by the exercise of mind is by nature intended to be lord and master, and that which can with its body give effect to such foresight is a subject, and by nature a
1252ᵇ slave; hence master and slave have the same interest. Now nature has distinguished between the female and the slave. For she is not niggardly, like the smith who fashions the Delphian knife for many uses; she makes each thing for a single use, and every instrument is best made when intended for one and not for many uses. But
5 among barbarians no distinction is made between women and slaves, because there is no natural ruler among them: they are a community of slaves, male and female. Wherefore the poets say—

'It is meet that Hellenes should rule over barbarians';

as if they thought that the barbarian and the slave were by nature one.

Out of these two relationships between man and woman, master and slave, the first thing to arise is the family, and Hesiod is right when he says— 10

'First house and wife and an ox for the plough',

for the ox is the poor man's slave. The family is the association established by nature for the supply of men's everyday wants, and the members of it are called by Charondas 'companions of the cupboard', and by Epimenides the Cretan, 'companions of the manger.' But when several families are united, and the association 15 aims at something more than the supply of daily needs, the first society to be formed is the village. And the most natural form of the village appears to be that of a colony from the family, composed of the children and grandchildren, who are said to be suckled 'with the same milk'. And this is the reason why Hellenic states were originally 20 governed by kings; because the Hellenes were under royal rule before they came together, as the barbarians still are. Every family is ruled by the eldest, and therefore in the colonies of the family the kingly form of government prevailed because they were of the same blood. As Homer says: [3]

'Each one gives law to his children and to his wives.'

For they lived dispersedly, as was the manner in ancient times. Wherefore men say that the Gods have a king, because they themselves either are or were in ancient 25 times under the rule of a king. For they imagine, not only the forms of the Gods, but their ways of life to be like their own.

When several villages are united in a single complete

[3] *Od.* ix. 114, quoted by Plato, *Laws*, iii. 680 ʙ, and in *N. Eth.* x. 1180ᵃ 28.

community, large enough to be nearly or quite self-sufficing, the state comes into existence, originating in the
bare needs of life, and continuing in existence for the
30 sake of a good life. And therefore, if the earlier forms of
society are natural, so is the state, for it is the end of
them, and the nature of a thing is its end. For what each
thing is when fully developed, we call its nature, whether
we are speaking of a man, a horse, or a family. Besides,
the final cause and end of a thing is the best, and to be
1253ᵃ self-sufficing is the end and the best.

Hence it is evident that the state is a creation of nature, and that man is by nature a political animal. And
he who by nature and not by mere accident is without a
state, is either a bad man or above humanity; he is like
the

'Tribeless, lawless, hearthless one,'

whom Homer[4] denounces—the natural outcast is forth-
with a lover of war; he may be compared to an isolated
piece at draughts.

Now, that man is more of a political animal than bees
or any other gregarious animals is evident. Nature, as
we often say, makes nothing in vain,[5] and man is the
only animal whom she has endowed with the gift of
10 speech.[6] And whereas mere voice is but an indication
of pleasure or pain, and is therefore found in other animals (for their nature attains to the perception of pleasure and pain and the intimation of them to one another,
and no further), the power of speech is intended to set
forth the expedient and inexpedient, and therefore like-
15 wise the just and the unjust. And it is a characteristic of
man that he alone has any sense of good and evil, of just

4 *Il*. ix. 63.                        5 Cp. 1256ᵇ 20.
8 Cp. vii. 1332ᵇ 5.

and unjust, and the like, and the association of living
beings who have this sense makes a family and a state.

Further, the state is by nature clearly prior to the
family and to the individual, since the whole is of neces- 20
sity prior to the part; for example, if the whole body be
destroyed, there will be no foot or hand, except in an
equivocal sense, as we might speak of a stone hand; for
when destroyed the hand will be no better than that.
But things are defined by their working and power; and
we ought not to say that they are the same when they
no longer have their proper quality, but only that they 25
have the same name. The proof that the state is a creation of nature and prior to the individual is that the individual, when isolated, is not self-sufficing; and therefore
he is like a part in relation to the whole. But he who is
unable to live in society, or who has no need because he
is sufficient for himself, must be either a beast or a god:
he is no part of a state. A social instinct is implanted in
all men by nature, and yet he who first founded the state 30
was the greatest of benefactors. For man, when per-
fected, is the best of animals, but, when separated from
law and justice, he is the worst of all; since armed injustice is the more dangerous, and he is equipped at birth
with arms, meant to be used by intelligence and virtue, 35
which he may use for the worst ends. Wherefore, if he
have not virtue, he is the most unholy and the most sav-
age of animals, and the most full of lust and gluttony.
But justice is the bond of men in states, for the administration of justice, which is the determination of what is
just,[7] is the principle of order in political society.

**3**  Seeing then that the state is made up of households,
before speaking of the state we must speak of the man-

[7] Cp. *Nic. Eth.* v. 1134ᵃ 31.

1253ᵇ agement of the household. The parts of household management correspond to the persons who compose the
household, and a complete household consists of slaves
and freemen. Now we should begin by examining every-
5 thing in its fewest possible elements; and the first and
fewest possible parts of a family are master and slave,
husband and wife, father and children. We have therefore to consider what each of these three relations is and
ought to be:—I mean the relation of master and servant,
10 the marriage relation (the conjunction of man and wife
has no name of its own), and thirdly, the procreative
relation (this also has no proper name). And there is another element of a household, the so-called art of getting
wealth, which, according to some, is identical with household management, according to others, a principal part
of it; the nature of this art will also have to be considered by us.

15    Let us first speak of master and slave, looking to the
needs of practical life and also seeking to attain some
better theory of their relation than exists at present. For
some are of opinion that the rule of a master is a science,
and that the management of a household, and the mas-
tership of slaves, and the political and royal rule, as I
20 was saying at the outset,[8] are all the same. Others affirm
that the rule of a master over slaves is contrary to nature,
and that the distinction between slave and freeman exists
by law only, and not by nature; and being an interfer-
ence with nature is therefore unjust.

**4**    Property is a part of the household, and the art of
acquiring property is a part of the art of managing the
25 household; for no man can live well, or indeed live at all,
unless he be provided with necessaries. And as in the

[8] Plato in *Pol.* 258 ᴇ–259 ᴅ, referred to already in 1252ᵃ 7–16.

arts which have a definite sphere the workers must have
their own proper instruments for the accomplishment of
their work, so it is in the management of a household.
Now instruments are of various sorts; some are living,
others lifeless; in the rudder, the pilot of a ship has a
lifeless, in the look-out man, a living instrument; for in
the arts the servant is a kind of instrument. Thus, too, a
possession is an instrument for maintaining life. And so, 30
in the arrangement of the family, a slave is a living possession, and property a number of such instruments; and
the servant is himself an instrument which takes preced-
ence of all other instruments. For if every instrument
could accomplish its own work, obeying or anticipating
the will of others, like the statues of Daedalus, or the 35
tripods of Hephaestus, which, says the poet,[9]

'of their own accord entered the assembly of the Gods';

if, in like manner, the shuttle would weave and the
plectrum touch the lyre without a hand to guide them,
chief workmen would not want servants, nor masters
slaves. Here, however, another distinction must be 1254ᵃ
drawn; the instruments commonly so called are instruments of production, whilst a possession is an instrument
of action. The shuttle, for example, is not only of use;
but something else is made by it, whereas of a garment or
of a bed there is only the use. Further, as production and 5
action are different in kind, and both require instruments, the instruments which they employ must likewise
differ in kind. But life is action and not production, and
therefore the slave is the minister of action. Again, a possession is spoken of as a part is spoken of; for the part
is not only a part of something else, but wholly belongs
to it; and this is also true of a possession. The master is 10

[9] Hom. *Il.* xviii. 376.

only the master of the slave; he does not belong to him, whereas the slave is not only the slave of his master, but wholly belongs to him. Hence we see what is the nature and office of a slave; he who is by nature not his own but
15 another's man, is by nature a slave; and he may be said to be another's man who, being a human being, is also a possession. And a possession may be defined as an instrument of action, separable from the possessor.

5    But is there any one thus intended by nature to be a slave, and for whom such a condition is expedient and right, or rather is not all slavery a violation of nature?
20    There is no difficulty in answering this question, on grounds both of reason and of fact. For that some should rule and others be ruled is a thing not only necessary, but expedient; from the hour of their birth, some are marked out for subjection, others for rule.

And there are many kinds both of rulers and subjects
25 (and that rule is the better which is exercised over better subjects—for example, to rule over men is better than to rule over wild beasts; for the work is better which is executed by better workmen, and where one man rules and another is ruled, they may be said to have a work); for in all things which form a composite whole and which
30 are made up of parts, whether continuous or discrete, a distinction between the ruling and the subject element comes to light. Such a duality exists in living creatures, but not in them only; it originates in the constitution of the universe; even in things which have no life there is a ruling principle, as in a musical mode. But we are wandering from the subject. We will therefore restrict ourselves to the living creature, which, in the first place,
35 consists of soul and body: and of these two, the one is by nature the ruler, and the other the subject. But then

we must look for the intentions of nature in things which
retain their nature, and not in things which are corrupted.
And therefore we must study the man who is in the most
perfect state both of body and soul, for in him we shall
see the true relation of the two; although in bad or corrupted natures the body will often appear to rule over 1254ᵃ
the soul, because they are in an evil and unnatural condition. At all events we may firstly observe in living creatures both a despotical and a constitutional rule; for the
soul rules the body with a despotical rule, whereas the
intellect rules the appetites with a constitutional and
royal rule. And it is clear that the rule of the soul over 5
the body, and of the mind and the rational element over
the passionate, is natural and expedient; whereas the
equality of the two or the rule of the inferior is always
hurtful. The same holds good of animals in relation to
men; for tame animals have a better nature than wild, 10
and all tame animals are better off when they are ruled
by man; for then they are preserved. Again, the male is
by nature superior, and the female inferior; and the one
rules, and the other is ruled; this principle, of necessity,
extends to all mankind. Where then there is such a dif- 15
ference as that between soul and body, or between men
and animals (as in the case of those whose business is to
use their body, and who can do nothing better), the
lower sort are by nature slaves, and it is better for them
as for all inferiors that they should be under the rule of
a master. For he who can be, and therefore is, another's, 20
and he who participates in rational principle enough to
apprehend, but not to have, such a principle, is a slave by
nature. Whereas the lower animals cannot even apprehend a principle; they obey their instincts. And indeed
the use made of slaves and of tame animals is not very
different; for both with their bodies minister to the needs

25 of life. Nature would like to distinguish between the bodies of freemen and slaves, making the one strong for servile labour, the other upright, and although useless 30 for such services, useful for political life in the arts both of war and peace. But the opposite often happens—that some have the souls and others have the bodies of freemen. And doubtless if men differed from one another in the mere forms of their bodies as much as the statues of 35 the Gods do from men, all would acknowledge that the inferior class should be slaves of the superior. And if this is true of the body, how much more just that a similar distinction should exist in the soul? but the beauty of the 1255ᵃ body is seen, whereas the beauty of the soul is not seen. It is clear, then, that some men are by nature free, and others slaves, and that for these latter slavery is both expedient and right.

6 But that those who take the opposite view have in a certain way right on their side, may be easily seen. For the words slavery and slave are used in two senses. There 5 is a slave or slavery by law as well as by nature. The law of which I speak is a sort of convention—the law by which whatever is taken in war is supposed to belong to the victors. But this right many jurists impeach, as they would an orator who brought forward an unconstitutional measure: they detest the notion that, because one man has the power of doing violence and is superior in brute strength, another shall be his slave and subject. 10 Even among philosophers there is a difference of opinion. The origin of the dispute, and what makes the views invade each other's territory, is as follows: in some sense virtue, when furnished with means, has actually the greatest power of exercising force: and as superior power is only found where there is superior excellence of

some kind, power seems to imply virtue, and the dispute
to be simply one about justice (for it is due to one party 15
identifying justice with goodwill,[10] while the other iden-
tifies it with the mere rule of the stronger). If these
views are thus set out separately, the other views [11] have
no force or plausibility against the view that the superior
in virtue ought to rule, or be master. Others, clinging, as 20
they think, simply to a principle of justice (for law and
custom are a sort of justice), assume that slavery in
accordance with the custom of war is justified by law,
but at the same moment they deny this. For what if the
cause of the war be unjust? And again, no one would ever 25
say that he is a slave who is unworthy to be a slave. Were
this the case, men of the highest rank would be slaves
and the children of slaves if they or their parents chance
to have been taken captive and sold. Wherefore Hellenes
do not like to call Hellenes slaves, but confine the term to
barbarians. Yet, in using this language, they really mean 30
the natural slave of whom we spoke at first; [12] for it must
be admitted that some are slaves everywhere, others nowhere. The same principle applies to nobility. Hellenes
regard themselves as noble everywhere, and not only in
their own country, but they deem the barbarians noble 35
only when at home, thereby implying that there are two
sorts of nobility and freedom, the one absolute, the other
relative. The Helen of Theodectes says:

'Who would presume to call me servant who am on
both sides sprung from the stem of the Gods?'

[10] i. e. mutual goodwill, which is held to be incompatible with the
relation of master and slave.

[11] i. e. those stated in ll. 5–12, that the stronger always has, and that
he never has, a right to enslave the weaker. Aristotle finds that these
views cannot maintain themselves against his intermediate view, that
the superior in *virtue* should rule.

[12] Chap. 5.

What does this mean but that they distinguish freedom
**40** and slavery, noble and humble birth, by the two princi-
**1255ᵇ** ples of good and evil? They think that as men and animals beget men and animals, so from good men a good
man springs. But this is what nature, though she may
intend it, cannot always accomplish.

We see then that there is some foundation for this dif-
**5** ference of opinion, and that all are not either slaves by
nature or freemen by nature, and also that there is in
some cases a marked distinction between the two classes,
rendering it expedient and right for the one to be slaves
and the others to be masters: the one practising obedience, the others exercising the authority and lordship
which nature intended them to have. The abuse of this
authority is injurious to both; for the interests of part
**10** and whole,[13] of body and soul, are the same, and the
slave is a part of the master, a living but separated part
of his bodily frame. Hence, where the relation of master
and slave between them is natural they are friends and
have a common interest, but where it rests merely on
**15** law and force the reverse is true.

**7** The previous remarks are quite enough to show that
the rule of a master is not a constitutional rule, and that
all the different kinds of rule are not, as some affirm, the
same with each other.[14] For there is one rule exercised
over subjects who are by nature free, another over subjects who are by nature slaves. The rule of a household
is a monarchy, for every house is under one head:
whereas constitutional rule is a government of freemen
**30** and equals. The master is not called a master because

---

[13] Cp. 1254ᵃ 8.
[14] Plato, *Polit.* 258 ᴇ–259 ᴅ, referred to already in 1252ᵃ 7–16, 1253ᵇ
18–20.

he has science,[15] but because he is of a certain character,
and the same remark applies to the slave and the freeman. Still there may be a science for the master and a
science for the slave. The science of the slave would be
such as the man of Syracuse taught, who made money
by instructing slaves in their ordinary duties. And such 25
a knowledge may be carried further, so as to include
cookery and similar menial arts. For some duties are of
the more necessary, others of the more honourable sort;
as the proverb says, 'slave before slave, master before
master'. But all such branches of knowledge are servile. 30
There is likewise a science of the master, which teaches
the use of slaves; for the master as such is concerned,
not with the acquisition, but with the use of them. Yet
this so-called science is not anything great or wonderful;
for the master need only know how to order that which
the slave must know how to execute. Hence those who are 35
in a position which places them above toil have stewards
who attend to their households while they occupy themselves with philosophy or with politics. But the art of acquiring slaves, I mean of justly acquiring them, differs
both from the art of the master and the art of the slave,
being a species of hunting or war.[16] Enough of the distinction between master and slave.
                                                    40

8  Let us now inquire into property generally, and into 1256ᵃ
the art of getting wealth, in accordance with our usual
method,[17] for a slave has been shown[18] to be a part of
property. The first question is whether the art of getting
wealth is the same with the art of managing a household
or a part of it, or instrumental to it; and if the last,

---

[15] *Polit.* 259 c, 293 c.                    [16] Cp. vii. 1333ᵇ 38.
[17] Of understanding the whole by the part, Cp. 1252ᵃ 17.
[18] Chap. 4.

whether in the way that the art of making shuttles is instrumental to the art of weaving, or in the way that the
5 casting of bronze is instrumental to the art of the statuary, for they are not instrumental in the same way, but
the one provides tools and the other material; and by
material I mean the substratum out of which any work
10 is made; thus wool is the material of the weaver, bronze
of the statuary. Now it is easy to see that the art of
household management is not identical with the art of
getting wealth, for the one uses the material which the
other provides. For the art which uses household stores
can be no other than the art of household management.
There is, however, a doubt whether the art of getting
wealth is a part of household management or a distinct
15 art. If the getter of wealth has to consider whence wealth
and property can be procured, but there are many sorts
of property and riches, then are husbandry, and the care
and provision of food in general, parts of the wealth-
getting art or distinct arts? Again, there are many sorts
of food, and therefore there are many kinds of lives both
20 of animals and men; they must all have food, and the
differences in their food have made differences in their
ways of life. For of beasts, some are gregarious, others
are solitary; they live in the way which is best adapted to
sustain them, accordingly as they are carnivorous or
25 herbivorous or omnivorous: and their habits are determined for them by nature in such a manner that they may
obtain with greater facility the food of their choice. But,
as different species have different tastes, the same things
are not naturally pleasant to all of them; and therefore
the lives of carnivorous or herbivorous animals further
10 differ among themselves. In the lives of men too there
is a great difference. The laziest are shepherds, who lead
an idle life, and get their subsistence without trouble

from tame animals; their flocks having to wander from
place to place in search of pasture, they are compelled to
follow them, cultivating a sort of living farm. Others 35
support themselves by hunting, which is of different
kinds. Some, for example, are brigands, others, who dwell
near lakes or marshes or rivers or a sea in which there are
fish, are fishermen, and others live by the pursuit of birds
or wild beasts. The greater number obtain a living from
the cultivated fruits of the soil. Such are the modes of 40
subsistence which prevail among those whose industry
springs up of itself, and whose food is not acquired by
exchange and retail trade—there is the shepherd, the 1256ᵇ
husbandman, the brigand, the fisherman, the hunter.
Some gain a comfortable maintenance out of two employments, eking out the deficiencies of one of them by
another: thus the life of a shepherd may be combined
with that of a brigand, the life of a farmer with that of a 5
hunter. Other modes of life are similarly combined in
any way which the needs of men may require. Property,
in the sense of a bare livelihood, seems to be given by
nature herself to all, both when they are first born, and
when they are grown up. For some animals bring forth, 10
together with their offspring, so much food as will last
until they are able to supply themselves; of this the
vermiparous or oviparous animals are an instance; and
the viviparous animals have up to a certain time a supply of food for their young in themselves, which is called
milk. In like manner we may infer that, after the birth of 15
animals, plants exist for their sake, and that the other
animals exist for the sake of man, the tame for use and
food, the wild, if not all, at least the greater part of them,
for food, and for the provision of clothing and various
instruments. Now if nature makes nothing incomplete, 20
and nothing in vain, the inference must be that she has

made all animals for the sake of man. And so, in one
point of view, the art of war is a natural art of acquisition, for the art of acquisition includes hunting, an art
which we ought to practise against wild beasts, and
25 against men who, though intended by nature to be governed, will not submit; for war of such a kind is naturally just.[19]

Of the art of acquisition then there is one kind which
by nature is a part of the management of a household, in
so far as the art of household management must either
find ready to hand, or itself provide. such things neces-
30 sary to life, and useful for the community of the family
or state, as can be stored. They are the elements of true
riches; for the amount of property which is needed for
a good life is not unlimited, although Solon in one of his
poems says that

'No bound to riches has been fixed for man'.

But there is a boundary fixed, just as there is in the other
35 arts; for the instruments of any art are never unlimited,
either in number or size, and riches may be defined as a
number of instruments to be used in a household or in a
state. And so we see that there is a natural art of acquisition which is practised by managers of households and
by statesmen. and what is the reason of this.

40 9   There is another variety of the art of acquisition
which is commonly and rightly called an art of wealth-
getting, and has in fact suggested the notion that riches
1257ª and property have no limit. Being nearly connected with
the preceding, it is often identified with it. But though
they are not very different, neither are they the same.

19 Cp. 1255ᵇ 38, 1333ᵇ 38.

The kind already described is given by nature, the other is gained by experience and art.

Let us begin our discussion of the question with the 5 following considerations:

Of everything which we possess there are two uses: both belong to the thing as such, but not in the same manner, for one is the proper, and the other the improper or secondary use of it. For example, a shoe is used for wear, and is used for exchange; both are uses of the shoe. He who gives a shoe in exchange for money or food to him 10 who wants one, does indeed use the shoe as a shoe, but this is not its proper or primary purpose, for a shoe is not made to be an object of barter. The same may be said of all possessions, for the art of exchange extends to all of 15 them, and it arises at first from what is natural, from the circumstance that some have too little, others too much. Hence we may infer that retail trade is not a natural part of the art of getting wealth; had it been so, men would have ceased to exchange when they had enough. In the first community, indeed, which is the family, this art is obviously of no use, but it begins to be useful when the 20 society increases. For the members of the family originally had all things in common; later, when the family divided into parts, the parts shared in many things, and different parts in different things, which they had to give in exchange for what they wanted, a kind of barter which is still practised among barbarous nations who exchange 25 with one another the necessaries of life and nothing more; giving and receiving wine, for example, in exchange for corn, and the like. This sort of barter is not part of the wealth-getting art and is not contrary to nature, but is needed for the satisfaction of men's natu- 30 ral wants. The other or more complex form of exchange grew, as might have been inferred, out of the simpler.

When the inhabitants of one country became more dependent on those of another, and they imported what they needed, and exported what they had too much of, 35 money necessarily came into use. For the various necessaries of life are not easily carried about, and hence men agreed to employ in their dealings with each other something which was intrinsically useful and easily applicable to the purposes of life, for example, iron, silver, and the like. Of this the value was at first measured simply by 40 size and weight, but in process of time they put a stamp upon it, to save the trouble of weighing and to mark the value.

**1257ᵇ** When the use of coin had once been discovered, out of the barter of necessary articles arose the other art of wealth-getting, namely, retail trade; which was at first probably a simple matter, but became more complicated as soon as men learned by experience whence and by what exchanges the greatest profit might be made. Origi-5 nating in the use of coin, the art of getting wealth is generally thought to be chiefly concerned with it, and to be the art which produces riches and wealth; having to consider how they may be accumulated. Indeed, riches is assumed by many to be only a quantity of coin, be-10 cause the arts of getting wealth and retail trade are concerned with coin. Others maintain that coined money is a mere sham, a thing not natural, but conventional only, because, if the users substitute another commodity for it, it is worthless, and because it is not useful as a means to any of the necessities of life, and, indeed, he who is rich in coin may often be in want of necessary food. But how can that be wealth of which a man may have a great 15 abundance and yet perish with hunger, like Midas in the fable, whose insatiable prayer turned everything that was set before him into gold?

Hence men seek after a better notion of riches and of the art of getting wealth than the mere acquisition of coin, and they are right. For natural riches and the natural art of wealth-getting are a different thing; in their true form they are part of the management of a house- 20 hold; whereas retail trade is the art of producing wealth, not in every way, but by exchange. And it is thought to be concerned with coin; for coin is the unit of exchange and the measure or limit of it. And there is no bound to the riches which spring from this art of wealth-getting.[20] As in the art of medicine there is no limit to the pursuit of 25 health, and as in the other arts there is no limit to the pursuit of their several ends, for they aim at accomplishing their ends to the uttermost (but of the means there is a limit, for the end is always the limit), so, too, in this art of wealth-getting there is no limit of the end, which is riches of the spurious kind, and the acquisition of wealth. 30 But the art of wealth-getting which consists in household management, on the other hand, has a limit; the unlimited acquisition of wealth is not its business. And, therefore, in one point of view, all riches must have a limit; nevertheless, as a matter of fact, we find the opposite to be the case; for all getters of wealth increase their hoard of coin without limit. The source of the confusion is the near connection between the two kinds of wealth-getting; in either, the instrument is the same, although the use is 35 different, and so they pass into one another; for each is a use of the same property, but with a difference: accumulation is the end in the one case, but there is a further end in the other. Hence some persons are led to believe that getting wealth is the object of household management, and the whole idea of their lives is that they ought either to increase their money without limit, or at any 40

[20] Cp. 1256b 32.

rate not to lose it. The origin of this disposition in men
is that they are intent upon living only, and not upon
1258ª living well; and, as their desires are unlimited, they also
desire that the means of gratifying them should be without limit. Those who do aim at a good life seek the means
5 of obtaining bodily pleasures; and, since the enjoyment
of these appears to depend on property, they are absorbed in getting wealth: and so there arises the second
species of wealth-getting. For, as their enjoyment is in
excess, they seek an art which produces the excess of
enjoyment; and, if they are not able to supply their
pleasures by the art of getting wealth, they try other arts,
using in turn every faculty in a manner contrary to na-
10 ture. The quality of courage, for example, is not intended
to make wealth, but to inspire confidence; neither is this
the aim of the general's or of the physician's art; but the
one aims at victory and the other at health. Nevertheless, some men turn every quality or art into a means of
getting wealth; this they conceive to be the end, and to
the promotion of the end they think all things must
contribute.

Thus, then, we have considered the art of wealth-get-
15 ting which is unnecessary, and why men want it; and
also the necessary art of wealth-getting, which we have
seen to be different from the other, and to be a natural
part of the art of managing a household, concerned with
the provision of food, not, however, like the former kind,
unlimited, but having a limit.

**10**  And we have found the answer to our original question,[21] Whether the art of getting wealth is the business
of the manager of a household and of the statesman or
20 not their business?—viz. that wealth is presupposed by

[21] 1256ª 3.

them. For as political science does not make men, but
takes them from nature and uses them, so too nature provides them with earth or sea or the like as a source of
food. At this stage begins the duty of the manager of a
household, who has to order the things which nature
supplies;—he may be compared to the weaver who has 25
not to make but to use wool, and to know, too, what sort
of wool is good and serviceable or bad and unserviceable.
Were this otherwise, it would be difficult to see why the
art of getting wealth is a part of the management of a
household and the art of medicine not; for surely the
members of a household must have health just as they
must have life or any other necessary. The answer is that 30
as from one point of view the master of the house and
the ruler of the state have to consider about health, from
another point of view not they but the physician; so in
one way the art of household management, in another way
the subordinate art, has to consider about wealth. But,
strictly speaking, as I have already said, the means of
life must be provided beforehand by nature; for the
business of nature is to furnish food to that which is 35
born, and the food of the offspring is always what remains over of that from which it is produced.[22] Wherefore the art of getting wealth out of fruits and animals is
always natural.

There are two sorts of wealth-getting, as I have said [23];
one is a part of household management, the other is retail
trade: the former necessary and honourable, while that 40
which consists in exchange is justly censured; for it is
unnatural, and a mode by which men gain from one an- 1258ᵇ
other. The most hated sort, and with the greatest reason,
is usury, which makes a gain out of money itself, and not
from the natural object of it. For money was intended to

[22] Cp. 1256ᵇ 10.                    [23] 1256ᵃ 15–1258ᵃ 18.

be used in exchange, but not to increase at interest. And
5 this term interest,[24] which means the birth of money
from money, is applied to the breeding of money because
the offspring resembles the parent. Wherefore of all
modes of getting wealth this is the most unnatural.

**11**    Enough has been said about the theory of wealth-
10 getting; we will now proceed to the practical part. The
discussion of such matters is not unworthy of philosophy,
but to be engaged in them practically is illiberal and irk-
some. The useful parts of wealth-getting are, first, the
knowledge of live-stock—which are most profitable, and
where, and how—as, for example, what sort of horses or
sheep or oxen or any other animals are most likely to
15 give a return. A man ought to know which of these pay
better than others, and which pay best in particular
places, for some do better in one place and some in another. Secondly, husbandry, which may be either tillage
or planting, and the keeping of bees and of fish, or fowl,
or of any animals which may be useful to man. These
20 are the divisions of the true or proper art of wealth-getting and come first. Of the other, which consists in exchange, the first and most important division is com-
merce (of which there are three kinds—the provision of
a ship, the conveyance of goods, exposure for sale—these
again differing as they are safer or more profitable), the
25 second is usury, the third, service for hire—of this, one
kind is employed in the mechanical arts, the other in
unskilled and bodily labour. There is still a third sort of
wealth-getting intermediate between this and the first or
natural mode which is partly natural, but is also concerned with exchange, viz., the industries that make their
30 profit from the earth, and from things growing from the

[24] *tokos,* lit. 'offspring'.

earth which, although they bear no fruit, are nevertheless profitable; for example, the cutting of timber and all mining. The art of mining, by which minerals are obtained, itself has many branches, for there are various kinds of things dug out of the earth. Of the several divisions of wealth-getting I now speak generally; a minute consideration of them might be useful in practice, but it would be tiresome to dwell upon them at greater length now.

Those occupations are most truly arts in which there 35 is the least element of chance; they are the meanest in which the body is most deteriorated, the most servile in which there is the greatest use of the body, and the most illiberal in which there is the least need of excellence.

Works have been written upon these subjects by various persons; for example, by Chares the Parian, and 40 Apollodorus the Lemnian, who have treated of Tillage and Planting, while others have treated of other 1259ª branches; any one who cares for such matters may refer to their writings. It would be well also to collect the scattered stories of the ways in which individuals have succeeded in amassing a fortune; for all this is useful to persons who value the art of getting wealth. There is the 5 anecdote of Thales the Milesian and his financial device, which involves a principle of universal application, but is attributed to him on account of his reputation for wisdom. He was reproached for his poverty, which was supposed to show that philosophy was of no use. According 10 to the story, he knew by his skill in the stars while it was yet winter that there would be a great harvest of olives in the coming year; so, having a little money, he gave deposits for the use of all the olive-presses in Chios and Miletus, which he hired at a low price because no one bid against him. When the harvest-time came, and many

15 were wanted all at once and of a sudden, he let them ouι
at any rate which he pleased, and made a quantity of
money. Thus he showed the world that philosophers can
easily be rich if they like, but that their ambition is of
another sort. He is supposed to have given a striking
proof of his wisdom, but, as I was saying, his device for
20 getting wealth is of universal application, and is nothing
but the creation of a monopoly. It is an art often practised by cities when they are in want of money; they
make a monopoly of provisions.

There was a man of Sicily, who, having money deposited with him, bought up all the iron from the iron mines;
25 afterwards, when the merchants from their various mar-
kets came to buy, he was the only seller, and without
much increasing the price he gained 200 per cent. Which
when Dionysius heard, he told him that he might take
away his money, but that he must not remain at Syracuse, for he thought that the man had discovered a way
30 of making money which was injurious to his own interests. He made the same discovery as Thales; they both
contrived to create a monopoly for themselves. And
statesmen as well ought to know these things; for a state
is often as much in want of money and of such devices
for obtaining it as a household, or even more so; hence
35 some public men devote themselves entirely to finance.

**12** Of household management we have seen[25] that
there are three parts—one is the rule of a master over
slaves, which has been discussed already,[26] another of a
father, and the third of a husband. A husband and
40 father, we saw, rules over wife and children, ɒoth free,
but the rule differs, the rule over his children being a
1259ᵇ royal, over his wife a constitutional rule. For although

[25] 1253ᵇ 3–11.       [26] 1253ᵇ 14–1255ᵇ 39.

there may be exceptions to the order of nature, the male
is by nature fitter for command than the female, just as
the elder and full-grown is superior to the younger and
more immature. But in most constitutional states the 5
citizens rule and are ruled by turns, for the idea of a
constitutional state implies that the natures of the citizens are equal, and do not differ at all.[27] Nevertheless,
when one rules and the other is ruled we endeavour to
create a difference of outward forms and names and titles
of respect, which may be illustrated by the saying of
Amasis about his foot-pan.[28] The relation of the male to
the female is of this kind, but there the inequality is
permanent. The rule of a father over his children is 10
royal, for he rules by virtue both of love and of the respect due to age, exercising a kind of royal power. And
therefore Homer has appropriately called Zeus 'father
of Gods and men', because he is the king of them all.
For a king is the natural superior of his subjects, but he
should be of the same kin or kind with them, and such 15
is the relation of elder and younger, of father and son.

**13**  Thus it is clear that household management attends
more to men than to the acquisition of inanimate things,
and to human excellence more than to the excellence of
property which we call wealth, and to the virtue of free- 20
men more than to the virtue of slaves. A question may
indeed be raised, whether there is any excellence at all
in a slave beyond and higher than merely instrumental
and ministerial qualities—whether he can have the virtues of temperance, courage, justice, and the like; or
whether slaves possess only bodily and ministerial quali- 25
ties. And, whichever way we answer the question, a difficulty arises; for, if they have virtue, in what will they

[27] Cp. ii. 1261ᵃ 39, iii. 1288ᵃ 12.          [28] Herod. ii. 172.

differ from freemen? On the other hand, since they are
men and share in rational principle, it seems absurd to
say that they have no virtue. A similar question may be
30 raised about women and children, whether they too have
virtues: ought a woman to be temperate and brave and
just, and is a child to be called temperate, and intemperate, or not? So in general we may ask about the natural
ruler, and the natural subject, whether they have the
same or different virtues. For if a noble nature is equally
35 required in both, why should one of them always rule,
and the other always be ruled? Nor can we say that this
is a question of degree, for the difference between ruler
and subject is a difference of kind, which the difference
of more and less never is. Yet how strange is the supposition that the one ought, and that the other ought not, to
40 have virtue! For if the ruler is intemperate and unjust,
1260ᵃ how can he rule well? if the subject, how can he obey
well? If he be licentious and cowardly, he will certainly
not do his duty. It is evident, therefore, that both of
them must have a share of virtue, but varying as natural
subjects also vary among themselves. Here the very con-
5 stitution of the soul has shown us the way; in it one part
naturally rules, and the other is subject, and the virtue
of the ruler we maintain to be different from that of the
subject;—the one being the virtue of the rational, and
the other of the irrational part. Now, it is obvious that
the same principle applies generally, and therefore almost all things rule and are ruled according to nature.
But the kind of rule differs;—the freeman rules over the
slave after another manner from that in which the male
rules over the female, or the man over the child; although
10 the parts of the soul are present in all of them, they are
present in different degrees. For the slave has no deliberative faculty at all; the woman has, but it is without au-

thority, and the child has, but it is immature. So it must necessarily be supposed to be with the moral virtues 15 also; all should partake of them, but only in such manner and degree as is required by each for the fulfilment of his duty. Hence the ruler ought to have moral virtue in perfection, for his function, taken absolutely, demands a master artificer, and rational principle is such an artificer; the subjects, on the other hand, require only that measure of virtue which is proper to each of them. 20 Clearly, then, moral virtue belongs to all of them; but the temperance of a man and of a woman, or the courage and justice of a man and of a woman, are not, as Socrates maintained,[29] the same; the courage of a man is shown in commanding, of a woman in obeying. And this holds of all other virtues, as will be more clearly seen if we look 25 at them in detail, for those who say generally that virtue consists in a good disposition of the soul, or in doing rightly, or the like, only deceive themselves. Far better than such definitions is their mode of speaking, who, like Gorgias,[30] enumerate the virtues. All classes must be deemed to have their special attributes; as the poet says of women,

> 'Silence is a woman's glory',     30

but this is not equally the glory of man. The child is imperfect, and therefore obviously his virtue is not relative to himself alone, but to the perfect man and to his teacher, and in like manner the virtue of the slave is relative to a master. Now we determined[31] that a slave is useful for the wants of life, and therefore he will obviously require only so much virtue as will prevent him 35 from failing in his duty through cowardice or lack of

---

[29] Plato, *Meno*, 72 A–73 C.          [30] *Meno*, 71 E, 72 A.
[31] 1254[b] 16–39, Cf. 1259[b] 25 sq.

self-control. Some one will ask whether, if what we are saying is true, virtue will not be required also in the artisans, for they often fail in their work through the lack of self-control? But is there not a great difference in the two cases? For the slave shares in his master's life; 40 the artisan is less closely connected with him, and only attains excellence in proportion as he becomes a slave. 1260ᵇ The meaner sort of mechanic has a special and separate slavery; and whereas the slave exists by nature, not so the shoemaker or other artisan. It is manifest, then, that the master ought to be the source of such excellence in the slave, and not a mere possessor of the art of mas- 5 tership which trains the slave in his duties.[32] Wherefore they are mistaken who forbid us to converse with slaves and say that we should employ command only,[33] for slaves stand even more in need of admonition than children.

So much for this subject; the relations of husband and wife, parent and child, their several virtues, what in their intercourse with one another is good, and what is 10 evil, and how we may pursue the good and escape the evil, will have to be discussed when we speak of the dif- ferent forms of government.[34] For, inasmuch as every family is a part of a state, and these relationships are the parts of a family, and the virtue of the part must have regard to the virtue of the whole, women and children 15 must be trained by education with an eye to the consti- tution,[35] if the virtues of either of them are supposed to make any difference in the virtues of the state. And they must make a difference: for the children grow up to be

[32] Cp. 1255ᵇ 23, 31–35.          [33] Plato, *Laws,* vi. 777 ᴇ.
[34] The question is not actually discussed in the *Politics*.
[35] Cp. v. 1310ᵃ 12–36, viii. 1337ᵃ 11–18.

citizens, and half the free persons in a state are women.[36] 20

Of these matters, enough has been said; of what remains, let us speak at another time. Regarding, then, our present inquiry as complete, we will make a new beginning. And, first, let us examine the various theories of a perfect state.

[36] Plato, *Laws,* vi. 781 A.

## BOOK II

**1** Our purpose is to consider what form of political community is best of all for those who are most able to realize their ideal of life. We must therefore examine not only this but other constitutions, both such as actually exist in well-governed states, and any theoretical forms which are held in esteem; that what is good and useful may be brought to light. And let no one suppose that in seeking for something beyond them we are anxious to make a sophistical display at any cost; we only undertake this inquiry because all the constitutions with which we are acquainted are faulty.

We will begin with the natural beginning of the subject. Three alternatives are conceivable: The members of a state must either have (1) all things or (2) nothing in common, or (3) some things in common and some not. That they should have nothing in common is clearly impossible, for the constitution is a community, and must at any rate have a common place—one city will be in one place, and the citizens are those who share in that one city. But should a well-ordered state have all things, as far as may be, in common, or some only and not others? For the citizens might conceivably have wives and children and property in common, as Socrates proposes in

80

the *Republic* of Plato.[1] Which is better, our present condition, or the proposed new order of society?

**2**    There are many difficulties in the community of women. And the principle on which Socrates rests the necessity of such an institution evidently is not established by his arguments. Further, as a means to the end which he ascribes to the state, the scheme, taken literally, is impracticable, and how we are to interpret it is nowhere precisely stated. I am speaking of the premiss from which the argument of Socrates proceeds, 'that the greater the unity of the state the better'. Is it not obvious that a state may at length attain such a degree of unity as to be no longer a state?—since the nature of a state is to be a plurality, and in tending to greater unity, from being a state, it becomes a family, and from being a family, an individual; for the family may be said to be more than the state, and the individual than the family. So that we ought not to attain this greatest unity even if we could, for it would be the destruction of the state. Again, a state is not made up only of so many men, but of different kinds of men; for similars do not constitute a state. It is not like a military alliance. The usefulness of the latter depends upon its quantity even where there is no difference in quality (for mutual protection is the end aimed at), just as a greater weight of anything is more useful than a less (in like manner, a state differs from a nation, when the nation has not its population organized in villages, but lives an Arcadian sort of life); but the elements out of which a unity is to be formed differ in kind. Wherefore the principle of compensation, as I have already remarked in the *Ethics*,[2] is the salvation of

---

[1] *Rep.* iv. 423 ᴇ, ᴠ. 457 ᴄ, 462 ʙ.        [2] *Nic. Eth.* ᴠ. 1132ᵇ 32.

states. Even among freemen and equals this is a principle
which must be maintained, for they cannot all rule together, but must change at the end of a year or some
other period of time or in some order of succession. The
result is that upon this plan they all govern; just as if
35 shoemakers and carpenters were to exchange their occupations, and the same persons did not always continue
shoemakers and carpenters. And since it is better that
this should be so in politics as well, it is clear that while
there should be continuance of the same persons in power
where this is possible, yet where this is not possible by
1261ᵇ reason of the natural equality of the citizens, and at the
same time it is just that all should share in the government (whether to govern be a good thing or a bad[3]), an
approximation to this is that equals should in turn re-
tire from office and should, apart from official position,
be treated alike.[4] Thus the one party rule and the others
5 are ruled in turn, as if they were no longer the same persons. In like manner when they hold office there is a variety in the offices held. Hence it is evident that a city is
not by nature one in that sense which some persons affirm; and that what is said to be the greatest good of
cities is in reality their destruction; but surely the good
10 of things must be that which preserves them.[5] Again, in
another point of view, this extreme unification of the
state is clearly not good; for a family is more self-sufficing than an individual, and a city than a family, and a city
only comes into being when the community is large
enough to be self-sufficing. If then self-sufficiency is to
be desired, the lesser degree of unity is more desirable
15 than the greater.

[3] Cp. Pl. *Rep.* i. 345–6.          [4] Cp. i. 1259ᵇ 4, iii. 1288ᵃ 12.
[5] Cp. Pl. *Rep.* i. 353.

**3**  But, even supposing that it were best for the community to have the greatest degree of unity, this unity is by no means proved to follow from the fact 'of all men saying "mine" and "not mine" at the same instant of time', which, according to Socrates,[6] is the sign of perfect unity in a state. For the word 'all' is ambiguous. If the meaning be that every individual says 'mine' and 'not mine' at the same time, then perhaps the result at which Socrates aims may be in some degree accomplished; each man will call the same person his own son and the same person his own wife, and so of his property and of all that falls to his lot. This, however, is not the way in which people would speak who had their wives and children in common; they would say 'all' but not 'each'. In like manner their property would be described as belonging to them, not severally but collectively. There is an obvious fallacy in the term 'all': like some other words, 'both', 'odd', 'even', it is ambiguous, and even in abstract argument becomes a source of logical puzzles. That all persons call the same thing mine in the sense in which each does so may be a fine thing, but it is impracticable; or if the words are taken in the other sense, such a unity in no way conduces to harmony. And there is another objection to the proposal. For that which is common to the greatest number has the least care bestowed upon it. Every one thinks chiefly of his own, hardly at all of the common interest; and only when he is himself concerned as an individual. For besides other considerations, everybody is more inclined to neglect the duty which he expects another to fulfil; as in families many attendants are often less useful than a few. Each citizen will have a thousand sons who will not be his sons

[6] Pl. *Rep.* v. 462 c.

1262ᵃ individually, but anybody will be equally the son of anybody, and will therefore be neglected by all alike. Further, upon this principle, every one will use the word
'mine' of one who is prospering or the reverse,[7] however
small a fraction he may himself be of the whole number;
the same boy will be 'my son', 'so and so's son', the son
of each of the thousand, or whatever be the number of
5 the citizens; and even about this he will not be positive;
for it is impossible to know who chanced to have a child,
or whether, if one came into existence, it has survived.
But which is better—for each to say 'mine' in this way,
making a man the same relation to two thousand or ten
thousand citizens, or to use the word 'mine' in the ordi-
10 nary and more restricted sense? For usually the same
person is called by one man his own son whom another
calls his own brother or cousin or kinsman—blood relation or connexion by marriage either of himself or of
some relation of his, and yet another his clansman or
tribesman; and how much better is it to be the real cousin
of somebody than to be a son after Plato's fashion! Nor
is there any way of preventing brothers and children and
15 fathers and mothers from sometimes recognizing one
another; for children are born like their parents, and
they will necessarily be finding indications of their relationship to one another. Geographers declare such to be
the fact; they say that in part of Upper Libya, where
20 the women are common, nevertheless the children who
are born are assigned to their respective fathers on the
ground of their likeness. And some women, like the fe-
males of other animals—for example, mares and cows—
have a strong tendency to produce offspring resembling
their parents, as was the case with the Pharsalian mare
called Honest.

[7] Cp. *Rep.* v. 463 ᴇ.

**4**  Other evils, against which it is not easy for the 25
authors of such a community to guard, will be assaults
and homicides, voluntary as well as involuntary, quarrels
and slanders, all which are most unholy acts when committed against fathers and mothers and near relations,
but not equally unholy when there is no relationship.
Moreover, they are much more likely to occur if the rela- 30
tionship is unknown, and, when they have occurred, the
customary expiations of them cannot be made. Again,
how strange it is that Socrates,[8] after having made the
children common, should hinder lovers from carnal intercourse only, but should permit love and familiarities 35
between father and son or between brother and brother,
than which nothing can be more unseemly, since even
without them love of this sort is improper. How strange,
too, to forbid intercourse for no other reason than the
violence of the pleasure, as though the relationship of
father and son or of brothers with one another made no
difference.

This community of wives and children seems better 40
suited to the husbandmen than to the guardians, for if 1262ᵃ
they have wives and children in common, they will be
bound to one another by weaker ties, as a subject class
should be, and they will remain obedient and not rebel.[9]
In a word, the result of such a law would be just the opposite of that which good laws ought to have, and the
intention of Socrates in making these regulations about 5
women and children would defeat itself. For friendship
we believe to be the greatest good of states[10] and the
preservative of them against revolutions; neither is there
anything which Socrates so greatly lauds as the unity of 10
the state which he and all the world declare to be cre-

---

[8] *Rep.* iii. 403 A–C.                    [9] Cp. vii. 1330ᵃ 28.
[10] Cp. *Nic. Eth.* viii. 1155ᵃ 22.

ated by friendship. But the unity which he commends [11] would be like that of the lovers in the *Symposium*,[12] who, as Aristophanes says, desire to grow together in the excess of their affection, and from being two to become one,
15 in which case one or both would certainly perish. Whereas in a state having women and children common, love will be watery; and the father will certainly not say 'my son', or the son 'my father'.[13] As a little sweet wine mingled with a great deal of water is imperceptible in the mixture, so, in this sort of community, the idea of rela-
20 tionship which is based upon these names will be lost; there is no reason why the so-called father should care about the son, or the son about the father, or brothers about one another. Of the two qualities which chiefly inspire regard and affection—that a thing is your own and that it is your only one—neither can exist in such a state as this.

Again, the transfer of children as soon as they are born
25 from the rank of husbandmen or of artisans to that of guardians, and from the rank of guardians into a lower rank,[14] will be very difficult to arrange; the givers or transferrers cannot but know whom they are giving and transferring, and to whom. And the previously men-
30 tioned [15] evils, such as assaults, unlawful loves, homicides, will happen more often amongst those who are transferred to the lower classes, or who have a place assigned to them among the guardians; for they will no longer call the members of the class they have left brothers, and children, and fathers, and mothers, and will not, therefore, be afraid of committing any crimes by reason of consanguinity. Touching the community of wives and
35 children, let this be our conclusion.

[11] Cp. c. 2.    [12] *Symp.* 191 A, 192 C.    [13] Cp. c. 3.
[14] *Rep.* iii. 415 B.    [15] a25–40.

**5**   Next let us consider what should be our arrangements about property: should the citizens of the perfect
state have their possessions in common or not? This 40
question may be discussed separately from the enact- 1263
ments about women and children. Even supposing that
the women and children belong to individuals, according
to the custom which is at present universal, may there
not be an advantage in having and using possessions in
common? Three cases are possible: (1) the soil may be
appropriated, but the produce may be thrown for con-
sumption into the common stock; and this is the practice
of some nations. Or (2), the soil may be common, and 5
may be cultivated in common, but the produce divided
among individuals for their private use; this is a form
of common property which is said to exist among certain
barbarians. Or (3), the soil and the produce may be
alike common.

When the husbandmen are not the owners, the case
will be different and easier to deal with; but when they 10
till the ground for themselves the question of ownership
will give a world of trouble. If they do not share equally
in enjoyments and toils, those who labour much and get
little will necessarily complain of those who labour little
and receive or consume much. But indeed there is always 15
a difficulty in men living together and having all human
relations in common, but especially in their having common property. The partnerships of fellow-travellers are
an example to the point; for they generally fall out over
everyday matters and quarrel about any trifle which
turns up. So with servants: we are most liable to take 20
offense at those with whom we most frequently come
into contact in daily life.

These are only some of the disadvantages which attend the community of property; the present arrange-

ment, if improved as it might be by good customs and laws, would be far better, and would have the advan-
25 tages of both systems. Property should be in a certain sense common, but, as a general rule, private; for, when every one has a distinct interest,[16] men will not complain of one another, and they will make more progress, because every one will be attending to his own business. And yet by reason of goodness, and in respect of use, 'Friends', as the proverb says, 'will have all things com-
30 mon.'[17] Even now there are traces of such a principle, showing that it is not impracticable, but, in well-ordered states, exists already to a certain extent and may be carried further. For, although every man has his own property, some things he will place at the disposal of his
35 friends, while of others he shares the use with them. The Lacedaemonians, for example, use one another's slaves, and horses, and dogs, as if they were their own; and when they lack provisions on a journey, they appropriate what they find in the fields throughout the country. It is clearly better that property should be private, but the use of it common; and the special business of the legislator is to
40 create in men this benevolent disposition. Again, how immeasurably greater is the pleasure, when a man feels a
1263ᵇ thing to be his own; for surely the love of self [18] is a feeling implanted by nature and not given in vain, although selfishness is rightly censured; this, however, is not the mere love of self, but the love of self in excess, like the miser's love of money; for all, or almost all, men love
5 money and other such objects in a measure. And further, there is the greatest pleasure in doing a kindness or service to friends or guests or companions, which can only be rendered when a man has private property. These

---

16 Cp. *Rep*. ii. 374.     17 Cp. *Rep*. iv. 424 A.
18 Cp. *Nic. Eth*. ix. 8.

advantages are lost by excessive unification of the state. The exhibition of two virtues, besides, is visibly anni- 10 hilated in such a state: first, temperance towards women (for it is an honourable action to abstain from another's wife for temperance sake); secondly, liberality in the matter of property. No one, when men have all things in common, will any longer set an example of liberality or do any liberal action; for liberality consists in the use which is made of property.[19]

Such legislation may have a specious appearance of 15 benevolence; men readily listen to it, and are easily in- duced to believe that in some wonderful manner every- body will become everybody's friend, especially when some one[20] is heard denouncing the evils now existing in states, suits about contracts, convictions for perjury, 20 flatteries of rich men and the like, which are said to arise out of the possession of private property. These evils, however, are due to a very different cause—the wicked- ness of human nature. Indeed, we see that there is much more quarrelling among those who have all things in com- mon, though there are not many of them when compared 25 with the vast numbers who have private property.

Again, we ought to reckon, not only the evils from which the citizens will be saved, but also the advantages which they will lose. The life which they are to lead ap- 30 pears to be quite impracticable. The error of Socrates must be attributed to the false notion of unity from which he starts.[21] Unity there should be, both of the family and of the state, but in some respects only. For there is a point at which a state may attain such a degree of unity as to be no longer a state, or at which, without actually ceasing to exist, it will become an inferior state, like har- 35

---

[19] Cp. *Nic. Eth.* iv. 1119[b] 22.          [20] *Rep.* v. 464, 465.
[21] Cp. c. 2.

mony passing into unison, or rhythm which has been reduced to a single foot. The state, as I was saying, is a
plurality,[22] which should be united and made into a community by education; and it is strange that the author of
a system of education which he thinks will make the
state virtuous, should expect to improve his citizens by
40 regulations of this sort, and not by philosophy or by
customs and laws, like those which prevail at Sparta and
1264ᵃ Crete respecting common meals, whereby the legislator
has made property common. Let us remember that we
should not disregard the experience of ages; in the multitude of years these things, if they were good, would
certainly not have been unknown; for almost everything
has been found out, although sometimes they are not put
together; in other cases men do not use the knowledge
5 which they have. Great light would be thrown on this
subject if we could see such a form of government in the
actual process of construction; for the legislator could
not form a state at all without distributing and dividing
its constituents into associations for common meals, and
into phratries and tribes. But all this legislation ends
10 only in forbidding agriculture to the guardians, a prohibition which the Lacedaemonians try to enforce already.

But, indeed, Socrates has not said, nor is it easy to
decide, what in such a community will be the general
form of the state. The citizens who are not guardians are
the majority, and about them nothing has been determined: are the husbandmen, too, to have their property
15 in common? Or is each individual to have his own? and
are the wives and children to be individual or common?
If, like the guardians, they are to have all things in common, in what do they differ from them, or what will they

22 Cp. 1261ᵃ 18.

gain by submitting to their government? Or, upon what
principle would they submit, unless indeed the govern- 20
ing class adopt the ingenious policy of the Cretans, who
give their slaves the same institutions as their own, but
forbid them gymnastic exercises and the possession of
arms. If, on the other hand, the inferior classes are to be
like other cities in respect of marriage and property,
what will be the form of the community? Must it not 25
contain two states in one,[23] each hostile to the other? He
makes the guardians into a mere occupying garrison,
while the husbandmen and artisans and the rest are the
real citizens. But if so the suits and quarrels, and all the
evils which Socrates affirms[24] to exist in other states,
will exist equally among them. He says indeed that, hav- 30
ing so good an education, the citizens will not need many
laws, for example laws about the city or about the mar-
kets;[25] but then he confines his education to the guardians. Again, he makes the husbandmen owners of the
property upon condition of their paying a tribute.[26] But
in that case they are likely to be much more unmanage-
able and conceited than the Helots, or Penestae, or slaves
in general.[27] And whether community of wives and prop- 35
erty be necessary for the lower equally with the higher
class or not, and the questions akin to this, what will be
the education, form of government, laws of the lower
class, Socrates has nowhere determined: neither is it
easy to discover this, nor is their character of small im-
portance if the common life of the guardians is to be 40
maintained.

Again, if Socrates makes the women common, and 1264ᵇ
retains private property, the men will see to the fields,
but who will see to the house? And who will do so if the

---

[23] Cp. *Rep.* iv. 422 E.                    [24] *Rep.* v. 464, 465.
[25] *Rep.* iv. 425 D.          [26] *Rep.* v. 464 C.          [27] Cp. 1269ᵃ 36.

agricultural class have both their property and their
wives in common? Once more: it is absurd to argue,
5 from the analogy of the animals, that men and women
should follow the same pursuits,[28] for animals have not
to manage a household. The government, too, as constituted by Socrates, contains elements of danger; for he
makes the same persons always rule. And if this is often
a cause of disturbance among the meaner sort, how much
10 more among high-spirited warriors? But that the persons
whom he makes rulers must be the same is evident; for
the gold which the God mingles in the souls of men is not
at one time given to one, at another time to another, but
always to the same: as he says, 'God mingles gold in
some, and silver in others, from their very birth; but
15 brass and iron in those who are meant to be artisans and
husbandmen.'[29] Again, he deprives the guardians even
of happiness, and says that the legislator ought to make
the whole state happy.[30] But the whole cannot be happy
unless most, or all, or some of its parts enjoy happiness.[31]
In this respect happiness is not like the even principle in
20 numbers, which may exist only in the whole, but in
neither of the parts; not so happiness. And if the guardians are not happy, who are? Surely not the artisans, or
the common people. The Republic of which Socrates dis-
25 courses has all these difficulties, and others quite as great.

**6** The same, or nearly the same, objections apply to
Plato's later work, the *Laws*, and therefore we had better
examine briefly the constitution which is therein described. In the *Republic*, Socrates has definitely settled
30 in all a few questions only; such as the community of
women and children, the community of property, and

[28] Cp. *Rep.* v. 451 D.                    [29] Cp. *Rep.* iii. 415 A.
[30] *Rep.* iv. 419, 420.                     [31] Cp. vii. 1329ᵃ 23.

the constitution of the state. The population is divided into two classes—one of husbandmen, and the other of warriors;[32] from this latter is taken a third class of counsellors and rulers of the state.[33] But Socrates has not determined whether the husbandmen and artisans are to have a share in the government, and whether they, too, are to carry arms and share in military service, or not. He certainly thinks[34] that the women ought to share in the education of the guardians, and to fight by their side. The remainder of the work is filled up with digressions foreign to the main subject, and with discussions about the education of the guardians. In the *Laws* there is hardly anything but laws; not much is said about the constitution. This, which he had intended to make more of the ordinary type, he gradually brings round to the other or ideal form. For with the exception of the community of women and property, he supposes everything to be the same in both states; there is to be the same education; the citizens of both are to live free from servile occupations, and there are to be common meals in both. The only difference is that in the *Laws,* the common meals are extended to women,[35] and the warriors number 5000,[36] but in the *Republic* only 1000.[37]

The discourses of Socrates are never commonplace; they always exhibit grace and originality and thought; but perfection in everything can hardly be expected. We must not overlook the fact that the number of 5000 citizens, just now mentioned, will require a territory as large as Babylon, or some other huge site, if so many persons are to be supported in idleness, together with their women and attendants, who will be a multitude many

---

[32] *Rep.* ii. 373 E.  [33] *Rep.* iii. 412 B.  [34] *Rep.* v. 451 E.
[35] *Laws*, vi. 780 E.  [36] *Laws*, v. 737 E.  [37] *Rep.* iv. 423 A.

times as great. In framing an ideal we may assume what we wish, but should avoid impossibilities.[38]

20 It is said that the legislator ought to have his eye directed to two points—the people and the country.[39] But neighbouring countries also must not be forgotten by him,[40] firstly because the state for which he legislates is to have a political and not an isolated life.[41] For a state must have such a military force as will be serviceable 25 against her neighbours, and not merely useful at home. Even if the life of action is not admitted to be the best, either for individuals or states,[42] still a city should be formidable to enemies, whether invading or retreating.

There is another point: Should not the amount of property be defined in some way which differs from this by being clearer? For Socrates says that a man should have so much property as will enable him to live tem-30 perately,[43] which is only a way of saying 'to live well'; this is too general a conception. Further, a man may live temperately and yet miserably. A better definition would be that a man must have so much property as will enable him to live not only temperately but liberally;[44] if the two are parted, liberality will combine with luxury; temperance will be associated with toil. For liberality and temperance are the only eligible qualities which have to 35 do with the use of property. A man cannot use property with mildness or courage, but temperately and liberally he may; and therefore the practice of these virtues is inseparable from property. There is an inconsistency, too, in equalizing the property and not regulating the number of the citizens;[45] the population is to remain unlim-

---

[38] Cp. vii. 1325[b] 38.  [39] Perhaps *Laws*, iv. 704–709, and v. 747 D.
[40] Cp. 1267[a] 19.  [41] Cp. vii. 1327[a] 41.
[42] Cp. vii. c. 2. and 3.  [43] *Laws*, v. 737 D.
[44] Cp. vii. 1326[b] 30.  [45] But see *Laws*, v. 740 B–741 A.

ited, and he thinks that it will be sufficiently equalized 40
by a certain number of marriages being unfruitful, how- 1265ᵉ
ever many are born to others, because he finds this to be
the case in existing states. But greater care will be required than now; for among ourselves, whatever may be
the number of citizens, the property is always distributed
among them, and therefore no one is in want; but, if the
property were incapable of division as in the *Laws,* the 5
supernumeraries, whether few or many, would get nothing. One would have thought that it was even more necessary to limit population than property; and that the
limit should be fixed by calculating the chances of mor-
tality in the children, and of sterility in married persons.
The neglect of this subject, which in existing states is so 10
common, is a never-failing cause of poverty among the
citizens; and poverty is the parent of revolution and
crime. Pheidon the Corinthian, who was one of the most
ancient legislators, thought that the families and the
number of citizens ought to remain the same, although 15
originally all the lots may have been of different sizes:
but in the *Laws* the opposite principle is maintained.
What in our opinion is the right arrangement will have
to be explained hereafter.[46]

There is another omission in the *Laws*: Socrates does
not tell us how the rulers differ from their subjects; he
only says that they should be related as the warp and the 20
woof, which are made out of different wools.[47] He allows
that a man's whole property may be increased fivefold,[48]
but why should not his land also increase to a certain
extent? Again, will the good management of a household
be promoted by his arrangement of homesteads? For he 25

---

[46] Cp. vii. 1326ᵇ 26–32, 1330ᵃ 9–18, 1335ᵇ 19–26; but the promise is
hardly fulfilled

[47] *Laws,* v. 734 ᴇ, 735 ᴀ.                    [48] *Laws,* v. 744 ᴇ.

assigns to each individual two homesteads in separate places,[49] and it is difficult to live in two houses.

The whole system of government tends to be neither democracy nor oligarchy, but something in a mean between them, which is usually called a polity, and is composed of the heavy-armed soldiers. Now, if he intended to frame a constitution which would suit the greatest number of states, he was very likely right, but not if he meant to say that this constitutional form came nearest to his first or ideal state; for many would prefer the Lacedaemonian, or, possibly, some other more aristocratic government. Some, indeed, say that the best constitution is a combination of all existing forms, and they praise the Lacedaemonian[50] because it is made up of oligarchy, monarchy, and democracy, the king forming the monarchy, and the council of elders the oligarchy, while the democratic element is represented by the Ephors; for the Ephors are selected from the people. Others, however, declare the Ephoralty to be a tyranny, and find the element of democracy in the common meals and in the habits of daily life. In the *Laws*[51] it is maintained that the best constitution is made up of democracy and tyranny, which are either not constitutions at all, or are the worst of all. But they are nearer the truth who combine many forms; for the constitution is better which is made up of more numerous elements. The constitution proposed in the *Laws* has no element of monarchy at all; it is nothing but oligarchy and democracy, leaning rather to oligarchy. This is seen in the mode of appointing magistrates;[52] for although the appointment of them by lot from among those who have been already selected

---

49 *Laws*, v. 745 c, but Cp. infra. vii. 1330ᵃ 9–18.

50 Cp. iv. 1293ᵇ 16, 1294ᵇ 18–34.

51 iii. 693 D, 701 E, iv. 710, vi. 756 E.     52 *Laws*, vi. 756, 763 E, 765.

combines both elements, the way in which the rich are 10
compelled by law to attend the assembly [53] and vote for
magistrates or discharge other political duties, while the
rest may do as they like, and the endeavour [54] to have
the greater number of the magistrates appointed out of
the richer classes and the highest officers selected from
those who have the greatest incomes, both these are
oligarchical features. The oligarchical principle prevails
also in the choice of the council,[55] for all are compelled 15
to choose, but the compulsion extends only to the choice
out of the first class, and of an equal number out of the
second class and out of the third class, but not in this
latter case to all the voters but to those of the first three
classes: and the selection of candidates out of the fourth
class is only compulsory on the first and second. Then,
from the persons so chosen, he says that there ought to
be an equal number of each class selected. Thus a pre- 20
ponderance will be given to the better sort of people, who
have the larger incomes, because many of the lower
classes, not being compelled, will not vote. These considerations, and others which will be adduced [56] when the 25
time comes for examining similar polities, tend to show
that states like Plato's should not be composed of democracy and monarchy. There is also a danger in electing the
magistrates out of a body who are themselves elected; [57]
for, if but a small number choose to combine, the elections will always go as they desire. Such is the constitu- 3
tion which is described in the *Laws*.

**7** Other constitutions have been proposed; some by
private persons, others by philosophers and statesmen,

---

[53] *Laws*, vi. 764 A; and *Pol.* iv. 1294$^a$ 37, 1298$^b$ 16.
[54] *Laws*, vi. 763 D E.                    [55] *Laws*, vi. 756 B–E.
[56] iv. 7–9, 12. 1296$^b$ 34–38, 1297$^a$ 7–13.          [57] *Laws*, vi. 753 D

which all come nearer to established or existing ones than
either of Plato's. No one else has introduced such novel-
85 ties as the community of women and children, or public
tables for women: other legislators begin with what is
necessary. In the opinion of some, the regulation of property is the chief point of all, that being the question upon
which all revolutions turn. This danger was recognized
by Phaleas of Chalcedon, who was the first to affirm that
the citizens of a state ought to have equal possessions.
40 He thought that in a new colony the equalization might
1266ᵇ be accomplished without difficulty, not so easily when a
state was already established; and that then the shortest
way of compassing the desired end would be for the rich
to give and not to receive marriage portions, and for the
poor not to give but to receive them.
5     Plato in the *Laws* ⁵⁸ was of opinion that, to a certain
extent, accumulation should be allowed, forbidding, as I
have already observed,⁵⁹ any citizen to possess more than
five times the minimum qualification. But those who
make such laws should remember what they are apt to
forget ⁶⁰—that the legislator who fixes the amount of
10 property should also fix the number of children; for, if
the children are too many for the property, the law must
be broken. And, besides the violation of the law, it is a
bad thing that many from being rich should become
poor; for men of ruined fortunes are sure to stir up revolutions. That the equalization of property exercises an
15 influence on political society was clearly understood even
by some of the old legislators. Laws were made by Solon
and others prohibiting an individual from possessing as
much land as he pleased; and there are other laws in
states which forbid the sale of property: among the
20 Locrians, for example, there is a law that a man is not

⁵⁸ v. 744 E.          ⁵⁹ 1265ᵇ 21.          ⁶⁰ Cp. 1265ᵃ 38–ᵇ 16.

to sell his property unless he can prove unmistakably that some misfortune has befallen him. Again, there have been laws which enjoin the preservation of the original lots. Such a law existed in the island of Leucas, and the abrogation of it made the constitution too democratic, for the rulers no longer had the prescribed qualification. Again, where there is equality of property, the amount may be either too large or too small, and the possessor 25 may be living either in luxury or penury. Clearly, then, the legislator ought not only to aim at the equalization of properties, but at moderation in their amount. Further, if he prescribe this moderate amount equally to all, he will be no nearer the mark; for it is not the possessions but the desires of mankind which require to be equalized,[61] and this is impossible, unless a sufficient educa- 30 tion is provided by the laws. But Phaleas will probably reply that this is precisely what he means; and that, in his opinion, there ought to be in states, not only equal property, but equal education. Still he should tell precisely what he means; and that, in his opinion, there ought to be in having one and the same for all, if it is of 35 a sort that predisposes men to avarice, or ambition, or both. Moreover, civil troubles arise, not only out of the inequality of property, but out of the inequality of honour, though in opposite ways. For the common people 40 quarrel about the inequality of property, the higher class 1267ᵃ about the equality of honour; as the poet says—

'The bad and good alike in honour share.'[62]

There are crimes of which the motive is want; and for these Phaleas expects to find a cure in the equalization of property, which will take away from a man the temptation to be a highwayman, because he is hungry or cold.

[61] Cp. 1263ᵇ 22.                                          [62] *Il.* ix. 319.

5 But want is not the sole incentive to crime; men also
wish to enjoy themselves and not to be in a state of desire
—they wish to cure some desire, going beyond the necessities of life, which preys upon them; nay, this is not the
only reason—they may desire superfluities in order to
enjoy pleasures unaccompanied with pain, and therefore
they commit crimes.

Now what is the cure of these three disorders? Of the
first, moderate possessions and occupation; of the sec-
10 ond, habits of temperance; as to the third, if any desire
pleasures which depend on themselves, they will find the
satisfaction of their desires nowhere but in philosophy;
for all other pleasures we are dependent on others. The
fact is that the greatest crimes are caused by excess and
not by necessity. Men do not become tyrants in order
that they may not suffer cold; and hence great is the
15 honour bestowed, not on him who kills a thief, but on him
who kills a tyrant. Thus we see that the institutions of
Phaleas avail only against petty crimes.

There is another objection to them. They are chiefly
designed to promote the internal welfare of the state.
But the legislator should consider also its relation to
neighbouring nations, and to all who are outside of it.[63]
20 The government must be organized with a view to military strength; and of this he has said not a word. And so
with respect to property: there should not only be enough
to supply the internal wants of the state, but also to meet
dangers coming from without. The property of the state
25 should not be so large that more powerful neighbours
may be tempted by it, while the owners are unable to
repel the invaders; nor yet so small that the state is unable to maintain a war even against states of equal power,
and of the same character. Phaleas has not laid down any

[63] Cp. 1265[a] 20.

rule; but we should bear in mind that abundance of wealth is an advantage. The best limit will probably be, that a more powerful neighbour must have no inducement to go to war with you by reason of the excess of 30 your wealth, but only such as he would have had if you had possessed less. There is a story that Eubulus, when Autophradates was going to besiege Atarneus, told him to consider how long the operation would take, and then reckon up the cost which would be incurred in the time. 'For', said he, 'I am willing for a smaller sum than that to leave Atarneus at once'. These words of Eubulus 35 made an impression on Autophradates, and he desisted from the siege.

The equalization of property is one of the things that tend to prevent the citizens from quarrelling. Not that the gain in this direction is very great. For the nobles will be dissatisfied because they think themselves worthy of more than an equal share of honours; and this is often 40 found to be a cause of sedition and revolution.[64] And the avarice of mankind is insatiable; at one time two obols 1267ᵇ was pay enough; but now, when this sum has become customary, men always want more and more without end; for it is of the nature of desire not to be satisfied, and most men live only for the gratification of it. The 5 beginning of reform is not so much to equalize property as to train the nobler sort of natures not to desire more, and to prevent the lower from getting more; that is to say, they must be kept down, but not ill-treated. Besides, the equalization proposed by Phaleas is imperfect; for 10 he only equalizes land, whereas a man may be rich also in slaves, and cattle, and money, and in the abundance of what are called his movables. Now either all these things must be equalized, or some limit must be imposed

64 Cp. l. 1.

on them, or they must all be let alone. It would appear
15 that Phaleas is legislating for a small city only, if, as he
supposes, all the artisans are to be public slaves and not
to form a supplementary part of the body of citizens. But
if there is a law that artisans are to be public slaves, it
should only apply to those engaged on public works, as at
Epidamnus, or at Athens on the plan which Diophantus
once introduced.

20     From these observations any one may judge how far
Phaleas was wrong or right in his ideas.

**8** Hippodamus, the son of Euryphon, a native of Miletus, the same who invented the art of planning cities, and
who also laid out the Piraeus—a strange man, whose
fondness for distinction led him into a general eccen-
25 tricity of life, which made some think him affected (for
he would wear flowing hair and expensive ornaments;
but these were worn on a cheap but warm garment both
in winter and summer); he, besides aspiring to be an
adept in the knowledge of nature, was the first person
not a statesman who made inquiries about the best form
of government.

30     The city of Hippodamus was composed of 10,000 citizens divided into three parts—one of artisans, one of
husbandmen, and a third of armed defenders of the state.
He also divided the land into three parts, one sacred, one
public, the third private:—the first was set apart to
maintain the customary worship of the gods, the second
was to support the warriors, the third was the property
35 of the husbandmen. He also divided laws into three
classes, and no more, for he maintained that there are
three subjects of lawsuits—insult, injury, and homicide.
He likewise instituted a single final court of appeal, to
40 which all causes seeming to have been improperly de-

cided might be referred; this court he formed of elders
chosen for the purpose. He was further of opinion that 126ᴀ
the decisions of the courts ought not to be given by the
use of a voting pebble, but that every one should have
a tablet on which he might not only write a simple condemnation, or leave the tablet blank for a simple acquittal; but, if he partly acquitted and partly condemned, he
was to distinguish accordingly. To the existing law he 5
objected that it obliged the judges to be guilty of perjury, whichever way they voted. He also enacted that
those who discovered anything for the good of the state
should be honoured; and he provided that the children
of citizens who died in battle should be maintained at the
public expense, as if such an enactment had never been
heard of before, yet it actually exists at Athens and in 10
other places. As to the magistrates, he would have them
all elected by the people, that is, by the three classes already mentioned, and those who were elected were to
watch over the interests of the public, of strangers, and
of orphans. These are the most striking points in the
constitution of Hippodamus. There is not much else.    15

The first of these proposals to which objection may be
taken is the threefold division of the citizens. The artisans, and the husbandmen, and the warriors, all have a
share in the government. But the husbandmen have no
arms, and the artisans neither arms nor land, and therefore they become all but slaves of the warrior class. That
they should share in all the offices is an impossibility; 20
for generals and guardians of the citizens, and nearly all
the principal magistrates, must be taken from the class
of those who carry arms. Yet, if the two other classes
have no share in the government, how can they be loyal
citizens? It may be said that those who have arms must 25
necessarily be masters of both the other classes, but this

is not so easily accomplished unless they are numerous; and if they are, why should the other classes share in the government at all, or have power to appoint magistrates?
30 Further, what use are farmers to the city? Artisans there must be, for these are wanted in every city, and they can live by their craft, as elsewhere; and the husbandmen, too, if they really provided the warriors with food, might fairly have a share in the government. But in the republic of Hippodamus they are supposed to have land of their
35 own, which they cultivate for their private benefit. Again, as to this common land out of which the soldiers are maintained, if they are themselves to be the cultivators of it, the warrior class will be identical with the husbandmen, although the legislator intended to make a distinction between them. If, again, there are to be other cultivators distinct both from the husbandmen, who have land of their own, and from the warriors, they will make a fourth class, which has no place in the state and no
40 share in anything. Or, if the same persons are to cultivate their own lands, and those of the public as well, they will have a difficulty in supplying the quantity of produce
1268$^b$ which will maintain two households: and why, in this case, should there be any division, for they might find food themselves and give to the warriors from the same land and the same lots? There is surely a great confusion in all this.

5 Neither is the law to be commended which says that the judges, when a simple issue is laid before them, should distinguish in their judgement; for the judge is thus converted into an arbitrator. Now, in an arbitration, although the arbitrators are many, they confer with one another about the decision, and therefore they can distinguish;
10 but in courts of law this is impossible, and, indeed, most legislators take pains to prevent the judges

from holding any communication with one another. Again, will there not be confusion if the judge thinks that damages should be given, but not so much as the suitor demands? He asks, say, for twenty minae, and the judge allows him ten minae (or in general the suitor asks for more and the judge allows less), while another judge allows five, another four minae. In this way they will go 15 on splitting up the damages, and some will grant the whole and others nothing: how is the final reckoning to be taken? Again, no one contends that he who votes for a simple acquittal or condemnation perjures himself, if the indictment has been laid in an unqualified form; and this is just, for the judge who acquits does not decide 20 that the defendant owes nothing, but that he does not owe the twenty minae. He only is guilty of perjury who thinks that the defendant ought not to pay twenty minae, and yet condemns him.

To honour those who discover anything which is useful to the state is a proposal which has a specious sound, but cannot safely be enacted by law, for it may encourage informers, and perhaps even lead to political commotions. This question involves another. It has been 25 doubted whether it is or is not expedient to make any changes in the laws of a country, even if another law be better. Now, if all changes are inexpedient, we can hardly assent to the proposal of Hippodamus; for, under pretence of doing a public service, a man may introduce 30 measures which are really destructive to the laws or to the constitution. But, since we have touched upon this subject, perhaps we had better go a little into detail, for, as I was saying, there is a difference of opinion, and it may sometimes seem desirable to make changes. Such changes in the other arts and sciences have certainly been 35 beneficial; medicine, for example, and gymnastic, and

every other art and craft have departed from traditional usage. And, if politics be an art, change must be necessary in this as in any other art. That improvement has occurred is shown by the fact that old customs are ex-
40 ceedingly simple and barbarous. For the ancient Hellenes went about armed and bought their brides of each other. The remains of ancient laws which have come down to 1269ª us are quite absurd; for example, at Cumae there is a law about murder, to the effect that if the accuser produce a certain number of witnesses from among his own kinsmen, the accused shall be held guilty. Again, men in general desire the good, and not merely what their fathers had. But the primeval inhabitants, whether they
5 were born of the earth or were the survivors of some destruction, may be supposed to have been no better than ordinary or even foolish people among ourselves (such is certainly the tradition[65] concerning the earth-born men); and it would be ridiculous to rest contented with their notions. Even when laws have been written down, they ought not always to remain unaltered. As in other
10 sciences, so in politics, it is impossible that all things should be precisely set down in writing; for enactments must be universal, but actions are concerned with particulars.[66] Hence we infer that sometimes and in certain cases laws may be changed; but when we look at the matter from another point of view, great caution would
15 seem to be required. For the habit of lightly changing the laws is an evil, and, when the advantage is small, some errors both of lawgivers and rulers had better be left; the citizen will not gain so much by making the change as he will lose by the habit of disobedience. The analogy of the arts[67] is false; a change in a law is a very different

---

[65] Cp. Plato, *Laws*, iii. 677 B; *Polit.* 274 C; *Tim.* 22 D.
[66] Cp. Plato, *Polit.* 295 A.      [67] 1268ᵇ 34 sqq.

thing from a change in an art. For the law has no power 2r
to command obedience except that of habit, which can
only be given by time, so that a readiness to change from
old to new laws enfeebles the power of the law. Even if
we admit that the laws are to be changed, are they all to
be changed, and in every state? And are they to be 25
changed by anybody who likes, or only by certain persons? These are very important questions; and therefore we had better reserve the discussion of them to a
more suitable occasion. [68]

**9** In the governments of Lacedaemon and Crete, and
indeed in all governments, two points have to be consid- 30
ered first, whether any particular law is good or bad,
when compared with the perfect state; secondly, whether
it is or is not consistent with the idea and character which
the lawgiver has set before his citizens. That in a well-
ordered state the citizens should have leisure and not
have to provide for their daily wants is generally ac- 35
knowledged, but there is a difficulty in seeing how this
leisure is to be attained. The Thessalian Penestae have
often risen against their masters, and the Helots in like
manner against the Lacedaemonians, for whose misfortunes they are always lying in wait. Nothing, however,
of this kind has as yet happened to the Cretans; the reason probably is that the neighbouring cities, even when 40
at war with one another, never form an alliance with 1269ᵇ
rebellious serfs, rebellions not being for their interest,
since they themselves have a dependent population. [69]
Whereas all the neighbours of the Lacedaemonians,
whether Argives, Messenians, or Arcadians, were their
enemies. In Thessaly, again, the original revolt of the 5

[68] These questions are not actually discussed in the *Politics*.
[69] Cp. 1271ᵇ 41.

slaves occurred because the Thessalians were still at war
with the neighbouring Achaeans, Perrhaebians and Magnesians. Besides, if there were no other difficulty, the
treatment or management of slaves is a troublesome affair; for, if not kept in hand, they are insolent, and think
10 that they are as good as their masters, and, if harshly
treated, they hate and conspire against them. Now it is
clear that when these are the results the citizens of a state
have not found out the secret of managing their subject
population.

Again, the licence of the Lacedaemonian women defeats the intention of the Spartan constitution, and is
15 adverse to the happiness of the state. For, a husband and
a wife being each a part of every family, the state may
be considered as about equally divided into men and
women; and, therefore, in those states in which the condition of the women is bad, half the city [70] may be regarded as having no laws. And this is what has actually
happened at Sparta; the legislator wanted to make the
20 whole state hardy and temperate, and he has carried out
his intention in the case of the men, but he has neglected
the women, who live in every sort of intemperance and
luxury. The consequence is that in such a state wealth
is too highly valued, especially if the citizens fall under
25 the dominion of their wives, after the manner of most
warlike races, except the Celts and a few others who
openly approve of male loves. The old mythologer would
seem to have been right in uniting Ares and Aphrodite,
for all warlike races are prone to the love either of men
30 or of women. This was exemplified among the Spartans
in the days of their greatness; many things were man-
aged by their women. But what difference does it make
whether women rule, or the rulers are ruled by women?

[70] Cp. i. 1260[b] 18.

The result is the same. Even in regard to courage, which
is of no use in daily life, and is needed only in war, the 35
influence of the Lacedaemonian women has been most
mischievous. The evil showed itself in the Theban invasion, when, unlike the women in other cities, they were
utterly useless and caused more confusion than the
enemy. This licence of the Lacedaemonian women existed from the earliest times, and was only what might be 40
expected. For, during the wars of the Lacedaemonians, 1270ᵃ
first against the Argives, and afterwards against the Arcadians and Messenians, the men were long away from
home, and, on the return of peace, they gave themselves
into the legislator's hand, already prepared by the dis- 5
cipline of a soldier's life (in which there are many elements of virtue), to receive his enactments. But, when
Lycurgus, as tradition says, wanted to bring the women
under his laws, they resisted, and he gave up the attempt.
These then are the causes of what then happened, and
this defect in the constitution is clearly to be attributed
to them. We are not, however, considering what is or is 10
not to be excused, but what is right or wrong, and the
disorder of the women, as I have already said,[71] not only
gives an air of indecorum to the constitution considered
in itself, but tends in a measure to foster avarice.

The mention of avarice naturally suggests a criticism 15
on the inequality of property. While some of the Spartan
citizens have quite small properties, others have very
large ones; hence the land has passed into the hands of a
few. And this is due also to faulty laws; for, although the
legislator rightly holds up to shame the sale or purchase 20
of an inheritance, he allows anybody who likes to give
or bequeath it. Yet both practices lead to the same result. And nearly two-fifths of the whole country are held

[71] 1269ᵇ 12, 23.

by women; this is owing to the number of heiresses and
25 to the large dowries which are customary. It would surely
have been better to have given no dowries at all, or, if
any, but small or moderate ones. As the law now stands,
a man may bestow his heiress on any one whom he
pleases, and, if he die intestate, the privilege of giving
her away descends to his heir.[72] Hence, although the
30 country is able to maintain 1500 cavalry and 30,000 hop-
lites, the whole number of Spartan citizens[73] fell below
1000. The result proves the faulty nature of their laws
respecting property; for the city sank under a single defeat; the want of men was their ruin. There is a tradition
that, in the days of their ancient kings, they were in the
35 habit of giving the rights of citizenship to strangers, and
therefore, in spite of their long wars, no lack of population was experienced by them; indeed, at one time Sparta
is said to have numbered not less than 10,000 citizens.
Whether this statement is true or not, it would certainly
have been better to have maintained their numbers by
the equalization of property. Again, the law which relates
40 to the procreation of children is adverse to the correction
1270ᵇ of this inequality. For the legislator, wanting to have as
many Spartans as he could, encouraged the citizens to
have large families; and there is a law at Sparta that the
father of three sons shall be exempt from military service, and he who has four from all the burdens of the state.
5 Yet it is obvious that, if there were many children, the
land being distributed as it is, many of them must necessarily fall into poverty.

The Lacedaemonian constitution is defective in another point; I mean the Ephoralty. This magistracy has
authority in the highest matters, but the Ephors are

---

[72] i. e. to the person who 'inherits' the heiress.
[73] At the time of the Theban invasion.

chosen from the whole people, and so the office is apt to
fall into the hands of very poor men, who, being badly 10
off, are open to bribes. There have been many examples
at Sparta of this evil in former times; and quite recently,
in the matter of the Andrians, certain of the Ephors who
were bribed did their best to ruin the state. And so great
and tyrannical is their power, that even the kings have
been compelled to court them, so that, in this way as well, 15
together with the royal office, the whole constitution has
deteriorated, and from being an aristocracy has turned
into a democracy. The Ephoralty certainly does keep
the state together; for the people are contented when
they have a share in the highest office, and the result,
whether due to the legislator or to chance, has been advantageous. For if a constitution is to be permanent, all 20
the parts of the state must wish that it should exist and
the same arrangements be maintained. This is the case
at Sparta, where the kings desire its permanence because
they have due honour in their own persons; the nobles
because they are represented in the council of elders (for
the office of elder is a reward of virtue); and the people, 25
because all are eligible to the Ephoralty. The election of
Ephors out of the whole people is perfectly right, but
ought not to be carried on in the present fashion, which
is too childish. Again, they have the decision of great
causes, although they are quite ordinary men, and therefore they should not determine them merely on their own
judgement, but according to written rules, and to the 30
laws. Their way of life, too, is not in accordance with
the spirit of the constitution—they have a deal too much
licence; whereas, in the case of the other citizens, the excess of strictness is so intolerable that they run away from
the law into the secret indulgence of sensual pleasures.

35    Again, the council of elders is not free from defects.
It may be said that the elders are good men and well
trained in manly virtue; and that, therefore, there is an
advantage to the state in having them. But that judges
of important causes should hold office for life is a dis-
40 putable thing, for the mind grows old as well as the body.
1271ᵃ And when men have been educated in such a manner that
even the legislator himself cannot trust them, there is
real danger. Many of the elders are well known to have
taken bribes and to have been guilty of partiality in
5 public affairs. And therefore they ought not to be irre-
sponsible; yet at Sparta they are so. But (it may be replied), 'All magistracies are accountable to the Ephors.'
Yes, but this prerogative is too great for them, and we
maintain that the control should be exercised in some
other manner. Further, the mode in which the Spartans
10 elect their elders is childish; and it is improper that the
person to be elected should canvass for the office; the
worthiest should be appointed, whether he chooses or not.
And here the legislator clearly indicates the same intention which appears in other parts of his constitution; he
would have his citizens ambitious, and he has reckoned
15 upon this quality in the election of the elders; for no one
would ask to be elected if he were not. Yet ambition and
avarice, almost more than any other passions, are the
motives of crime.

Whether kings are or are not an advantage to states,
20 I will consider at another time [74]; they should at any rate
be chosen, not as they are now, but with regard to their
personal life and conduct. The legislator himself obviously did not suppose that he could make them really
good men; at least he shows a great distrust of their vir-
25 tue. For this reason the Spartans used to join enemies

[74] iii. 14–17.

with them in the same embassy, and the quarrels between
the kings were held to be conservative of the state.

Neither did the first introducer of the common meals,
called 'phiditia', regulate them well. The entertainment
ought to have been provided at the public cost, as in
Crete[75]; but among the Lacedaemonians every one is
expected to contribute, and some of them are too poor to 30
afford the expense; thus the intention of the legislator is
frustrated. The common meals were meant to be a popular institution, but the existing manner of regulating
them is the reverse of popular. For the very poor can
scarcely take part in them; and, according to ancient 35
custom, those who cannot contribute are not allowed to
retain their rights of citizenship.

The law about the Spartan admirals has often been
censured, and with justice; it is a source of dissension,
for the kings are perpetual generals, and this office of 40
admiral is but the setting up of another king.

The charge which Plato brings, in the *Laws*,[76] against 1271ᵇ
the intention of the legislator, is likewise justified; the
whole constitution has regard to one part of virtue only—
the virtue of the soldier, which gives victory in war. So
long as they were at war, therefore, their power was preserved, but when they had attained empire they fell,[77] 5
for of the arts of peace they knew nothing, and had never
engaged in any employment higher than war. There is
another error, equally great, into which they have fallen.
Although they truly think that the goods for which men
contend are to be acquired by virtue rather than by vice,
they err in supposing that these goods are to be preferred
to the virtue which gains them.

Once more: the revenues of the state are ill-managed; 10

[75] Cp. 1272ᵃ 13–21.        [76] *Laws*, i. 625 ᴇ, 630.
[77] Cp. vii. 1334ᵃ 6.

there is no money in the treasury, although they are obliged to carry on great wars, and they are unwilling to pay taxes. The greater part of the land being in the hands of the Spartans, they do not look closely into one 15 another's contributions. The result which the legislator has produced is the reverse of beneficial; for he has made his city poor, and his citizens greedy.

Enough respecting the Spartan constitution, of which these are the principal defects.

20 **10** The Cretan constitution nearly resembles the Spartan, and in some few points is quite as good; but for the most part less perfect in form. The older constitutions are generally less elaborate than the later, and the Lacedaemonian is said to be, and probably is, in a very great measure, a copy of the Cretan. According to tradition, 25 Lycurgus, when he ceased to be the guardian of King Charillus, went abroad and spent most of his time in Crete. For the two countries are nearly connected; the Lyctians are a colony of the Lacedaemonians, and the colonists, when they came to Crete, adopted the constitution which they found existing among the inhabitants. 30 Even to this day the Perioeci, or subject population of Crete, are governed by the original laws which Minos is supposed to have enacted. The island seems to be intended by nature for dominion in Hellas, and to be well situated; it extends right across the sea, around which nearly all the Hellenes are settled; and while one end is 35 not far from the Peloponnese, the other almost reaches to the region of Asia about Triopium and Rhodes. Hence Minos acquired the empire of the sea, subduing some of the islands and colonizing others; at last he invaded Sicily, where he died near Camicus.

The Cretan institutions resemble the Lacedaemonian.

The Helots are the husbandmen of the one, the Perioeci 40
of the other, and both Cretans and Lacedaemonians have
common meals, which were anciently called by the Lace- 1272ᵇ
daemonians not 'phiditia' but 'andria'; and the Cretans
have the same word, the use of which proves that the
common meals originally came from Crete. Further, the
two constitutions are similar; for the office of the Ephors 5
is the same as that of the Cretan Cosmi, the only difference being that whereas the Ephors are five, the Cosmi
are ten in number. The elders, too, answer to the elders
in Crete, who are termed by the Cretans the council.
And the kingly office once existed in Crete, but was abol-
ished, and the Cosmi have now the duty of leading them
in war. All classes share in the ecclesia, but it can only 10
ratify the decrees of the elders and the Cosmi.

The common meals of Crete are certainly better man-
aged than the Lacedaemonian; for in Lacedaemon every
one pays so much per head, or, if he fails, the law, as I 15
have already explained,[78] forbids him to exercise the
rights of citizenship. But in Crete they are of a more
popular character. There, of all the fruits of the earth
and cattle raised on the public lands, and of the tribute
which is paid by the Perioeci, one portion is assigned to
the gods and to the service of the state, and another to
the common meals, so that men, women, and children are 20
all supported out of a common stock.[79] The legislator has
many ingenious ways of securing moderation in eating,
which he conceives to be a gain; he likewise encourages
the separation of men from women, lest they should have
too many children, and the companionship of men with
one another—whether this is a good or bad thing I shall 25
have an opportunity of considering at another time.[80]

---

[78] 1271ᵃ 35.                    [79] Cp. vii. 1330ᵃ 5.
[80] The question is nowhere discussed by Aristotle.

But that the Cretan common meals are better ordered than the Lacedaemonian there can be no doubt.

On the other hand, the Cosmi are even a worse institution than the Ephors, of which they have all the evils 30 without the good. Like the Ephors, they are any chance persons, but in Crete this is not counterbalanced by a corresponding political advantage. At Sparta every one is eligible, and the body of the people, having a share in the highest office, want the constitution to be permanent.[81] But in Crete the Cosmi are elected out of certain families, and not out of the whole people, and the elders out of those who have been Cosmi.

35 The same criticism may be made about the Cretan, which has been already made about the Lacedaemonian elders.[82] Their irresponsibility and life tenure is too great a privilege, and their arbitrary power of acting upon their own judgement, and dispensing with written law, is dangerous. It is no proof of the goodness of the institution 40 that the people are not discontented at being excluded from it. For there is no profit to be made out of the office 1272b as out of the Ephoralty, since, unlike the Ephors, the Cosmi, being in an island, are removed from temptation.

The remedy by which they correct the evil of this institution is an extraordinary one, suited rather to a close oligarchy than to a constitutional state. For the Cosmi are often expelled by a conspiracy of their own colleagues, or of private individuals; and they are allowed also to resign before their term of office has expired. Surely all matters of this kind are better regulated by 5 law than by the will of man, which is a very unsafe rule. Worst of all is the suspension of the office of Cosmi, a device to which the nobles often have recourse when they will not submit to justice. This shows that the Cretan

[81] Cp. *supra,* 1270b 25.          [82] 1270b 35–1271a 18.

government, although possessing some of the characteris- 10
tics of a constitutional state, is really a close oligarchy.

The nobles have a habit, too, of setting up a chief; they
get together a party among the common people and their
own friends and then quarrel and fight with one another.
What is this but the temporary destruction of the state
and dissolution of society? A city is in a dangerous con- 15
dition when those who are willing are also able to attack
her. But, as I have already said,[83] the island of Crete is
saved by her situation; distance has the same effect as
the Lacedaemonian prohibition of strangers; and the
Cretans have no foreign dominions. This is the reason
why the Perioeci are contented in Crete, whereas the
Helots are perpetually revolting. But when lately foreign 20
invaders found their way into the island, the weakness of
the Cretan constitution was revealed. Enough of the
government of Crete.

**11**   The Carthaginians are also considered to have an
excellent form of government, which differs from that of
any other state in several respects, though it is in some
very like the Lacedaemonian. Indeed, all three states— 25
the Lacedaemonian, the Cretan, and the Carthaginian
—nearly resemble one another, and are very different
from any others. Many of the Carthaginian institutions
are excellent. The superiority of their constitution is
proved by the fact that the common people remain 30
loyal to the constitution; the Carthaginians have never
had any rebellion worth speaking of, and have never
been under the rule of a tyrant.

Among the points in which the Carthaginian constitution resembles the Lacedaemonian are the following:--
The common tables of the clubs answer to the Spartan

[83] ᵃ41 sq.

35 phiditia, and their magistracy of the 104 to the Ephors;
but, whereas the Ephors are any chance persons, the
magistrates of the Carthaginians are elected according
to merit—this is an improvement. They have also their
kings and their gerusia, or council of elders, who correspond to the kings and elders of Sparta. Their kings, unlike the Spartan, are not always of the same family, nor
40 that an ordinary one, but if there is some distinguished
family they are selected out of it and not appointed by
1273ᵃ seniority—this is far better. Such officers have great
power, and therefore, if they are persons of little worth,
do a great deal of harm, and they have already done harm
at Lacedaemon.

Most of the defects or deviations from the perfect
state, for which the Carthaginian constitution would be
censured, apply equally to all the forms of government
which we have mentioned. But of the deflections from
5 aristocracy and constitutional government, some incline
more to democracy and some to oligarchy. The kings and
elders, if unanimous, may determine whether they will
or will not bring a matter before the people, but when
they are not unanimous, the people decide on such matters as well. And whatever the kings and elders bring
10 before the people is not only heard but also determined
by them, and any one who likes may oppose it; now this
is not permitted in Sparta and Crete. That the magistracies of five who have under them many important
matters should be co-opted, that they should choose the
15 supreme council of 100, and should hold office longer
than other magistrates (for they are virtually rulers both
before and after they hold office)—these are oligarchical features; their being without salary and not elected
by lot, and any similar points, such as the practice of

having all suits tried by the magistrates,[84] and not some 20
by one class of judges or jurors and some by another, as
at Lacedaemon, are characteristic of aristocracy. The
Carthaginian constitution deviates from aristocracy and
inclines to oligarchy, chiefly on a point where popular
opinion is on their side. For men in general think that
magistrates should be chosen not only for their merit,
but for their wealth: a man, they say, who is poor cannot
rule well—he has not the leisure. If, then, election of
magistrates for their wealth be characteristic of oli- 25
garchy, and election for merit of aristocracy, there will
be a third form under which the constitution of Carthage
is comprehended; for the Carthaginians choose their
magistrates, and particularly the highest of them—their
kings and generals—with an eye both to merit and to 30
wealth.

But we must acknowledge that, in thus deviating from
aristocracy, the legislator has committed an error. Nothing is more absolutely necessary than to provide that the
highest class, not only when in office, but when out of office, should have leisure and not disgrace themselves in
any way; and to this his attention should be first directed.
Even if you must have regard to wealth, in order to se- 35
cure leisure, yet it is surely a bad thing that the greatest
offices, such as those of kings and generals, should be
bought. The law which allows this abuse makes wealth
of more account than virtue, and the whole state becomes
avaricious. For, whenever the chiefs of the state deem
anything honourable, the other citizens are sure to fol- 40
low their example; and, where virtue has not the first 1273[b]
place, their aristocracy cannot be firmly established.
Those who have been at the expense of purchasing their
places will be in the habit of repaying themselves; and

[84] Cp. iii. 1275[b] 8–12.

it is absurd to suppose that a poor and honest man will
be wanting to make gains, and that a lower stamp of man
who has incurred a great expense will not. Wherefore
5 they should rule who are able to rule best. And even if
the legislator does not care to protect the good from
poverty, he should at any rate secure leisure for them
when in office.[85]

It would seem also to be a bad principle that the same
person should hold many offices, which is a favourite
practice among the Carthaginians, for one business is
10 better done by one man.[86] The legislator should see to this
and should not appoint the same person to be a flute-
player and a shoemaker. Hence, where the state is large,
it is more in accordance both with constitutional and
with democratic principles that the offices of state should
be distributed among many persons. For, as I said,[87] this
arrangement is fairer to all, and any action familiarized
by repetition is better and sooner performed. We have a
15 proof in military and naval matters; the duties of command and of obedience in both these services extend
to all.

The government of the Carthaginians is oligarchical,
but they successfully escape the evils of oligarchy by
enriching one portion of the people after another by sending them to their colonies. This is their panacea and the
20 means by which they give stability to the state. Accident
favours them, but the legislator should be able to provide against revolution without trusting to accidents. As
things are, if any misfortune occurred, and the bulk of
the subjects revolted, there would be no way of restoring
peace by legal methods.

25    Such is the character of the Lacedaemonian, Cretan,

---

[85] Cp. 1269[a] 34.        [86] Cp. Plato, *Rep.* ii. 374 A.        [87] 1261[b] 1.

and Carthaginian constitutions, which are justly celebrated.

**12**  Of those who have treated of governments, some
have never taken any part at all in public affairs, but have
passed their lives in a private station; about most of
them, what was worth telling has been already told.[88]
Others have been lawgivers, either in their own or in 30
foreign cities, whose affairs they have administered; and
of these some have only made laws, others have framed
constitutions; for example, Lycurgus and Solon did both.
Of the Lacedaemonian constitution I have already
spoken.[89] As to Solon, he is thought by some to have been 35
a good legislator, who put an end to the exclusiveness of
the oligarchy, emancipated the people, established the
ancient Athenian democracy, and harmonized the different elements of the state. According to their view, the
council of Areopagus was an oligarchical element, the
elected magistracy, aristocratical, and the courts of law, 40
democratical. The truth seems to be that the council and 1274*
the elected magistracy existed before the time of Solon,
and were retained by him, but that he formed the courts
of law out of all the citizens, thus creating the democracy,
which is the very reason why he is sometimes blamed.
For in giving the supreme power to the law courts, which
are elected by lot, he is thought to have destroyed the 5
non-democratic element. When the law courts grew powerful, to please the people who were now playing the
tyrant the old constitution was changed into the existing
democracy. Ephialtes and Pericles curtailed the power
of the Areopagus; Pericles also instituted the payment of
the juries, and thus every demagogue in turn increased 10
the power of the democracy until it became what we now

----

[88] cc. 1–8.                                    [89] c. 9.

see. All this is true; it seems, however, to be the result of
circumstances, and not to have been intended by Solon.
For the people, having been instrumental in gaining the
empire of the sea in the Persian War,[90] began to get a
notion of itself, and followed worthless demagogues,
whom the better class opposed. Solon, himself, appears to
15 have given the Athenians only that power of electing to
offices and calling to account the magistrates which was
absolutely necessary; [91] for without it they would have
been in a state of slavery and enmity to the government.
All the magistrates he appointed from the notables and
the men of wealth, that is to say, from the pentacosio-
20 medimni, or from the class called zeugitae, or from a
third class of so-called knights or cavalry. The fourth
class were labourers who had no share in any magistracy.

Mere legislators were Zaleucus, who gave laws to the
Epizephyrian Locrians, and Charondas, who legislated
for his own city of Catana, and for the other Chalcidian
25 cities in Italy and Sicily. Some people attempt to make
out that Onomacritus was the first person who had any
special skill in legislation, and that he, although a Locrian
by birth, was trained in Crete, where he lived in the
exercise of his prophetic art; that Thales was his companion, and that Lycurgus and Zaleucus were disciples
30 of Thales, as Charondas was of Zaleucus. But their
account is quite inconsistent with chronology.

There was also Philolaus, the Corinthian, who gave
laws to the Thebans. This Philolaus was one of the family of the Bacchiadae, and a lover of Diocles, the Olympic
victor, who left Corinth in horror of the incestuous passion which his mother Halcyone had conceived for him,
35 and retired to Thebes, where the two friends together
ended their days. The inhabitants still point out their

[90] Cp. v. 1304[a] 20, viii. 1341[a] 29.          [91] Cp. iii. 1281[b] 32.

tombs, which are in full view of one another, but one is
visible from the Corinthian territory, the other not. Tradition says the two friends arranged them thus, Diocles
out of horror at his misfortunes, so that the land of 40
Corinth might not be visible from his tomb; Philolaus 1274ᵇ
that it might. This is the reason why they settled at
Thebes, and so Philolaus legislated for the Thebans, and,
besides some other enactments, gave them laws about the
procreation of children, which they call the 'Laws of
Adoption'. These laws were peculiar to him, and were
intended to preserve the number of the lots.

In the legislation of Charondas there is nothing re- 5
markable, except the suits against false witnesses. He
is the first who instituted denunciation for perjury. His
laws are more exact and more precisely expressed than
even those of our modern legislators.

(Characteristic of Phaleas is the equalization of property; of Plato, the community of women, children, and 10
property, the common meals of women, and the law about
drinking, that the sober shall be masters of the feast; [92]
also the training of soldiers to acquire by practice equal
skill with both hands, so that one should be as useful as
the other.) [93]

Draco has left laws, but he adapted them to a constitu- 15
tion which already existed, and there is no peculiarity in
them which is worth mentioning, except the greatness
and severity of the punishments.

Pittacus, too, was only a lawgiver, and not the author
of a constitution; he has a law which is peculiar to him,
that, if a drunken man do something wrong, he shall be 20
more heavily punished than if he were sober; [94] he looked
not to the excuse which might be offered for the drunkard,

[92] Cp. *Laws*, i. 640 ᴅ, ii. 671 ᴅ–672 ᴀ.      [93] Cp. *Laws*, vii. 794 ᴅ.
[94] Cp. *Nic. Eth.* 1113ᵇ 31.

but only to expediency, for drunken more often than sober people commit acts of violence.

Androdamas of Rhegium gave laws to the Chalcidians 25 of Thrace. Some of them relate to homicide, and to heiresses; but there is nothing remarkable in them.

And here let us conclude our inquiry into the various constitutions which either actually exist, or have been devised by theorists.

## BOOK III

**1**  He who would inquire into the essence and attributes
of various kinds of governments must first of all determine 'What is a state?' At present this is a disputed question. Some say that the state has done a certain act;
others, no, not the state,[1] but the oligarchy or the tyrant. 35
And the legislator or statesman is concerned entirely
with the state; a constitution or government being an
arrangement of the inhabitants of a state. But a state is
composite, like any other whole made up of many parts;
—these are the citizens, who compose it. It is evident, 40
therefore, that we must begin by asking, Who is the citi- 1275ᵃ
zen, and what is the meaning of the term? For here again
there may be a difference of opinion. He who is a citizen
in a democracy will often not be a citizen in an oligarchy. 5
Leaving out of consideration those who have been made
citizens, or who have obtained the name of citizen in any
other accidental manner, we may say, first, that a citizen
is not a citizen because he lives in a certain place, for
resident aliens and slaves share in the place; nor is he a
citizen who has no legal right except that of suing and
being sued; for this right may be enjoyed under the pro- 10
visions of a treaty. Nay, resident aliens in many places do
not possess even such rights completely, for they are

<hr>

¹ Cp. 1276ᵃ 8

125

obliged to have a patron, so that they do but imperfectly participate in citizenship, and we call them citizens only in a qualified sense, as we might apply the term to chil-
15 dren who are too young to be on the register, or to old men who have been relieved from state duties. Of these we do not say quite simply that they are citizens, but add in the one case that they are not of age, and in the other, that they are past the age, or something of that
20 sort; the precise expression is immaterial, for our meaning is clear. Similar difficulties to those which I have mentioned may be raised and answered about deprived citizens and about exiles. But the citizen whom we are seeking to define is a citizen in the strictest sense, against whom no such exception can be taken, and his special characteristic is that he shares in the administration of justice, and in offices. Now of offices some are discontinuous, and the same persons are not allowed to hold them
45 twice, or can only hold them after a fixed interval; others have no limit of time—for example, the office of dicast or ecclesiast.[2] It may, indeed, be argued that these are not magistrates at all, and that their functions give them no share in the government. But surely it is ridiculous to say that those who have the supreme power do not govern. Let us not dwell further upon this, which is a purely
30 verbal question; what we want is a common term including both dicast and ecclesiast. Let us, for the sake of distinction, call it 'indefinite office', and we will assume that those who share in such office are citizens. This is the most comprehensive definition of a citizen, and best suits all those who are generally so called.

35 But we must not forget that things of which the underlying principles differ in kind, one of them being first,

---

[2] 'Dicast' = juryman and judge in one: 'ecclesiast' = member of the ecclesia or assembly of the citizens.

another second, another third, have, when regarded in this relation, nothing, or hardly anything, worth mentioning in common. Now we see that governments differ in kind, and that some of them are prior and that others are posterior; those which are faulty or perverted are 1275ᵇ necessarily posterior to those which are perfect. (What we mean by perversion will be hereafter explained.[3]) The citizen then of necessity differs under each form of government; and our definition is best adapted to the citizen 5 of a democracy; but not necessarily to other states. For in some states the people are not acknowledged, nor have they any regular assembly, but only extraordinary ones; and suits are distributed by sections among the magistrates. At Lacedaemon, for instance, the Ephors determine suits about contracts, which they distribute among 10 themselves, while the elders are judges of homicide, and other causes are decided by other magistrates. A similar principle prevails at Carthage;[4] there certain magistrates decide all causes. We may, indeed, modify our definition of the citizen so as to include these states. In them it is the holder of a definite, not of an indefinite 15 office, who legislates and judges, and to some or all such holders of definite offices is reserved the right of deliberating or judging about some things or about all things. The conception of the citizen now begins to clear up.

He who has the power to take part in the deliberative or judicial administration of any state is said by us to be a citizen of that state; and, speaking generally, a state is 20 a body of citizens sufficing for the purposes of life.

**2**  But in practice a citizen is defined to be one of whom both the parents are citizens; others insist on going further back; say to two or three or more ancestors. This is 25

---

[3] Cp. 1279ᵃ 19.                    [4] Cp. ii. 1273ᵃ 19.

a short and practical definition; but there are some who
raise the further question: How this third or fourth an-
cestor came to be a citizen? Gorgias of Leontini, partly
because he was in a difficulty, partly in irony, said—
'Mortars are what is made by the mortar-makers, and the
citizens of Larissa are those who are made by the magistrates; [5] for it is their trade to make Larissaeans.' Yet
30 the question is really simple, for, if according to the definition just given they shared in the government, they
were citizens. This is a better definition than the other.
For the words, 'born of a father or mother who is a citizen', cannot possibly apply to the first inhabitants or
founders of a state.

There is a greater difficulty in the case of those who
35 have been made citizens after a revolution, as by Cleisthenes at Athens after the expulsion of the tyrants, for
he enrolled in tribes many metics, both strangers and
slaves. The doubt in these cases is, not who is, but
1276ᵃ whether he who is ought to be a citizen; and there will
still be a furthering the state, whether a certain act is
or is not an act of the state; for what ought not to be is
what is false. Now, there are some who hold office, and
yet ought not to hold office, whom we describe as ruling,
but ruling unjustly. And the citizen was defined [6] by the
fact of his holding some kind of rule or office—he who
holds a judicial or legislative office fulfils our definition
5 of a citizen. It is evident, therefore, that the citizens
about whom the doubt has arisen must be called citizens.

**3** Whether they ought to be so or not is a question
which is bound up with the previous inquiry.[7] For a par-

---

[5] An untranslatable play upon the word *demiourgos*, which means
either 'a magistrate' or 'an artisan'.

[6] 1275ᵃ 22 sqq.

[7] Cp. 1274ᵇ 34.

allel question is raised respecting the state, whether a certain act is or is not an act of the state; for example, in the transition from an oligarchy or a tyranny to a democracy. In such cases persons refuse to fulfil their contracts or any other obligations, on the ground that the tyrant, and not the state, contracted them; they argue that some constitutions are established by force, and not for the sake of the common good. But this would apply equally to democracies, for they too may be founded on violence, and then the acts of the democracy will be neither more nor less acts of the state in question than those of an oligarchy or of a tyranny. This question runs up into another:—on what principle shall we ever say that the state is the same, or different? It would be a very superficial view which considered only the place and the inhabitants (for the soil and the population may be separated, and some of the inhabitants may live in one place and some in another). This, however, is not a very serious difficulty; we need only remark that the word 'state' is ambiguous.[8]

It is further asked: When are men, living in the same place, to be regarded as a single city—what is the limit? Certainly not the wall of the city, for you might surround all Peloponnesus with a wall. Like this, we may say, is Babylon,[9] and every city that has the compass of a nation rather than a city; Babylon, they say, had been taken for three days before some part of the inhabitants became aware of the fact. This difficulty may, however, with advantage be deferred[10] to another occasion; the statesman has to consider the size of the state, and whether it should consist of more than one nation or not.

---

[8] i. e. *Polis* means both 'state' and 'city'.          [9] Cp. ii. 1265ᵃ 14.

[10] The size of the state is discussed in vii. 1326ᵃ 8–1327ᵃ 3; the question whether it should consist of more than one nation is barely touched upon, in v. 1303ᵃ 25–ᵇ 3.

35 Again, shall we say that while the race of inhabitants, as well as their place of abode, remain the same, the city is also the same, although the citizens are always dying and being born, as we call rivers and fountains the same, although the water is always flowing away and coming again? Or shall we say that the generations of men, like 40 the rivers, are the same, but that the state changes? For, 1276ᵇ since the state is a partnership, and is a partnership of citizens in a constitution, when the form of the government changes, and becomes different, then it may be supposed that the state is no longer the same, just as a 5 tragic differs from a comic chorus, although the members of both may be identical. And in this manner we speak of every union or composition of elements as different when the form of their composition alters; for example, a scale containing the same sounds is said to be different, 10 accordingly as the Dorian or the Phrygian mode is employed. And if this is true it is evident that the sameness of the state consists chiefly in the sameness of the constitution, and it may be called or not called by the same name, whether the inhabitants are the same or entirely different. It is quite another question, whether a state 15 ought or ought not to fulfil engagements when the form of government changes.

**4** There is a point nearly allied to the preceding: Whether the virtue of a good man and a good citizen is the same or not.[11] But, before entering on this discussion, we must certainly first obtain some general notion 20 of the virtue of the citizen. Like the sailor, the citizen is a member of a community. Now, sailors have different functions, for one of them is a rower, another a pilot, and a third a look-out man, a fourth is described by some

---

11 Cp. *Nic. Eth.* v. 1130ᵇ 28.

similar term; and while the precise definition of each individual's virtue applies exclusively to him, there is, at 25
the same time, a common definition applicable to them
all. For they have all of them a common object, which is
safety in navigation. Similarly, one citizen differs from
another, but the salvation of the community is the common business of them all. This community is the constitution; the virtue of the citizen must therefore be rela- 30
tive to the constitution of which he is a member. If, then,
there are many forms of government, it is evident that
there is not one single virtue of the good citizen which is
perfect virtue. But we say that the good man is he who
has one single virtue which is perfect virtue. Hence it is
evident that the good citizen need not of necessity possess the virtue which makes a good man.                   35

The same question may also be approached by another
road, from a consideration of the best constitution. If
the state cannot be entirely composed of good men, and
yet each citizen is expected to do his own business well,
and must therefore have virtue, still, inasmuch as all the 40
citizens cannot be alike, the virtue of the citizen and of 1277ᵇ
the good man cannot coincide. All must have the virtue
of the good citizen—thus, and thus only, can the state be
perfect; but they will not have the virtue of a good man,
unless we assume that in the good state all the citizens
must be good.

Again, the state, as composed of unlikes, may be com- 5
pared to the living being: as the first elements into which
a living being is resolved are soul and body, as soul is
made up of rational principle and appetite, the family of
husband and wife, property of master and slave, so of
all these, as well as other dissimilar elements, the state is
composed; and, therefore, the virtue of all the citizens 10
cannot possibly be the same, any more than the excel-

lence of the leader of a chorus is the same as that of the
performer who stands by his side. I have said enough to
show why the two kinds of virtue cannot be absolutely
and always the same.

But will there then be no case in which the virtue of
15 the good citizen and the virtue of the good man coincide?
To this we answer that the good *ruler* is a good and wise
man, and that he who would be a statesman must be a
wise man. And some persons say that even the education of the ruler should be of a special kind; for are not
the children of kings instructed in riding and military
exercises? As Euripides says:

'No subtle arts for me, but what the state requires.'

As though there were a special education needed by a
20 ruler. If then the virtue of a good ruler is the same as that
of a good man, and we assume further that the subject is
a citizen as well as the ruler, the virtue of the good citizen
and the virtue of the good man cannot be absolutely the
same, although in some cases they may; for the virtue
of a ruler differs from that of a citizen. It was the sense
of this difference which made Jason say that 'he felt
hungry when he was not a tyrant', meaning that he could
not endure to live in a private station. But, on the other
25 hand, it may be argued that men are praised for knowing
both how to rule and how to obey, and he is said to be a
citizen of approved virtue who is able to do both. Now if
we suppose the virtue of a good man to be that which
rules, and the virtue of the citizen to include ruling and
obeying, it cannot be said that they are equally worthy
30 of praise. Since, then, it is sometimes thought that the
ruler and the ruled must learn different things and not
the same, but that the citizen must know and share in
them both, the inference is obvious. There is, indeed, the

rule of a master, which is concerned with menial offices [12]
—the master need not know how to perform these, but
may employ others in the execution of them: the other 3
would be degrading; and by the other I mean the power
actually to do menial duties, which vary much in character and are executed by various classes of slaves, such,
for example, as handicraftsmen, who, as their name sig-
nifies, live by the labour of their hands:—under these **1277**
the mechanic is included. Hence in ancient times, and
among some nations, the working classes had no share in
the government—a privilege which they only acquired
under the extreme democracy. Certainly the good man
and the statesman and the good citizen ought not to learn
the crafts of inferiors except for their own occasional
use; [13] if they habitually practice them, there will cease 5
to be a distinction between master and slave.

This is not the rule of which we are speaking; but
there is a rule of another kind, which is exercised over
freemen and equals by birth—a constitutional rule,
which the ruler must learn by obeying, as he would learn 10
the duties of a general of cavalry by being under the
orders of a general of cavalry, or the duties of a general
of infantry by being under the orders of a general of
infantry, and by having had the command of a regiment
and of a company. It has been well said that 'he who has
never learned to obey cannot be a good commander'. The
two are not the same, but the good citizen ought to be
capable of both; he should know how to govern like a
freeman, and how to obey like a freeman—these are the 15
virtues of a citizen. And, although the temperance and
justice of a ruler are distinct from those of a subject, the
virtue of a good man will include both; for the virtue of
the good man who is free and also a subject, e. g. his jus-

[12] Cp. i. 1255^b 20–37.          [13] Cp. viii. 1337^b 15.

tice, will not be one but will comprise distinct kinds, the one qualifying him to rule, the other to obey, and differing as the temperance and courage of men and women
20 differ.[14] For a man would be thought a coward if he had no more courage than a courageous woman, and a woman would be thought loquacious if she imposed no more restraint on her conversation than the good man; and indeed their part in the management of the household is different, for the duty of the one is to acquire, and of
25 the other to preserve. Practical wisdom only is characteristic of the ruler: [15] it would seem that all other virtues must equally belong to ruler and subject. The virtue of the subject is certainly not wisdom, but only true opinion; he may be compared to the maker of the flute, while his master is like the flute-player or user of the flute.[16]

30 From these considerations may be gathered the answer to the question, whether the virtue of the good man is the same as that of the good citizen, or different, and how far the same, and how far different.[17]

**5** There still remains one more question about the citi-
35 zen: Is he only a true citizen who has a share of office, or is the mechanic to be included? If they who hold no office are to be deemed citizens, not every citizen can have this virtue of ruling and obeying; for this man is a citizen. And if none of the lower class are citizens, in which part of the state are they to be placed? For they
1278ᵃ are not resident aliens, and they are not foreigners. May we not reply, that as far as this objection goes there is no more absurdity in excluding them than in excluding slaves and freedmen from any of the above-mentioned classes? It must be admitted that we cannot consider all

---

[14] Cp. i. 1260ᵃ 20.     [15] Cp. *Rep.* iv. 428.
[16] Cp. *Rep.* x. 601 D, E.
[17] Cp. 1278ᵃ 40, 1288ᵃ 39, iv. 1293ᵇ 5, vii. 1333ᵃ 11.

those to be citizens who are necessary to the existence of the state; for example, children are not citizens equally with grown-up men, who are citizens absolutely, but children, not being grown up, are only citizens on a certain 5 assumption.[18] Nay, in ancient times, and among some nations, the artisan class *were* slaves or foreigners, and therefore the majority of them are so now. The best form of state will not admit them to citizenship; but if they are admitted, then our definition of the virtue of a citizen will not apply to every citizen, nor to every free man as such, but only to those who are freed from necessary 10 services. The necessary people are either slaves who minister to the wants of individuals, or mechanics and labourers who are the servants of the community. These reflections carried a little further will explain their position; and indeed what has been said already [19] is of itself, when understood, explanation enough.

Since there are many forms of government there must 15 be many varieties of citizens, and especially of citizens who are subjects; so that under some governments the mechanic and the labourer will be citizens, but not in others, as, for example, in aristocracy or the so-called government of the best (if there be such an one), in which honours are given according to virtue and merit; for no 20 man can practise virtue who is living the life of a mechanic or labourer. In oligarchies the qualification for office is high, and therefore no labourer can ever be a citizen; but a mechanic may, for an actual majority of them are rich. At Thebes [20] there was a law that no man 25 could hold office who had not retired from business for ten years. But in many states the law goes to the length of admitting aliens; for in some democracies a man is a citi-

---

[18] *sc.* that they grow up to be men.  [19] 1275ᵃ 38 sqq.
[20] Cp. vi. 1321ᵃ 28.

zen though his mother only be a citizen; and a similar principle is applied to illegitimate children; the law is
30 relaxed when there is a dearth of population. But when the number of citizens increases, first the children of a male or a female slave are excluded; then those whose mothers only are citizens; and at last the right of citizenship is confined to those whose fathers and mothers are both citizens.

35    Hence, as is evident, there are different kinds of citizens; and he is a citizen in the highest sense who shares in the honours of the state. Compare Homer's words 'like some dishonoured stranger'; [21] he who is excluded from the honours of the state is no better than an alien. But when this exclusion is concealed, then the object is that the privileged class may deceive their fellow inhabitants.
40    As to the question whether the virtue of the good man
1278b is the same as that of the good citizen, the considerations already adduced prove that in some states the good man and the good citizen are the same, and in others different. When they are the same it is not every citizen who is a good man, but only the statesman and those who have or
5 may have, alone or in conjunction with others, the conduct of public affairs.

6    Having determined these questions, we have next to consider whether there is only one form of government or many, and if many, what they are, and how many, and what are the differences between them.
10    A constitution is the arrangement of magistracies in a state,[22] especially of the highest of all. The government is everywhere sovereign in the state, and the constitution is in fact the government. For example, in de-

---

[21] Achilles complains of Agamemnon's so treating him, *Il.* ix. 648, xvi. 59.     [22] Cp. 1274b 38, iv. 1289a 15.

mocracies the people are supreme, but in oligarchies, the few; and, therefore, we say that these two forms of government also are different: and so in other cases.

First, let us consider what is the purpose of a state, and how many forms of government there are by which human society is regulated. We have already said, in the first part of this treatise,[23] when discussing household management and the rule of a master, that man is by nature a political animal. And therefore, men, even when they do not require one another's help, desire to live together; not but that they are also brought together by their common interests in proportion as they severally attain to any measure of well-being. This is certainly the chief end, both of individuals and of states. And also for the sake of mere life (in which there is possibly some noble element so long as the evils of existence do not greatly overbalance the good) mankind meet together and maintain the political community. And we all see that men cling to life even at the cost of enduring great misfortune, seeming to find in life a natural sweetness and happiness.

There is no difficulty in distinguishing the various kinds of authority; they have been often defined already in discussions outside the school. The rule of a master, although the slave by nature and the master by nature have in reality the same interests, is nevertheless exercised primarily with a view to the interest of the master, but accidentally considers the slave, since, if the slave perish, the rule of the master perishes with him. On the other hand, the government of a wife and children and of a household, which we have called household management, is exercised in the first instance for the good of the governed or for the common good of both parties, but

[23] Cp. i. 1253[a] 2.

40 essentially for the good of the governed, as we see to be
1279ᵇ the case in medicine, gymnastic, and the arts in general,
which are only accidentally concerned with the good of
the artists themselves.[24] For there is no reason why the
trainer may not sometimes practise gymnastics, and the
helmsman is always one of the crew. The trainer or
the helmsman considers the good of those committed to
5 his care. But, when he is one of the persons taken care
of, he accidentally participates in the advantage, for the
helmsman is also a sailor, and the trainer becomes one
of those in training. And so in politics: when the state is
framed upon the principle of equality and likeness, the
10 citizens think that they ought to hold office by turns.
Formerly, as is natural, every one would take his turn
of service; and then again, somebody else would look
after his interest, just as he, while in office, had looked
after theirs.[25] But nowadays, for the sake of the advantage which is to be gained from the public revenues and
from office, men want to be always in office. One might
15 imagine that the rulers, being sickly, were only kept in
health while they continued in office; in that case we may
be sure that they would be hunting after places. The conclusion is evident: that governments which have a regard
to the common interest are constituted in accordance
with strict principles of justice, and are therefore true
forms; but those which regard only the interest of the
20 rulers are all defective and perverted forms, for they are
despotic, whereas a state is a community of freemen.

**7** Having determined these points, we have next to
consider how many forms of government there are, and
what they are; and in the first place what are the true
forms, for when they are determined the perversions of

[24] Cᴅ. Pl. *Rep*. i. 341 ᴅ.  [25] Cᴘ. ii. 1261ᵃ 37—ᵇ 6.

them will at once be apparent. The words constitution 25 and government have the same meaning, and the government, which is the supreme authority in states, must be in the hands of one, or of a few, or of the many. The true forms of government, therefore, are those in which the one, or the few, or the many, govern with a view to the common interest; but governments which rule with a 30 view to the private interest, whether of the one, or of the few, or of the many, are perversions.[26] For the members of a state, if they are truly citizens, ought to participate in its advantages. Of forms of government in which one rules, we call that which regards the common interests, kingship or royalty; that in which more than one, 35 but not many, rule, aristocracy; and it is so called, either because the rulers are the best men, or because they have at heart the best interests of the state and of the citizens. But when the citizens at large administer the state for the common interest, the government is called by the generic name—a constitution. And there is a reason for this use of language. One man or a few may excel in virtue; but 40 as the number increases it becomes more difficult for 1279ᵇ them to attain perfection in every kind of virtue, though they may in military virtue, for this is found in the masses. Hence in a constitutional government the fighting-men have the supreme power, and those who possess arms are the citizens.

Of the above-mentioned forms, the perversions are as follows:—of royalty, tyranny; of aristocracy, oligarchy; 5 of constitutional government, democracy. For tyranny is a kind of monarchy which has in view the interest of the monarch only; oligarchy has in view the interest of the wealthy; democracy, of the needy: none of them the common good of all. 10

---

[26] Cp. *Nic. Eth.* viii. 10.

**8**  But there are difficulties about these forms of government, and it will therefore be necessary to state a little more at length the nature of each of them. For he who would make a philosophical study of the various sciences, and does not regard practice only, ought not to
15 overlook or omit anything, but to set forth the truth in every particular. Tyranny, as I was saying, is monarchy exercising the rule of a master over the political society; oligarchy is when men of property have the government in their hands; democracy, the opposite, when the indigent, and not the men of property, are the rulers. And here arises the first of our difficulties, and it relates to
20 the distinction just drawn. For democracy is said to be the government of the many. But what if the many are men of property and have the power in their hands? In like manner oligarchy is said to be the government of the few; but what if the poor are fewer than the rich,
25 and have the power in their hands because they are stronger? In these cases the distinction which we have drawn between these different forms of government would no longer hold good.

Suppose, once more, that we add wealth to the few and poverty to the many, and name the governments accordingly—an oligarchy is said to be that in which the few and the wealthy, and a democracy that in which the many
30 and the poor are the rulers—there will still be a difficulty. For, if the only forms of government are the ones already mentioned, how shall we describe those other governments also just mentioned by us, in which the rich are the more numerous and the poor are the fewer, and both govern in their respective states?

35    The argument seems to show that, whether in oligarchies or in democracies, the number of the governing body, whether the greater number, as in a democracy, or

the smaller number, as in an oligarchy, is an accident due
to the fact that the rich everywhere are few, and the poor
numerous. But if so, there is a misapprehension of the
causes of the difference between them. For the real differ- 40
ence between democracy and oligarchy is poverty and 1280ᵃ
wealth. Wherever men rule by reason of their wealth,
whether they be few or many, that is an oligarchy, and
where the poor rule, that is a democracy. But as a fact the
rich are few and the poor many; for few are well-to-do,
whereas freedom is enjoyed by all, and wealth and free- 5
dom are the grounds on which the oligarchical and democratical parties respectively claim power in the state.

**9** Let us begin by considering the common definitions
of oligarchy and democracy, and what is justice oligarchical and democratical. For all men cling to justice
of some kind, but their conceptions are imperfect and 10
they do not express the whole idea. For example, justice
is thought by them to be, and is, equality, not, however,
for all, but only for equals. And inequality is thought to
be, and is, justice; neither is this for all, but only for
unequals. When the persons are omitted, then men judge
erroneously. The reason is that they are passing judgement on themselves, and most people are bad judges in 15
their own case. And whereas justice implies a relation to
persons as well as to things, and a just distribution, as I
have already said in the *Ethics*,[27] implies the same ratio
between the persons and between the things, they agree
about the equality of the things, but dispute about the
equality of the persons, chiefly for the reason which I 20
have just given—because they are bad judges in their
own affairs; and secondly, because both the parties to
the argument are speaking of a limited and partial jus-

[27] v. 1131ᵃ 15.

tice, but imagine themselves to be speaking of absolute
justice. For the one party, if they are unequal in one
respect, for example wealth, consider themselves to be
unequal in all; and the other party, if they are equal in
one respect, for example free birth, consider themselves
25 to be equal in all. But they leave out the capital point.
For if men met and associated out of regard to wealth
only, their share in the state would be proportioned to
their property, and the oligarchical doctrine would then
seem to carry the day. It would not be just that he who
paid one mina should have the same share of a hundred
30 minae, whether of the principal or of the profits, as he
who paid the remaining ninety-nine. But a state exists
for the sake of a good life, and not for the sake of life
only: if life only were the object, slaves and brute animals might form a state, but they cannot, for they have
no share in happiness or in a life of free choice. Nor does
35 a state exist for the sake of alliance and security from injustice, nor yet for the sake of exchange and mutual
intercourse; for then the Tyrrhenians and the Carthaginians, and all who have commercial treaties with one
another,[28] would be the citizens of one state. True, they
have agreements about imports, and engagements that
40 they will do no wrong to one another, and written articles
1280ᵇ of alliance. But there are no magistracies common to the
contracting parties who will enforce their engagements;
different states have each their own magistracies. Nor
does one state take care that the citizens of the other are
such as they ought to be, nor see that those who come
under the terms of the treaty do no wrong or wickedness
at all, but only that they do no injustice to one another.
5 Whereas, those who care for good government take into
consideration virtue and vice in states. Whence it may

---

[28] Cp. 1275ᵃ 10.

be further inferred that virtue must be the care of a state which is truly so called, and not merely enjoys the name: for without this end the community becomes a mere alliance which differs only in place from alliances of which the members live apart; and law is only a convention, 'a surety to one another of justice,' as the sophist Lycophron says, and has no real power to make the citizens good and just.

This is obvious; for suppose distinct places, such as Corinth and Megara, to be brought together so that their walls touched, still they would not be one city, not even if the citizens had the right to intermarry, which is one of the rights peculiarly characteristic of states. Again, if men dwelt at a distance from one another, but not so far off as to have no intercourse, and there were laws among them that they should not wrong each other in their exchanges, neither would this be a state. Let us suppose that one man is a carpenter, another a husbandman, another a shoemaker, and so on, and that their number is ten thousand: nevertheless, if they have nothing in common but exchange, alliance, and the like, that would not constitute a state. Why is this? Surely not because they are at a distance from one another: for even supposing that such a community were to meet in one place, but that each man had a house of his own, which was in a manner his state, and that they made alliance with one another, but only against evil-doers; still an accurate thinker would not deem this to be a state, if their intercourse with one another was of the same character after as before their union. It is clear then that a state is not a mere society, having a common place, established for the prevention of mutual crime and for the sake of exchange.[29] These are conditions without which a state cannot exist;

[29] Cp. *Protag.* 322 в.

but all of them together do not constitute a state, which
is a community of families and aggregations of families
in well-being, for the sake of a perfect and self-sufficing
35 life. Such a community can only be established among
those who live in the same place and intermarry. Hence
arise in cities family connexions, brotherhoods, common
sacrifices, amusements which draw men together. But
these are created by friendship, for the will to live together is friendship. The end of the state is the good life,
40 and these are the means towards it. And the state is the
1281ᵃ union of families and villages in a perfect and self-sufficing life, by which we mean a happy and honourable life.[30]

Our conclusion, then, is that political society exists for
the sake of noble actions, and not of mere companionship.
5 Hence they who contribute most to such a society have
a greater share in it than those who have the same or a
greater freedom or nobility of birth but are inferior to
them in political virtue; or than those who exceed them
in wealth but are surpassed by them in virtue.

From what has been said it will be clearly seen that all
the partisans of different forms of government speak of
10 a part of justice only.

**10**　　There is also a doubt as to what is to be the supreme
power in the state:—Is it the multitude? Or the wealthy?
Or the good? Or the one best man? Or a tyrant? Any of
these alternatives seems to involve disagreeable consequences. If the poor, for example, because they are more
in number, divide among themselves the property of the
15 rich—is not this unjust? No, by heaven (will be the reply), for the supreme authority justly willed it. But if
this is not injustice, pray what is? Again, when in the
first division all has been taken, and the majority divide

[30] Cp. i. 1252ᵇ 27; *Nic. Eth.* i. 1097ᵇ 6.

anew the property of the minority, is it not evident, if this
goes on, that they will ruin the state? Yet surely, virtue
is not the ruin of those who possess her, nor is justice
destructive of a state; and therefore this law of confiscation clearly cannot be just. If it were, all the acts of a 20
tyrant must of necessity be just; for he only coerces
other men by superior power, just as the multitude coerce
the rich. But is it just then that the few and the wealthy 25
should be the rulers? And what if they, in like manner,
rob and plunder the people—is this just? If so, the other
case will likewise be just. But there can be no doubt that
all these things are wrong and unjust.

Then ought the good to rule and have supreme power?
But in that case everybody else, being excluded from 30
power, will be dishonoured. For the offices of a state are
posts of honour; and if one set of men always hold them,
the rest must be deprived of them. Then will it be well
that the one best man should rule? Nay, that is still more
oligarchical, for the number of those who are dishonoured is thereby increased. Some one may say that it is
bad in any case for a man, subject as he is to all the accidents of human passion, to have the supreme power, 35
rather than the law. But what if the law itself be democratical or oligarchical, how will that help us out of our
difficulties? [31] Not at all; the same consequences [32] will
follow.

**11**    Most of these questions may be reserved for another
occasion.[33] The principle that the multitude ought to be 40
supreme rather than the few best is one that is maintained, and, though not free from difficulty, yet seems to
contain an element of truth. For the many, of whom each
individual is but an ordinary person, when they meet **1281**ᵇ

[31] Cp. 1282ᵇ 6.    [32] Cp. ll. 11–34.    [33] cc. 12–17, iv., vi.

together may very likely be better than the few good, if regarded not individually but collectively, just as a feast to which many contribute is better than a dinner provided out of a single purse. For each individual among the many has a share of virtue and prudence, and when
5 they meet together, they become in a manner one man, who has many feet, and hands, and senses; that is a figure of their mind and disposition. Hence the many are better judges than a single man of music and poetry; for some understand one part, and some another, and among them
10 they understand the whole. There is a similar combination of qualities in good men, who differ from any individual of the many, as the beautiful are said to differ from those who are not beautiful, and works of art from realities, because in them the scattered elements are combined, although, if taken separately, the eye of one person or some other feature in another person would be
15 fairer than in the picture. Whether this principle can apply to every democracy, and to all bodies of men, is not clear. Or rather, by heaven, in some cases it is impossible of application; for the argument would equally hold about brutes; and wherein, it will be asked, do some
20 men differ from brutes? But there may be bodies of men about whom our statement is nevertheless true. And if so, the difficulty which has been already raised,[34] and also another which is akin to it—viz. what power should be assigned to the mass of freemen and citizens, who are
25 not rich and have no personal merit—are both solved. There is still a danger in allowing them to share the great offices of state; for their folly will lead them into error, and their dishonesty into crime. But there is a danger also
30 in not letting them share, for a state in which many poor men are excluded from office will necessarily be full of

[34] c. 10.

enemies. The only way of escape is to assign to them
some deliberative and judicial functions. For this reason Solon [35] and certain other legislators give them the
power of electing to offices, and of calling the magistrates
to account, but they do not allow them to hold office
singly. When they meet together their perceptions are
quite good enough, and combined with the better class 35
they are useful to the state (just as impure food when
mixed with what is pure sometimes makes the entire mass
more wholesome than a small quantity of the pure would
be), but each individual, left to himself, forms an imperfect judgement. On the other hand, the popular form of
government involves certain difficulties. In the first place,
it might be objected that he who can judge of the healing 40
of a sick man would be one who could himself heal his
disease, and make him whole—that is, in other words, 1282ª
the physician; and so in all professions and arts. As,
then, the physician ought to be called to account by physicians, so ought men in general to be called to account
by their peers. But physicians are of three kinds:—there
is the ordinary practitioner, and there is the physician of
the higher class, and thirdly the intelligent man who has
studied the art: in all arts there is such a class; and we
attribute the power of judging to them quite as much as 5
to professors of the art. Secondly, does not the same
principle apply to elections? For a right election can
only be made by those who have knowledge; those who
know geometry, for example, will choose a geometrician
rightly, and those who know how to steer, a pilot; and,
even if there be some occupations and arts in which 10
private persons share in the ability to choose, they certainly cannot choose better than those who know. So
that, according to this argument, neither the election of

[35] Cp. ii. 1274ª 15.

magistrates, nor the calling of them to account, should
be entrusted to the many. Yet possibly these objections
15 are to a great extent met by our old answer,[36] that if the
people are not utterly degraded, although individually
they may be worse judges than those who have special
knowledge—as a body they are as good or better. Moreover, there are some arts whose products are not judged
of solely, or best, by the artists themselves, namely those
arts whose products are recognized even by those who
20 do not possess the art; for example, the knowledge of
the house is not limited to the builder only; the user, or,
in other words, the master, of the house will be even a
better judge than the builder, just as the pilot will judge
better of a rudder than the carpenter, and the guest will
judge better of a feast than the cook.

This difficulty seems now to be sufficiently answered,
25 but there is another akin to it. That inferior persons
should have authority in greater matters than the good
would appear to be a strange thing, yet the election and
calling to account of the magistrates is the greatest of all.
And these, as I was saying,[37] are functions which in some
states are assigned to the people, for the assembly is
30 supreme in all such matters. Yet persons of any age, and
having but a small property qualification, sit in the assembly and deliberate and judge, although for the great
officers of state, such as treasurers and generals, a high
qualification is required. This difficulty may be solved
in the same manner as the preceding, and the present
practice of democracies may be really defensible. For
35 the power does not reside in the dicast, or senator, or
ecclesiast, but in the court, and the senate, and the
assembly, of which individual senators, or ecclesiasts, or
dicasts, are only parts or members. And for this reason

36 1281ᵃ 40–ᵇ 21.                         37 1281ᵇ 32.

the many may claim to have a higher authority than the few; for the people, and the senate, and the courts consist of many persons, and their property collectively is greater than the property of one or of a few individuals 40 holding great offices. But enough of this.

The discussion of the first question [38] shows nothing 1282ᵇ so clearly as that laws, when good, should be supreme; and that the magistrate or magistrates should regulate those matters only on which the laws are unable to speak with precision owing to the difficulty of any general prin- 5 ciple embracing all particulars.[39] But what are good laws has not yet been clearly explained; the old difficulty remains.[40] The goodness or badness, justice or injustice, of laws varies of necessity with the constitutions of states. This, however, is clear, that the laws must be adapted to 10 the constitutions. But if so, true forms of government will of necessity have just laws, and perverted forms of government will have unjust laws.

**12**   In all sciences and arts the end is a good, and the 14 greatest good and in the highest degree a good in the most authoritative of all [41]—this is the political science of which the good is justice, in other words, the common interest. All men think justice to be a sort of equality; and to a certain extent [42] they agree in the philosophical distinctions which have been laid down by us about Ethics.[43] For they admit that justice is a thing and has 20 a relation to persons, and that equals ought to have equality. But there still remains a question: equality or inequality of what? Here is a difficulty which calls for political speculation. For very likely some persons will

[38] c. 10.

[39] Cp. *Nic. Eth.* v. 1137ᵇ 19.

[40] Cp. 1281ᵃ 36.

[41] Cp. i. 1252ᵃ 2 ; *N. Eth.* i. 1094ᵃ 1.

[42] Cp. 1280ᵃ 9.

[43] Cp. *Nic. Eth.* v. 3.

say that offices of state ought to be unequally distributed
25 according to superior excellence, in whatever respect, of
the citizen, although there is no other difference between
him and the rest of the community; for that those who
differ in any one respect have different rights and claims.
But, surely, if this is true, the complexion or height of a
man, or any other advantage, will be a reason for his
30 obtaining a greater share of political rights. The error
here lies upon the surface, and may be illustrated from
the other arts and sciences. When a number of flute-
players are equal in their art, there is no reason why
those of them who are better born should have better
flutes given to them; for they will not play any better
on the flute, and the superior instrument should be reserved for him who is the superior artist. If what I am
saying is still obscure, it will be made clearer as we pro-
35 ceed. For if there were a superior flute-player who was
far inferior in birth and beauty, although either of these
may be a greater good than the art of flute-playing, and
40 may excel flute-playing in a greater ratio than he excels
1283ª the others in his art, still he ought to have the best flutes
given to him, unless the advantages of wealth and birth
contribute to excellence in flute-playing, which they do
not. Moreover, upon this principle any good may be compared with any other. For if a given height may be meas-
5 ured against wealth and against freedom, height in general may be so measured. Thus if A excels in height more
than B in virtue, even if virtue in general excels height
still more, all goods will be commensurable; for if a certain amount is better than some other, it is clear that
10 some other will be equal. But since no such comparison
can be made, it is evident that there is good reason why
in politics men do not ground their claim to office on every
sort of inequality any more than in the arts. For if some

be slow, and others swift, that is no reason why the one
should have little and the others much; it is in gymnastic
contests that such excellence is rewarded. Whereas the
rival claims of candidates for office can only be based on 15
the possession of elements which enter into the composition of a state. And therefore the noble, or free-born, or
rich, may with good reason claim office; for holders of
offices must be freemen and tax-payers: a state can be
no more composed entirely of poor men than entirely of
slaves. But if wealth and freedom are necessary elements,
justice and valour are equally so; [44] for without the former qualities a state cannot exist at all, without the
latter not well.

20

**13** If the existence of the state is alone to be considered, then it would seem that all, or some at least, of
these claims are just; but, if we take into account a good
life, then, as I have already said,[45] education and virtue 25
have superior claims. As, however, those who are equal
in one thing ought not to have an equal share in all,
nor those who are unequal in one thing to have an
unequal share in all, it is certain that all forms of
government which rest on either of these principles
are perversions. All men have a claim in a certain sense,
as I have already admitted,[46] but all have not an abso- 30
lute claim. The rich claim because they have a greater
share in the land, and land is the common element of the
state; also they are generally more trustworthy in contracts. The free claim under the same title as the noble;
for they are nearly akin. For the noble are citizens in a
truer sense than the ignoble, and good birth is always
valued in a man's own home and country.[47] Another rea- 35

[44] Cp. iv. 1291ᵃ 19–33.                    [45] Cp. 1281ᵃ 4.
[46] 1280ᵃ 9 sqq.                    [47] Cp. i. 1255ᵃ 32.

son is, that those who are sprung from better ancestors
are likely to be better men, for nobility is excellence of
race. Virtue, too, may be truly said to have a claim, for
justice has been acknowledged by us to be a social [48] vir-
40 tue, and it implies all others.[49] Again, the many may urge
their claim against the few; for, when taken collectively,
and compared with the few, they are stronger and richer
1283ᵇ and better. But, what if the good, the rich, the noble, and
the other classes who make up a state, are all living together in the same city, will there, or will there not, be
any doubt who shall rule?—No doubt at all in determining who ought to rule in each of the above-mentioned
5 forms of government. For states are characterized by differences in their governing bodies—one of them has a
government of the rich, another of the virtuous, and so
on. But a difficulty arises when all these elements co-
exist. How are we to decide? Suppose the virtuous to be
10 very few in number: may we consider their numbers in
relation to their duties, and ask whether they are enough
to administer the state, or so many as will make up a
state? Objections may be urged against all the aspirants
to political power. For those who found their claims on
15 wealth or family might be thought to have no basis of
justice; on this principle, if any one person were richer
than all the rest, it is clear that he ought to be ruler of
them. In like manner he who is very distinguished by his
birth ought to have the superiority over all those who
claim on the ground that they are freeborn. In an aris-
20 tocracy, or government of the best, a like difficulty occurs
about virtue; for if one citizen be better than the other
members of the government, however good they may be,
he too, upon the same principle of justice, should rule
over them. And if the people are to be supreme because

---

[48] Cp. i. 1253ᵃ 37.           [49] Cp. *N. Eth.* v. 1129ᵇ 25.

they are stronger than the few, then if one man, or more
than one, but not a majority, is stronger than the many, 25
they ought to rule, and not the many.

All these considerations appear to show that none of
the principles on which men claim to rule and to hold
all other men in subjection to them are strictly right. To
those who claim to be masters of the government on the 30
ground of their virtue or their wealth, the many might
fairly answer that they themselves are often better and
richer than the few—I do not say individually, but collectively. And another ingenious objection which is some- 35
times put forward may be met in a similar manner. Some
persons doubt whether the legislator who desires to make
the justest laws ought to legislate with a view to the
good of the higher classes or of the many, when the case
which we have mentioned occurs.[50] Now what is just or 40
right is to be interpreted in the sense of 'what is equal';
and that which is right in the sense of being equal is to
be considered with reference to the advantage of the
state, and the common good of the citizens. And a citizen
is one who shares in governing and being governed. He
differs under different forms of government, but in the 1284ª
best state he is one who is able and willing to be governed and to govern with a view to the life of virtue.

If, however, there be some one person, or more than
one, although not enough to make up the full complement
of a state, whose virtue is so pre-eminent that the virtues 5
or the political capacity of all the rest admit of no comparison with his or theirs, he or they can be no longer
regarded as part of a state; for justice will not be done
to the superior, if he is reckoned only as the equal of
those who are so far inferior to him in virtue and in
political capacity. Such an one may truly be deemed a 10

[50] i. e. when the many collectively are better than the few.

God among men. Hence we see that legislation is necessarily concerned only with those who are equal in birth
and in capacity; and that for men of pre-eminent virtue
there is no law—they are themselves a law. Any one
would be ridiculous who attempted to make laws for
15 them: they would probably retort what, in the fable of
Antisthenes, the lions said to the hares,[51] when in the
council of the beasts the latter began haranguing and
claiming equality for all. And for this reason democratic
states have instituted ostracism; equality is above all
20 things their aim, and therefore they ostracized and ban-
ished from the city for a time those who seemed to pre-
dominate too much through their wealth, or the number
of their friends, or through any other political influence.
Mythology tells us that the Argonauts left Heracles behind for a similar reason; the ship Argo would not take
25 him because she feared that he would have been too
much for the rest of the crew. Wherefore those who de-
nounce tyranny and blame the counsel which Periander
gave to Thrasybulus cannot be held altogether just in
their censure. The story is that Periander, when the
herald was sent to ask counsel of him, said nothing, but
30 only cut off the tallest ears of corn till he had brought the
field to a level. The herald did not know the meaning of
the action, but came and reported what he had seen to
Thrasybulus, who understood that he was to cut off the
principal men in the state; [52] and this is a policy not only
35 expedient for tyrants or in practice confined to them, but
equally necessary in oligarchies and democracies. Ostracism [53] is a measure of the same kind, which acts by
disabling and banishing the most prominent citizens.
Great powers do the same to whole cities and nations, as

[51] i. e. 'where are your claws and teeth?'     [52] Cp. v. 1311ᵃ 20.
[53] Cp. v. 1302ᵇ 18.

the Athenians did to the Samians, Chians, and Lesbians;
no sooner had they obtained a firm grasp of the empire, 40
than they humbled their allies contrary to treaty; and **1284ᵇ**
the Persian king has repeatedly crushed the Medes,
Babylonians, and other nations, when their spirit has
been stirred by the recollection of their former greatness.

The problem is a universal one, and equally concerns
all forms of government, true as well as false; for,
although perverted forms with a view to their own interests may adopt this policy, those which seek the com- 5
mon interest do so likewise. The same thing may be observed in the arts and sciences; [54] for the painter will not
allow the figure to have a foot which, however beautiful,
is not in proportion, nor will the ship-builder allow the 10
stern or any other part of the vessel to be unduly large,
any more than the chorus-master will allow any one who
sings louder or better than all the rest to sing in the
choir. Monarchs, too, may practise compulsion and still
live in harmony with their cities, if their own government 15
is for the interest of the state. Hence where there is an
acknowledged superiority the argument in favour of ostracism is based upon a kind of political justice. It would
certainly be better that the legislator should from the
first so order his state as to have no need of such a remedy. But if the need arises, the next best thing is that he
should endeavour to correct the evil by this or some
similar measure. The principle, however, has not been 20
fairly applied in states; for, instead of looking to the
good of their own constitution, they have used ostracism
for factious purposes. It is true that under perverted
forms of government, and from their special point of
view, such a measure is just and expedient, but it is also
clear that it is not absolutely just. In the perfect state 25

[54] Cp. v. 1302ᵇ 34, 1309ᵇ 21; vii. 1326ᵃ 35; *Rep.* iv. 420.

there would be great doubts about the use of it, not when
applied to excess in strength, wealth, popularity, or the
like, but when used against some one who is pre-eminent
in virtue—what is to be done with him? Mankind will
not say that such an one is to be expelled and exiled; on
30 the other hand, he ought not to be a subject—that would
be as if mankind should claim to rule over Zeus, dividing
his offices among them. The only alternative is that all
should joyfully obey such a ruler, according to what
seems to be the order of nature, and that men like him
should be kings in their state for life.

35 **14** The preceding discussion, by a natural transition,
leads to the consideration of royalty, which we admit to
be one of the true forms of government. Let us see
whether in order to be well governed a state or country
should be under the rule of a king or under some other
form of government; and whether monarchy, although
good for some, may not be bad for others. But first we
40 must determine whether there is one species of royalty
1285ª or many. It is easy to see that there are many, and that
the manner of government is not the same in all of them.

Of royalties according to law, (1) the Lacedaemonian
is thought to answer best to the true pattern; but there
5 the royal power is not absolute, except when the kings
go on an expedition, and then they take the command.
Matters of religion are likewise committed to them. The
kingly office is in truth a kind of generalship, irrespon-
sible and perpetual. The king has not the power of life
and death, except in a specified case, as for instance, in
ancient times, he had it when upon a campaign, by right
10 of force. This custom is described in Homer. For Agamemnon is patient when he is attacked in the assembly,
but when the army goes out to battle he has the power

even of life and death. Does he not say?—'When I find a man skulking apart from the battle, nothing shall save him from the dogs and vultures, for in my hands is death.' [55]

This, then, is one form of royalty—a generalship for 15 life: and of such royalties some are hereditary and others elective.

(2) There is another sort of monarchy not uncommon among the barbarians, which nearly resembles tyranny. But this is both legal and hereditary. For bar- 20 barians, being more servile in character than Hellenes, and Asiatics than Europeans, do not rebel against a despotic government. Such royalties have the nature of tyrannies because the people are by nature slaves; [56] but there is no danger of their being overthrown, for they are hereditary and legal. Wherefore also their guards are such as a king and not such as a tyrant would employ, 25 that is to say, they are composed of citizens, whereas the guards of tyrants are mercenaries.[57] For kings rule according to law over voluntary subjects, but tyrants over involuntary; and the one are guarded by their fellow-citizens, the others are guarded against them.

These are two forms of monarchy, and there was a 30 third (3) which existed in ancient Hellas, called an Aesymnetia or dictatorship. This may be defined generally as an elective tyranny, which, like the barbarian monarchy, is legal, but differs from it in not being hereditary. Sometimes the office was held for life, sometimes for a term of years, or until certain duties had been per- 35 formed. For example, the Mytilenaeans elected Pittacus leader against the exiles, who were headed by Antimenides and Alcaeus the poet. And Alcaeus himself

---

[55] *Il.* ii. 391–393. The last clause is not found in our Homer.
[56] Cp. i. 1252ᵇ 7.                              [57] Cp. v. 1311ᵃ 7.

shows in one of his banquet odes that they chose Pittacus tyrant, for he reproaches his fellow-citizens for 'having made the low-born Pittacus tyrant of the spiritless and **1285ᵇ** ill-fated city, with one voice shouting his praises'.

These forms of government have always had the character of tyrannies, because they possess despotic power; but inasmuch as they are elective and acquiesced in by their subjects, they are kingly.

(4) There is a fourth species of kingly rule—that of the heroic times—which was hereditary and legal, and 5 was exercised over willing subjects. For the first chiefs were benefactors of the people [58] in arts or arms; they either gathered them into a community, or procured land for them; and thus they became kings of voluntary subjects, and their power was inherited by their descend-10 ants. They took the command in war and presided over the sacrifices, except those which required a priest. They also decided causes either with or without an oath; and when they swore, the form of the oath was the stretching out of their sceptre. In ancient times their power extended continuously to all things whatsoever, in city and 15 country, as well as in foreign parts; but at a later date they relinquished several of these privileges, and others the people took from them, until in some states nothing was left to them but the sacrifices; and where they retained more of the reality they had only the right of leadership in war beyond the border.

20 These, then, are the four kinds of royalty. First the monarchy of the heroic ages; this was exercised over voluntary subjects, but limited to certain functions; the king was a general and a judge, and had the control of religion. The second is that of the barbarians, which is an hereditary despotic government in accordance with

[58] Cp. v. 1310ᵇ 10.

law. A third is the power of the so-called Aesymnete or 25
Dictator; this is an elective tyranny. The fourth is the
Lacedaemonian, which is in fact a generalship, hereditary and perpetual. These four forms differ from one
another in the manner which I have described.

(5) There is a fifth form of kingly rule in which one
has the disposal of all, just as each nation or each state 30
has the disposal of public matters; this form corresponds to the control of a household. For as household
management is the kingly rule of a house, so kingly rule
is the household management of a city, or of a nation,
or of many nations.

**15** Of these forms we need only consider two, the
Lacedaemonian and the absolute royalty; for most of 35
the others lie in a region between them, having less
power than the last, and more than the first. Thus the
inquiry is reduced to two points: first, is it advantageous
to the state that there should be a perpetual general, and
if so, should the office be confined to one family, or open 1286ᵃ
to the citizens in turn? Secondly, is it well that a single
man should have the supreme power in all things? The
first question falls under the head of laws rather than of
constitutions; for perpetual generalship might equally
exist under any form of government, so that this matter
may be dismissed for the present.[59] The other kind of 5
royalty is a sort of constitution; this we have now to consider, and briefly to run over the difficulties involved in
it. We will begin by inquiring whether it is more advantageous to be ruled by the best man or by the best laws.[60]

The advocates of royalty maintain that the laws speak 10
only in general terms, and cannot provide for circumstances; and that for any science to abide by written

<hr>

[59] It is not discussed later.        [60] Cp. Plato, *Polit.* 294 ᴀ–295 ᴄ.

rules is absurd. In Egypt the physician is allowed to alter
his treatment after the fourth day, but if sooner, he takes
15 the risk. Hence it is clear that a government acting according to written laws is plainly not the best. Yet surely
the ruler cannot dispense with the general principle
which exists in law; and that is a better ruler which is
free from passion than that in which it is innate. Whereas
the law is passionless, passion must ever sway the heart
20 of man. Yes, it may be replied, but then on the other
hand an individual will be better able to deliberate in
particular cases.

The best man, then, must legislate, and laws must be
passed, but these laws will have no authority when they
25 miss the mark, though in all other cases retaining their
authority. But when the law cannot determine a point
at all, or not well, should the one best man or should all
decide? According to our present practice assemblies
meet, sit in judgment, deliberate, and decide, a    their
judgements all relate to individual cases. Now any member of the assembly, taken separately, is certainly inferior to the wise man. But the state is made up of many
individuals. And as a feast to which all the guests contribute is better than a banquet furnished by a single
30 man,[61] so a multitude is a better judge of many things
than any individual.

Again, the many are more incorruptible than the few;
they are like the greater quantity of water which is less
easily corrupted than a little. The individual is liable to
be overcome by anger or by some other passion, and then
35 his judgement is necessarily perverted; but it is hardly
to be supposed that a great number of persons would all
get into a passion and go wrong at the same moment. Let
us assume that they are the freemen, and that they never

[61] Cp. 1281ᵃ 42.

act in violation of the law, but fill up the gaps which the law is obliged to leave. Or, if such virtue is scarcely attainable by the multitude, we need only suppose that the majority are good men and good citizens, and ask which will be the more incorruptible, the one good ruler, or the [40] many who are all good? Will not the many? But, you [1286] will say, there may be parties among them, whereas the one man is not divided against himself. To which we may answer that their character is as good as his. If we call the rule of many men, who are all of them good, aristoc- [5] racy, and the rule of one man royalty, then aristocracy will be better for states than royalty, whether the government is supported by force or not,[62] provided only that a number of men equal in virtue can be found.

The first governments were kingships, probably for this reason, because of old, when cities were small, men of eminent virtue were few. Further, they were made [10] kings because they were benefactors,[63] and benefits can only be bestowed by good men. But when many persons equal in merit arose, no longer enduring the pre-eminence of one, they desired to have a commonwealth, and set up a constitution. The ruling class soon deteriorated and enriched themselves out of the public treasury; riches became the path to honour, and so oligarchies [15] naturally grew up. These passed into tyrannies and tyrannies into democracies; for love of gain in the ruling classes was always tending to diminish their number, and so to strengthen the masses, who in the end set upon their masters and established democracies. Since cities [20] have increased in size, no other form of government appears to be any longer even easy to establish.[64]

Even supposing the principle to be maintained that kingly power is the best thing for states, how about the

[62] Cp. l. 27.      [63] Cp. 1285ᵇ 6.      [64] Cp. iv. 1293ᵃ 1, 1297ᵇ 22.

family of the king? Are his children to succeed him? If
they are no better than anybody else, that will be mis-
25 chievous. But, says the lover of royalty, the king, though
he might, will not hand on his power to his children.
That, however, is hardly to be expected, and is too much
to ask of human nature. There is also a difficulty about
the force which he is to employ; should a king have
guards about him by whose aid he may be able to coerce
30 the refractory? If not, how will he administer his kingdom? Even if he be the lawful sovereign who does nothing arbitrarily or contrary to law, still he must have some
force wherewith to maintain the law. In the case of a
limited monarchy there is not much difficulty in answer-
35 ing this question; the king must have such force as will
be more than a match for one or more individuals, but
not so great as that of the people. The ancients observe
this principle when they have guards to any one whom
they appointed dictator or tyrant. Thus, when Dionysius
40 asked the Syracusans to allow him guards, somebody
advised that they should give him only such a number.

1287ᵃ 16    At this place in the discussion there impends the
inquiry respecting the king who acts solely according
to his own will; he has now to be considered. The so-
called limited monarchy, or kingship according to law,
as I have already remarked,[65] is not a distinct form of
5 government, for under all governments, as, for example,
in a democracy or aristocracy, there may be a general
holding office for life, and one person is often made supreme over the administration of a state. A magistracy
of this kind exists at Epidamnus,[66] and also at Opus, but
10 in the latter city has a more limited power. Now, absolute monarchy, or the arbitrary rule of a sovereign over

[65] 1286ᵃ 2.                    [66] Cp. v. 1301ᵇ 21.

all the citizens, in a city which consists of equals, is
thought by some to be quite contrary to nature; it is
argued that those who are by nature equals must have
the same natural right and worth, and that for unequals
to have an equal share, or for equals to have an uneven
share, in the offices of state, is as bad as for different 15
bodily constitutions to have the same food and clothing.
Wherefore it is thought to be just that among equals
every one be ruled as well as rule, and therefore that all
should have their turn. We thus arrive at law; for an
order of succession implies law. And the rule of the law,
it is argued, is preferable to that of any individual. On 20
the same principle, even if it be better for certain individuals to govern, they should be made only guardians
and ministers of the law. For magistrates there must be
—this is admitted; but then men say that to give authority to any one man when all are equal is unjust. Nay,
there may indeed be cases which the law seems unable
to determine, but in such cases can a man? Nay, it will 25
be replied, the law trains officers for this express purpose,
and appoints them to determine matters which are left
undecided by it, to the best of their judgement. Further,
it permits them to make any amendment of the existing
laws which experience suggests. Therefore he who bids
the law rule may be deemed to bid God and Reason alone
rule, but he who bids man rule adds an element of the
beast; for desire is a wild beast, and passion perverts the 30
minds of rulers, even when they are the best of men. The
law is reason unaffected by desire. We are told [67] that a
patient should call in a physician; he will not get better
if he is doctored out of a book. But the parallel of the
arts is clearly not in point; for the physician does noth- 35
ing contrary to rule from motives of friendship; he only

[67] Cp. 1286ᵃ 12–14, *Polit.* 296 B.

cures a patient and takes a fee; whereas magistrates do many things from spite and partiality. And, indeed, if a man suspected the physician of being in league with his
40 enemies to destroy him for a bribe, he would rather have recourse to the book. But certainly physicians, when they
1287ᵇ are sick, call in other physicians, and training-masters, when they are in training, other training-masters, as if they could not judge truly about their own case and might be influenced by their feelings. Hence it is evident that in seeking for justice men seek for the mean or neutral,⁶⁸
5 for the law is the mean. Again, customary laws have more weight, and relate to more important matters, than written laws, and a man may be a safer ruler than the written law, but not safer than the customary law.

Again, it is by no means easy for one man to superintend many things; he will have to appoint a number of
10 subordinates, and what difference does it make whether these subordinates always existed or were appointed by him because he needed them? If, as I said before,⁶⁹ the good man has a right to rule because he is better, still two good men are better than one: this is the old saying—

'two going together',⁷⁰

and the prayer of Agamemnon—

'would that I had ten such counsellors!'⁷¹

15 And at this day there are magistrates, for example judges, who have authority to decide some matters which the law is unable to determine, since no one doubts that the law would command and decide in the best manner whatever it could. But some things can, and other things
20 cannot, be comprehended under the law, and this is the

⁶⁸ Cp. *Nic. Eth.* v. 1132ᵃ 22.　　　⁶⁹ 1283ᵇ 21, 1284ᵇ 32.
⁷⁰ *Il.* x. 224.　　　⁷¹ *Il.* ii. 372.

origin of the vexed question whether the best law or the best man should rule. For matters of detail about which men deliberate cannot be included in legislation. Nor does any one deny that the decision of such matters must be left to man, but it is argued that there should be many judges, and not one only. For every ruler who has been 25 trained by the law judges well; and it would surely seem strange that a person should see better with two eyes, or hear better with two ears, or act better with two hands or feet, than many with many; indeed, it is already the practice of kings to make to themselves many eyes and ears and hands and feet. For they make colleagues of 30 those who are the friends of themselves and their governments. They must be friends of the monarch and of his government; if not his friends, they will not do what he wants; but friendship implies likeness and equality; and, therefore, if he thinks that his friends ought to rule, he must think that those who are equal to himself and like 35 himself ought to rule equally with himself. These are the principal controversies relating to monarchy.

**17**   But may not all this be true in some cases and not in others? for there is by nature both a justice and an advantage appropriate to the rule of a master, another to kingly rule, another to constitutional rule; but there is none naturally appropriate to tyranny, or to any other perverted form of government; for these come into being contrary to nature. Now, to judge at least from what 40 has been said, it is manifest that, where men are alike and equal, it is neither expedient nor just that one man 1288ᵃ should be lord of all, whether there are laws, or whether there are no laws, but he himself is in the place of law. Neither should a good man be lord over good men, nor a bad man over bad; nor, even if he excels in virtue,

should he have a right to rule, unless in a particular case,
at which I have already hinted, and to which I will once
5 more recur.[72] But first of all, I must determine what
natures are suited for government by a king, and what
for an aristocracy, and what for a constitutional government.

A people who are by nature capable of producing a
race superior in the virtue needed for political rule are
fitted for kingly government; and a people submitting
10 to be ruled as freemen by men whose virtue renders
them capable of political command are adapted for an
aristocracy; while the people who are suited for constitutional freedom are those among whom there naturally
exists a warlike multitude[73] able to rule and to obey in
turn by a law which gives office to the well-to-do accord-
15 ing to their desert. But when a whole family, or some
individual, happens to be so pre-eminent in virtue as to
surpass all others, then it is just that they should be the
royal family and supreme over all, or that this one citizen
should be king of the whole nation. For, as I said be-
20 fore,[74] to give them authority is not only agreeable to
that ground of right which the founders of all states,
whether aristocratical, or oligarchical, or again democratical, are accustomed to put forward (for these all
recognize the claim of excellence, although not the same
25 excellence), but accords with the principle already laid
down. For surely it would not be right to kill, or ostra-
cize, or exile such a person, or require that he should take
his turn in being governed. The whole is naturally superior to the part, and he who has this pre-eminence is
in the relation of a whole to a part. But if so, the only
alternative is that he should have the supreme power,

[72] 1284ᵃ 3, and 1288ᵃ 15.　　　　　　　　　　[73] Cp. 1279ᵇ 2.
[74] 1283ᵇ 20, 1284ᵃ 3-17, ᵇ25.

and that mankind should obey him, not in turn, but 30
always. These are the conclusions at which we arrive
respecting royalty and its various forms, and this is the
answer to the question, whether it is or is not advantageous to states, and to which, and how.

**18** We maintain [75] that the true forms of government
are three, and that the best must be that which is ad- 35
ministered by the best, and in which there is one man,
or a whole family, or many persons, excelling all the
others together in virtue, and both rulers and subjects
are fitted, the one to rule, the others to be ruled, in such
a manner as to attain the most eligible life. We showed
at the commencement of our inquiry [76] that the virtue of
the good man is necessarily the same as the virtue of the
citizen of the perfect state. Clearly then in the same
manner, and by the same means through which a man 40
becomes truly good, he will frame a state that is to be 1288[b]
ruled by an aristocracy or by a king, and the same education and the same habits will be found to make a good
man and a man fit to be a statesman or king.

Having arrived at these conclusions, we must proceed
to speak of the perfect state, and describe how it comes 5
into being and is established.

[75] Cp. 1279[a] 22–[b]4.                          [76] cc. 4, 5.

## BOOK IV

10 **1** In all arts and sciences which embrace the whole of any subject, and do not come into being in a fragmentary way, it is the province of a single art or science to consider all that appertains to a single subject. For example, the art of gymnastic considers not only the suitableness of different modes of training to different bodies (2), but what sort is absolutely the best (1); (for the absolutely best must suit that which is by nature best and best furnished with the means of life), and also 15 what common form of training is adapted to the great majority of men (4). And if a man does not desire the best habit of body, or the greatest skill in gymnastics, which might be attained by him, still the trainer or the teacher of gymnastic should be able to impart any lower degree of either (3). The same principle equally holds in medicine and ship-building, and the making of clothes, 20 and in the arts generally.[1]

Hence it is obvious that government too is the subject of a single science, which has to consider what government is best and of what sort it must be, to be most in accordance with our aspirations, if there were no external impediment, and also what kind of government 25 is adapted to particular states. For the best is often un-

[1] The numbers in this paragraph are made to correspond with the numbers in the next.

attainable, and therefore the true legislator and states·
man ought to be acquainted, not only with (1) that which
is best in the abstract, but also with (2) that which is
best relatively to circumstances. We should be able further to say how a state may be constituted under any
given conditions (3); both how it is originally formed
and, when formed, how it may be longest preserved; the
supposed state being so far from having the best consti-  30
tution that it is unprovided even with the conditions
necessary for the best; neither is it the best under the
circumstances, but of an inferior type.

He ought, moreover, to know (4) the form of government which is best suited to states in general; for politi-  35
cal writers, although they have excellent ideas, are often
unpractical. We should consider, not only what form of
government is best, but also what is possible and what is
easily attainable by all. There are some who would have
none but the most perfect; for this many natural advan-  40
tages are required. Others, again, speak of a more attainable form, and, although they reject the constitution
under which they are living, they extol some one in particular, for example the Lacedaemonian.[2] Any change
of government which has to be introduced should be one  1289ᵃ
which men, starting from their existing constitutions,
will be both willing and able to adopt, since there is quite
as much trouble in the reformation of an old constitution as in the establishment of a new one, just as to un-
learn is as hard as to learn. And therefore, in addition  5
to the qualifications of the statesman already mentioned,
he should be able to find remedies for the defects of
existing constitutions, as has been said before.[3] This he
cannot do unless he knows how many forms of government there are. It is often supposed that there is only

[2] Cp. ii. 1265ᵇ 35.                    [3] Cp. 1288ᵇ 29.

10 one kind of democracy and one of oligarchy. But this is a mistake; and, in order to avoid such mistakes, we must ascertain what differences there are in the constitutions of states, and in how many ways they are combined. The same political insight will enable a man to know which laws are the best, and which are suited to different constitutions; for the laws are, and ought to be, relative to the constitution, and not the constitution to the laws. A 15 constitution is the organization of offices in a state, and determines what is to be the governing body, and what is the end of each community. But laws are not to be confounded with the principles of the constitution; they are the rules according to which the magistrates should administer the state, and proceed against offenders. So that 20 we must know the varieties, and the number of varieties, of each form of government, if only with a view to making laws. For the same laws cannot be equally suited to all oligarchies or to all democracies, since there is certainly more than one form both of democracy and of oli-25 garchy.

2 In our original discussion[4] about governments we divided them into three true forms: kingly rule, aristocracy, and constitutional government, and three corresponding perversions—tyranny, oligarchy, and de-30 mocracy. Of kingly rule and of aristocracy we have already spoken,[5] for the inquiry into the perfect state is the same thing with the discussion of the two forms thus named, since both imply a principle of virtue provided with external means. We have already determined in what aristocracy and kingly rule differ from one another, 35 and when the latter should be established.[6] In what

[4] iii. 7; Cp. *Nic. Eth*. viii. 10.　　　　　　　　　[5] iii. 14–18.
[6] iii. 1279ª 32–37, 1286ᵇ 3–5, 1284ª 3–ᵇ34, ch. 17.

follows we have to describe the so-called constitutional government, which bears the common name of all constitutions, and the other forms, tyranny, oligarchy, and democracy.

It is obvious which of the three perversions is the worst, and which is the next in badness. That which is 40 the perversion of the first and most divine is necessarily the worst. And just as a royal rule, if not a mere name, 1289ᵇ must exist by virtue of some great personal superiority in the king,⁷ so tyranny, which is the worst of governments, is necessarily the farthest removed from a well-constituted form; oligarchy is little better, for it is a long way from aristocracy, and democracy is the most tolerable of the three.

A writer⁸ who preceded me has already made these 5 distinctions, but his point of view is not the same as mine. For he lays down the principle that when all the constitutions are good (the oligarchy and the rest being virtuous), democracy is the worst, but the best when all are bad. Whereas we maintain that they are in any case defective, and that one oligarchy is not to be accounted 10 better than another, but only less bad.

Not to pursue this question further at present, let us begin by determining (1)⁹ how many varieties of constitution there are (since of democracy and oligarchy there are several): (2)¹⁰ what constitution is the most 15 generally acceptable, and what is eligible in the next degree after the perfect state; and besides this what other there is which is aristocratical and well-constituted, and at the same time adapted to states in general; (3)¹¹ of the other forms of government to whom each is suited.

⁷ Cp. iii. 1284ᵃ 3–ᵇ34, chs. 17, 18, v. 1310ᵇ 10 sq., vii. 1325ᵇ 10–12.
⁸ Plato, *Polit.* 302 E, 303 A.          ⁹ C. 3–10.          ¹⁰ C. 11.
¹¹ C. 12.

For democracy may meet the needs of some better than
20 oligarchy, and conversely. In the next place (4)[12] we
have to consider in what manner a man ought to proceed
who desires to establish some one among these various
forms, whether of democracy or of oligarchy; and lastly,
(5)[13] having briefly discussed these subjects to the best
of our power, we will endeavour to ascertain the modes
of ruin and preservation both of constitutions generally
and of each separately, and to what causes they are to be
25 attributed.

**3** The reason why there are many forms of government is that every state contains many elements. In the
first place we see that all states are made up of families,
30 and in the multitude of citizens there must be some rich
and some poor, and some in a middle condition; the rich
are heavy-armed, and the poor not. Of the common
people, some are husbandmen, and some traders, and
some artisans. There are also among the notables differences of wealth and property—for example, in the
35 number of horses which they keep, for they cannot afford
to keep them unless they are rich. And therefore in old
times the cities whose strength lay in their cavalry were
oligarchies, and they used cavalry in wars against their
neighbours; as was the practice of the Eretrians and
Chalcidians, and also of the Magnesians on the river
40 Maeander, and of other peoples in Asia. Besides differ-
1290ᵃ ences of wealth there are differences of rank and merit,
and there are some other elements which were mentioned
by us when in treating of aristocracy we enumerated the
essentials of a state.[14] Of these elements, sometimes all,
sometimes the lesser and sometimes the greater number,

---

[12] Book vi. 1–7.     [13] Book v.
[14] iii. 1283ᵃ 14 sq., and Cp. vii. 8, 9.

have a share in the government. It is evident then that ₅ there must be many forms of government, differing in kind, since the parts of which they are composed differ from each other in kind. For a constitution is an organization of offices, which all the citizens distribute among themselves, according to the power which different classes possess, for example the rich or the poor, or according to some principle of equality which includes ₁₀ both. There must therefore be as many forms of government as there are modes of arranging the offices, according to the superiorities and the differences of the parts of the state.

There are generally thought to be two principal forms: as men say of the winds that there are but two—north and south, and that the rest of them are only variations ₁₅ of these, so of governments there are said to be only two forms—democracy and oligarchy. For aristocracy is considered to be a kind of oligarchy, as being the rule of a few, and the so-called constitutional government to be really a democracy, just as among the winds we make the west a variation of the north, and the east of the south wind. Similarly of musical modes there are said ₂₀ to be two kinds, the Dorian and the Phrygian; the other arrangements of the scale are comprehended under one or other of these two. About forms of government this is a very favourite notion. But in either case the better and more exact way is to distinguish, as I have done,[15] the one or two which are true forms, and to regard the ₂₅ others as perversions, whether of the most perfectly attempered mode or of the best form of government: we may compare the severer and more overpowering modes to the oligarchical forms, and the more relaxed and gentler ones to the democratic.

[15] 1289ᵃ 31–33, 40 sqq., Cp. viii. 1340ᵃ 40–ᵇ5, 1342ᵃ 28 sqq., ᵇ29 sqq.

40 **4** It must not be assumed, as some are fond of saying, that democracy is simply that form of government in which the greater number are sovereign,[16] for in oligarchies, and indeed in every government, the majority rules; nor again is oligarchy that form of government in which a few are sovereign. Suppose the whole population

35 of a city to be 1300, and that of these 1000 are rich, and do not allow the remaining 300 who are poor, but free, and in all other respects their equals, a share of the government—no one will say that this is a democracy. In like manner, if the poor were few and the masters of the rich who outnumber them, no one would ever call such a government, in which the rich majority have no share of office, an oligarchy. Therefore we should rather say

40 that democracy is the form of government in which the

1290ᵇ free are rulers, and oligarchy in which the rich; it is only an accident that the free are the many and the rich are the few. Otherwise a government in which the offices

5 were given according to stature, as is said to be the case in Ethiopia, or according to beauty, would be an oligarchy; for the number of tall or good-looking men is small. And yet oligarchy and democracy are not sufficiently distinguished merely by these two characteristics of wealth and freedom. Both of them contain many other elements, and therefore we must carry our analysis further, and say that the government is not a democracy in

10 which the freemen, being few in number, rule over the many who are not free, as at Apollonia, on the Ionian Gulf, and at Thera; (for in each of these states the nobles, who were also the earliest settlers, were held in chief honour, although they were but a few out of many). Neither is it a democracy when the rich have the government because they exceed in number; as was the case

[16] Cp. iii. 1279ᵇ 21.

formerly at Colophon, where the bulk of the inhabitants  15
were possessed of large property before the Lydian War.
But the form of government is a democracy when the
free, who are also poor and the majority, govern, and
an oligarchy when the rich and the noble govern, they
being at the same time few in number.                    20

I have said that there are many forms of government,
and have explained to what causes the variety is due.
Why there are more than those already mentioned,[17]
and what they are, and whence they arise, I will now
proceed to consider, starting from the principle already
admitted,[18] which is that every state consists, not of one,
but of many parts. If we were going to speak of the dif-  25
ferent species of animals, we should first of all determine
the organs which are indispensable to every animal, as
for example some organs of sense and the instruments
of receiving and digesting food, such as the mouth and
the stomach, besides organs of locomotion. Assuming
now that there are only so many kinds of organs,  30
but that there may be differences in them—I mean
different kinds of mouths, and stomachs, and per-
ceptive and locomotive organs—the possible combinations of these differences will necessarily furnish many
varieties of animals. (For animals cannot be the same
which have different kinds of mouths or of ears.) And
when all the combinations are exhausted, there will be  35
as many sorts of animals as there are combinations of
the necessary organs. The same, then, is true of the forms
of government which have been described; states, as I
have repeatedly said,[19] are composed, not of one, but of

---

[17] i. e. democracy and oligarchy, Cp. 1290ᵃ 13.

[18] 1289ᵇ 27 sq.

[19] ii. 1261ᵃ 22 sqq., iii. 1283ᵃ 14 sqq., iv. 1289ᵇ 27–1290ᵃ 5, 1290ᵇ
23 sq., Cp. iii. 1277ᵃ 5 sqq.

.ο many elements. One element is the food-producing class,
1291ᵃ who are called husbandmen; a second, the class of mechanics who practise the arts without which a city cannot
exist;—of these arts some are absolutely necessary,
others contribute to luxury or to the grace of life. The
third class is that of traders, and by traders I mean those
5 who are engaged in buying and selling, whether in com-
merce or in retail trade. A fourth class is that of the
serfs or labourers. The warriors make up the fifth class,
and they are as necessary as any of the others, if the
country is not to be the slave of every invader. For how
can a state which has any title to the name be of a slavish
nature? The state is independent and self-sufficing, but
10 a slave is the reverse of independent. Hence we see that
this subject, though ingeniously, has not been satisfac-
torily treated in the *Republic*.²⁰ Socrates says that a
state is made up of four sorts of people who are absolutely necessary; these are a weaver, a husbandman, a
15 shoemaker, and a builder; afterwards, finding that they
are not enough, he adds a smith, and again a herdsman,
to look after the necessary animals; then a merchant,
and then a retail trader. All these together form the
complement of the first state, as if a state were established merely to supply the necessaries of life, rather
than for the sake of the good, or stood equally in need of
shoemakers and of husbandmen. But he does not admit
20 into the state a military class until the country has increased in size, and is beginning to encroach on its neighbour's land, whereupon they go to war. Yet even amongst
his four original citizens, or whatever be the number of
those whom he associates in the state, there must be some
one who will dispense justice and determine what is just.
And as the soul may be said to be more truly part of an

²⁰ *Rep.* ii. 369.

animal than the body, so the higher parts of states, that 25
is to say, the warrior class, the class engaged in the administration of justice, and that engaged in deliberation,
which is the special business of political common sense—
these are more essential to the state than the parts which
minister to the necessaries of life. Whether their several
functions are the functions of different citizens, or of the 30
same—for it may often happen that the same persons are
both warriors and husbandmen—is immaterial to the
argument. The higher as well as the lower elements are
to be equally considered parts of the state, and if so, the
military element at any rate must be included. There are
also the wealthy who minister to the state with their
property; these form the seventh class. The eighth class
is that of magistrates and of officers; for the state cannot
exist without rulers. And therefore some must be able to 35
take office and to serve the state, either always or in
turn. There only remains the class of those who deliberate and who judge between disputants; we were just
now distinguishing them. If presence of all these elements, and their fair and equitable organization, is nec- 40
essary to states, then there must also be persons who 1291ᵃ
have the ability of statesmen. Different functions appear
to be often combined in the same individual; for example, the warrior may also be a husbandman, or an artisan; or, again, the counsellor a judge. And all claim to 5
possess political ability, and think that they are quite
competent to fill most offices. But the same persons cannot be rich and poor at the same time. For this reason
the rich and the poor are regarded in an especial sense
as parts of a state. Again, because the rich are generally
few in number, while the poor are many, they appear to 10
be antagonistic, and as the one or the other prevails they
form the government. Hence arises the common opinion

that there are two kinds of government—democracy and oligarchy.

I have already explained [21] that there are many forms of constitution, and to what causes the variety is due.

15 Let me now show that there are different forms both of democracy and oligarchy, as will indeed be evident from what has preceded. For both in the common people and in the notables various classes are included; of the common people, one class are husbandmen, another artisans;

20 another traders, who are employed in buying and selling; another are the seafaring class, whether engaged in war or in trade, as ferrymen or as fishermen. (In many places any one of these classes forms quite a large population; for example, fishermen at Tarentum and Byzantium, crews of triremes at Athens, merchant seamen at

25 Aegina and Chios, ferrymen at Tenedos.) To the classes already mentioned may be added day-labourers, and those who, owing to their needy circumstances, have no leisure, or those who are not of free birth on both sides; and there may be other classes as well. The notables again may be divided according to their wealth, birth, virtue, education, and similar differences.

30 Of forms of democracy first comes that which is said to be based strictly on equality. In such a democracy the law says that it is just for the poor to have no more advantage than the rich; and that neither should be masters, but both equal. For if liberty and equality, as

35 is thought by some, are chiefly to be found in democracy, they will be best attained when all persons alike share in the government to the utmost. And since the people are the majority, and the opinion of the majority is decisive, such a government must necessarily be a democracy. Here then is one sort of democracy. There is

[21] Cp. iii. c. 6.

another, in which the magistrates are elected according to
a certain property qualification, but a low one; he who 40
has the required amount of property has a share in the
government, but he who loses his property loses his rights.
Another kind is that in which all the citizens who are 1292ᵃ
under no disqualification share in the government, but
still the law is supreme. In another, everybody, if he be
only a citizen, is admitted to the government, but the law
is supreme as before. A fifth form of democracy, in other
respects, the same, is that in which, not the law, but the 5
multitude, have the supreme power, and supersede the
law by their decrees. This is a state of affairs brought
about by the demagogues. For in democracies which are
subject to the law the best citizens hold the first place,
and there are no demagogues; but where the laws are not 10
supreme, there demagogues spring up. For the people becomes a monarch, and is many in one; and the many have
the power in their hands, not as individuals, but collectively. Homer says that 'it is not good to have a rule of
many',²² but whether he means this corporate rule, or the
rule of many individuals, is uncertain. At all events this
sort of democracy, which is now a monarch, and no longer 15
under the control of law, seeks to exercise monarchical
sway, and grows into a despot; the flatterer is held in
honour; this sort of democracy being relatively to other
democracies what tyranny is to other forms of monarchy.
The spirit of both is the same, and they alike exercise a
despotic rule over the better citizens. The decrees of the
demos correspond to the edicts of the tyrant; and the 20
demagogue is to the one what the flatterer is to the other.
Both have great power;—the flatterer with the tyrant,
the demagogue with democracies of the kind which we
are describing. The demagogues make the decrees of the

²² *Il.* ii. 204.

25 people override the laws, by referring all things to the
popular assembly. And therefore they grow great, because the people have all things in their hands, and they
hold in their hands the votes of the people, who are too
ready to listen to them. Further, those who have any
complaint to bring against the magistrates say, 'let the
people be judges'; the people are too happy to accept the
invitation; and so the authority of every office is under-
30 mined. Such a democracy is fairly open to the objection
that it is not a constitution at all; for where the laws have
no authority, there is no constitution. The law ought to
be supreme over all, and the magistracies should judge of
particulars, and only this should be considered a constitution. So that if democracy be a real form of govern-
35 ment, the sort of system in which all things are regulated
by decrees is clearly not even a democracy in the true
sense of the word, for decrees relate only to particulars.[23]

These then are the different kinds of democracy.

5  Of oligarchies, too, there are different kinds:—one
40 where the property qualification for office is such that the
poor, although they form the majority, have no share in
the government, yet he who acquires a qualification may
1292ᵇ obtain a share. Another sort is when there is a qualification for office, but a high one, and the vacancies in the
governing body are filled by co-optation. If the election is
made out of all the qualified persons, a constitution of
this kind inclines to an aristocracy, if out of a privileged
class, to an oligarchy. Another sort of oligarchy is when
5 the son succeeds the father. There is a fourth form, likewise hereditary, in which the magistrates are supreme
and not the law. Among oligarchies this is what tyranny
is among monarchies, and the last-mentioned form of

[23] Cp. *Nic. Eth.* v. 1137ᵇ 27.

democracy among democracies; and in fact this sort of
oligarchy receives the name of a dynasty (or rule 10
of powerful families).

These are the different sorts of oligarchies and democracies. It should however be remembered that in
many states [24] the constitution which is established by
law, although not democratic, owing to the education and
habits of the people may be administered democratically,
and conversely in other states the established constitu- 15
tion may incline to democracy, but may be administered
in an oligarchical spirit. This most often happens after a
revolution: for governments do not change at once; at
first the dominant party are content with encroaching a 20
little upon their opponents. The laws which existed previously continue in force, but the authors of the revolution
have the power in their hands.

**6**  From what has been already said we may safely infer
that there are so many different kinds of democracies and
of oligarchies. For it is evident that either all the classes
whom we mentioned [25] must share in the government, or 25
some only and not others. When the class of husbandmen
and of those who possess moderate fortunes have the supreme power, the government is administered according
to law. For the citizens being compelled to live by their
labour have no leisure; and so they set up the authority
of the law, and attend assemblies only when necessary.
They all obtain a share in the government when they
have acquired the qualification which is fixed by the law
—the absolute exclusion of any class would be a step 30
towards oligarchy; hence all who have acquired the property qualification are admitted to a share in the constitution. But leisure cannot be provided for them unless there

**24** Cp. v. 1301$^b$ 10.                    **25** 1291$^b$ 17–30.

are revenues to support them. This is one sort of democracy, and these are the causes which give birth to it.
Another kind is based on the distinction which naturally
35 comes next in order; in this, every one to whose birth
there is no objection is eligible, but actually shares in the
government only if he can find leisure. Hence in such a
democracy the supreme power is vested in the laws, because the state has no means of paying the citizens. A
third kind is when all freemen have a right to share in the
government, but do not actually share, for the reason
40 which has been already given; so that in this form again
the law must rule. A fourth kind of democracy is that
1293ᵃ which comes latest in the history of states. In our own
day, when cities have far outgrown their original size,
and their revenues have increased, all the citizens have a
place in the government, through the great preponderance of the multitude; and they all, including the poor
5 who receive pay, and therefore have leisure to exercise
their rights, share in the administration. Indeed, when
they are paid, the common people have the most leisure,
for they are not hindered by the care of their property,
which often fetters the rich, who are thereby prevented
from taking part in the assembly or in the courts, and so
the state is governed by the poor, who are a majority, and
10 not by the laws. So many kinds of democracies there are,
and they grow out of these necessary causes.

Of oligarchies, one form is that in which the majority
of the citizens have some property, but not very much;
and this is the first form, which allows to any one who
obtains the required amount the right of sharing in the
15 government. The sharers in the government being a
numerous body, it follows that the law must govern, and
not individuals. For in proportion as they are further removed from a monarchical form of government, and in

respect of property have neither so much as to be able
to live without attending to business, nor so little as to
need state support, they must admit the rule of law and 20
not claim to rule themselves. But if the men of property
in the state are fewer than in the former case, and own
more property, there arises a second form of oligarchy.
For the stronger they are, the more power they claim,
and having this object in view, they themselves select
those of the other classes who are to be admitted to the
government; but, not being as yet strong enough to rule 25
without the law, they make the law represent their
wishes.[26] When this power is intensified by a further
diminution of their numbers and increase of their property, there arises a third and further stage of oligarchy,
in which the governing class keep the offices in their own
hands, and the law ordains that the son shall succeed the 30
father. When, again, the rulers have great wealth and
numerous friends, this sort of family despotism ap-
proaches a monarchy; individuals rule and not the law.
This is the fourth sort of oligarchy, and is analogous to
the last sort of democracy.

7   There are still two forms besides democracy and oli- 35
garchy; one of them is universally recognized and included among the four principal forms of government,
which are said to be (1) monarchy, (2) oligarchy, (3)
democracy, and (4) the so-called aristocracy or government of the best. But there is also a fifth, which retains
the generic name of polity or constitutional government;
this is not common, and therefore has not been noticed 40
by writers who attempt to enumerate the different kinds

---

[26] i. e. they make a law that the governing class shall have the power
of co-optation from other classes.

of government; like Plato,[27] in their books about the
1293[b] state, they recognize four only. The term 'aristocracy' is
rightly applied to the form of government which is described in the first part of our treatise; [28] for that only
can be rightly called aristocracy which is a government
formed of the best men absolutely, and not merely of
men who are good when tried by any given standard. In
5 the perfect state the good man is absolutely the same as
the good citizen; whereas in other states the good citizen
is only good relatively to his own form of government.
But there are some states differing from oligarchies and
also differing from the so-called polity or constitutional
government; these are termed aristocracies, and in them
magistrates are certainly chosen, both according to their
10 wealth and according to their merit. Such a form of government differs from each of the two just now mentioned, and is termed an aristocracy. For indeed in states
which do not make virtue the aim of the community, men
of merit and reputation for virtue may be found. And so
where a government has regard to wealth, virtue, and
15 numbers, as at Carthage,[29] that is aristocracy; and also
where it has regard only to two out of the three, as at
Lacedaemon, to virtue and numbers, and the two principles of democracy and virtue temper each other. There
are these two forms of aristocracy in addition to the first
20 and perfect state, and there is a third form, viz. the constitutions which incline more than the so-called polity
towards oligarchy.

**8** I have yet to speak of the so-called polity and of
tyranny. I put them in this order, not because a polity or
constitutional government is to be regarded as a perver-

---

[27] *Rep*. viii, ix.　　　　[28] iii. 1279[a] 34, 1286[b] 3, Cp. vii. 1328[b] 37.
[29] Cp. ii. 1273[a] 21–30.

sion any more than the above-mentioned aristocracies.
The truth is, that they all fall short of the most perfect 25
form of government, and so they are reckoned among
perversions, and the really perverted forms are perversions of these, as I said in the original discussion.[30] Last
of all I will speak of tyranny, which I place last in the
series because I am inquiring into the constitutions of
states, and this is the very reverse of a constitution.

Having explained why I have adopted this order, I will 30
proceed to consider constitutional government; of which
the nature will be clearer now that oligarchy and democracy have been defined. For polity or constitutional
government may be described generally as a fusion of
oligarchy and democracy; but the term is usually applied
to those forms of government which incline towards de- 35
mocracy, and the term aristocracy to those which incline
towards oligarchy, because birth and education are commonly the accompaniments of wealth. Moreover, the rich
already possess the external advantages the want of
which is a temptation to crime, and hence they are called
noblemen and gentlemen. And inasmuch as aristocracy
seeks to give predominance to the best of the citizens, 40
people say also of oligarchies that they are composed of
noblemen and gentlemen. Now it appears to be an impos- 1294ᵇ
sible thing that the state which is governed not by the
best citizens but by the worst should be well-governed,
and equally impossible that the state which is ill-gov-
erned should be governed by the best. But we must remember that good laws, if they are not obeyed, do not
constitute good government. Hence there are two parts of
good government; one is the actual obedience of citizens 5
to the laws, the other part is the goodness of the laws
which they obey; they may obey bad laws as well as

[30] iii. 7.

good. And there may be a further subdivision; they may obey either the best laws which are attainable to them, or the best absolutely.

The distribution of offices according to merit is a spe-
10 cial characteristic of aristocracy, for the principle of an aristocracy is virtue, as wealth is of an oligarchy, and freedom of a democracy. In all of them there of course exists the right of the majority, and whatever seems good to the majority of those who share in the government has
15 authority. Now in most states the form called polity exists, for the fusion goes no further than the attempt to unite the freedom of the poor and the wealth of the rich, who commonly take the place of the noble. But as there are three grounds on which men claim an equal share in the government, freedom, wealth, and virtue (for the
20 fourth or good birth is the result of the two last, being only ancient wealth and virtue), it is clear that the admixture of the two elements, that is to say, of the rich and poor, is to be called a polity or constitutional government; and the union of the three is to be called aristocracy or the government of the best, and more than any other form of government, except the true and ideal, has a right to this name.

25 Thus far I have shown the existence of forms of states other than monarchy, democracy, and oligarchy, and what they are, and in what aristocracies differ from one another, and polities from aristocracies—that the two latter are not very unlike is obvious.

30 9 Next we have to consider how by the side of oligarchy and democracy the so-called polity or constitutional government springs up, and how it should be organized. The nature of it will be at once understood from a comparison of oligarchy and democracy; we must ascertain their dif-

ferent characteristics, and taking a portion from each,
put the two together, like the parts of an indenture. Now
there are three modes in which fusions of government 35
may be affected. In the first mode we must combine the
laws made by both governments, say concerning the administration of justice. In oligarchies they impose a fine
on the rich if they do not serve as judges, and to the poor
they give no pay; but in democracies they give pay to the
poor and do not fine the rich. Now (1) the union of these 40
two modes [31] is a common or middle term between them,
and is therefore characteristic of a constitutional govern- 1294ᵇ
ment, for it is a combination of both. This is one mode of
uniting the two elements. Or (2) a mean may be taken
between the enactments of the two: thus democracies
require no property qualification, or only a small one,
from members of the assembly, oligarchies a high one;
here neither of these is the common term, but a mean be- 5
tween them. (3) There is a third mode, in which something is borrowed from the oligarchical and something
from the democratical principle. For example, the
appointment of magistrates by lot is thought to be democratical, and the election of them oligarchical; democratical again when there is no property qualification,
oligarchical when there is. In the aristocratical or consti- 10
tutional state, one element will be taken from each—
from oligarchy the principle of electing to offices, from
democracy the disregard of qualification. Such are the
various modes of combination.

There is a true union of oligarchy and democracy
when the same state may be termed either a democracy or 15
an oligarchy; those who use both names evidently feel
that the fusion is complete. Such a fusion there is also in
the mean; for both extremes appear in it. The Lacedae-

[31] Cp. 1297ᵃ 38.

monian constitution, for example, is often described as
20 a democracy, because it has many democratical features.
In the first place the youth receive a democratical education. For the sons of the poor are brought up with the
sons of the rich, who are educated in such a manner as to
make it possible for the sons of the poor to be educated
like them. A similar equality prevails in the following
25 period of life, and when the citizens are grown up to man-
hood the same rule is observed; there is no distinction
between the rich and poor. In like manner they all have
the same food at their public tables, and the rich wear
only such clothing as any poor man can afford. Again, the
people elect to one of the two greatest offices of state, and
in the other they share; [32] for they elect the Senators and
30 share in the Ephoralty. By others the Spartan constitution is said to be an oligarchy, because it has many oligarchical elements. That all offices are filled by election
and none by lot, is one of these oligarchical characteristics; that the power of inflicting death or banishment
rests with a few persons is another; and there are others.
35 In a well attempered polity there should appear to be
both elements and yet neither; also the government
should rely on itself, and not on foreign aid, and on itself
not through the good will of a majority—they might be
equally well-disposed when there is a vicious form of
government—but through the general willingness of all
classes in the state to maintain the constitution.

40 Enough of the manner in which a constitutional government, and in which the so-called aristocracies ought
to be framed.

1295ª **10** Of the nature of tyranny I have still to speak, in
order that it may have its place in our inquiry (since even

[32] Cp. ii. 1270ᵇ 17.

tyranny is reckoned by us to be a form of government),
although there is not much to be said about it. I have already in the former part of this treatise[33] discussed
royalty or kingship according to the most usual meaning  5
of the term, and considered whether it is or is not advantageous to states, and what kind of royalty should be
established, and from what source, and how.

When speaking of royalty we also spoke[34] of two
forms of tyranny, which are both according to law, and  10
therefore easily pass into royalty. Among Barbarians
there are elected monarchs who exercise a despotic
power; despotic rulers were also elected in ancient Hellas, called Aesymnetes or dictators. These monarchies,
when compared with one another, exhibit certain differ-  15
ences. And they are, as I said before,[35] royal, in so far as
the monarch rules according to law over willing subjects;
but they are tyrannical in so far as he is despotic and
rules according to his own fancy. There is also a third
kind of tyranny, which is the most typical form, and is
the counterpart of the perfect monarchy. This tyranny
is just that arbitrary power of an individual which is re-  20
sponsible to no one, and governs all alike, whether equals
or better, with a view to its own advantage, not to that of
its subjects, and therefore against their will. No freeman,
if he can escape from it, will endure such a government.

The kinds of tyranny are such and so many, and for
the reasons which I have given.

**11**  We have now to inquire what is the best constitution  25
for most states, and the best life for most men, neither assuming a standard of virtue which is above ordinary persons, nor an education which is exceptionally favoured
by nature and circumstances, nor yet an ideal state

[33] iii. 14–17.          [34] iii. 1285ᵃ 16–ᵇ3.          [35] iii. 1285ᵇ 2.

which is an aspiration only, but having regard to the life
30 in which the majority are able to share, and to the form of
government which states in general can attain. As to
those aristocracies, as they are called, of which we were
just now speaking,[36] they either lie beyond the possibilities of the greater number of states, or they approxi-
mate to the so-called constitutional government, and
therefore need no separate discussion. And in fact the
35 conclusion at which we arrive respecting all these forms
rests upon the same grounds. For if what was said in the
*Ethics*[37] is true, that the happy life is the life according
to virtue lived without impediment, and that virtue is a
mean, then the life which is in a mean, and in a mean
attainable by every one, must be the best. And the same
40 principles of virtue and vice are characteristic of cities
and of constitutions; for the constitution is in a figure the
1295ᵇ life of the city.

Now in all states there are three elements: one class is
very rich, another very poor, and a third in a mean. It is
admitted that moderation and the mean are best, and
therefore it will clearly be best to possess the gifts of for-
5 tune in moderation; for in that condition of life men are
most ready to follow rational principle. But he who
greatly excels in beauty, strength, birth, or wealth, or on
the other hand who is very poor, or very weak, or very
much disgraced, finds it difficult to follow rational principle.[38] Of these two the one sort grow into violent and
10 great criminals, the others into rogues and petty rascals.
And two sorts of offences correspond to them, the one
committed from violence, the other from roguery. Again,
the middle class is least likely to shrink from rule, or to

36 1293ᵇ 7–21, Cp. 1293ᵇ 36–1294ᵃ 25.

37 *Nic. Eth*. i. 1098ᵃ 16. vii. 1153ᵇ 10, x. 1177ᵃ 12.

38 Cp. Pl. *Rep*. iv. 421 ᴅ ff.

be over-ambitious for it; both of which are injuries to
the state. Again, those who have too much of the goods of
fortune, strength, wealth, friends, and the like, are 15
neither willing nor able to submit to authority. The evil
begins at home; for when they are boys, by reason of the
luxury in which they are brought up,[39] they never learn,
even at school, the habit of obedience. On the other hand,
the very poor, who are in the opposite extreme, are too
degraded. So that the one class cannot obey, and can only
rule despotically; the other knows not how to command 20
and must be ruled like slaves. Thus arises a city, not of
freemen, but of masters and slaves, the one despising, the
other envying; and nothing can be more fatal to friendship and good fellowship in states than this: for good fellowship springs from friendship; when men are at
enmity with one another, they would rather not even
share the same path. But a city ought to be composed, as 25
far as possible, of equals and similars; and these are generally the middle classes. Wherefore the city which is
composed of middle-class citizens is necessarily best constituted in respect of the elements of which we say the
fabric of the state naturally consists.[40] And this is the
class of citizens which is most secure in a state, for they 30
do not, like the poor, covet their neighbours' goods; nor
do others covet theirs, as the poor covet the goods of the
rich; and as they neither plot against others, nor are
themselves plotted against, they pass through life safely.
Wisely then did Phocylides pray—'Many things are best
in the mean; I desire to be of a middle condition in my
city.'

Thus it is manifest that the best political community 35
is formed by citizens of the middle class, and that those
states are likely to be well-administered, in which the

---

[39] Cp. v. 1310ᵃ 22.                    [40] Cp. ll. 1–3.

middle class is large, and stronger if possible than both the other classes, or at any rate than either singly; for the addition of the middle class turns the scale, and prevents
40 either of the extremes from being dominant. Great then
1296ᵃ is the good fortune of a state in which the citizens have a moderate and sufficient property; for where some possess much, and the others nothing, there may arise an extreme democracy, or a pure oligarchy; or a tyranny may grow out of either extreme—either out of the most rampant democracy, or out of an oligarchy; but it is not so likely
5 to arise out of the middle constitutions and those akin to them. I will explain the reason of this hereafter, when I speak of the revolutions of states.[41] The mean condition of states is clearly best, for no other is free from faction; and where the middle class is large, there are least likely to be factions and dissensions. For a similar reason large
10 states are less liable to faction than small ones, because in them the middle class is large; whereas in small states it is easy to divide all the citizens into two classes who are either rich or poor, and to leave nothing in the middle. And democracies are safer [42] and more permanent than
15 oligarchies, because they have a middle class which is more numerous and has a greater share in the government; for when there is no middle class, and the poor greatly exceed in number, troubles arise, and the state soon comes to an end. A proof of the superiority of the middle class is that the best legislators have been of a
20 middle condition; for example, Solon, as his own verses testify; and Lycurgus, for he was not a king; and Charondas, and almost all legislators.

These considerations will help us to understand why most governments are either democratical or oligarchical. The reason is that the middle class is seldom numerous in

[41] v. 1308ᵃ 18–24.  [42] Cp. v. 1302ᵃ 8, 1307ᵃ 16.

them, and whichever party, whether the rich or the common people, transgresses the mean and predominates, 25
draws the constitution its own way, and thus arises either
oligarchy or democracy. There is another reason—the
poor and the rich quarrel with one another, and whichever side gets the better, instead of establishing a just or
popular government, regards political supremacy as the 30
prize of victory, and the one party sets up a democracy
and the other an oligarchy. Further, both the parties
which had the supremacy in Hellas looked only to the
interest of their own form of government, and established
in states, the one, democracies, and the other, oligarchies;
they thought of their own advantage, of the public not 35
at all. For these reasons the middle form of government
has rarely, if ever, existed, and among a very few only.
One man alone of all who ever ruled in Hellas was in-
duced to give this middle constitution to states. But it has 40
now become a habit among the citizens of states, not even 1296
to care about equality; all men are seeking for dominion,
or, if conquered, are willing to submit.

What then is the best form of government, and what
makes it the best, is evident; and of other constitutions,
since we say [43] that there are many kinds of democracy
and many of oligarchy, it is not difficult to see which has
the first and which the second or any other place in the 5
order of excellence, now that we have determined which
is the best. For that which is nearest to the best must of
necessity be better, and that which is furthest from it
worse, if we are judging absolutely and not relatively to
given conditions: I say 'relatively to given conditions', 10
since a particular government may be preferable, but
another form may be better for some people.

[43] 1289ᵃ 8, ᵇ13, 1291ᵇ 15–1292ᵇ 10, 1292ᵇ 22–1293ᵃ 10.

**12** We have now to consider what and what kind of government is suitable to what and what kind of men. I 15 may begin by assuming, as a general principle common to all governments, that the portion of the state which desires the permanence of the constitution ought to be stronger than that which desires the reverse. Now every city is composed of quality and quantity. By quality I mean freedom, wealth, education, good birth, and by 20 quantity, superiority of numbers. Quality may exist in one of the classes which make up the state, and quantity in the other. For example, the meanly-born may be more in number than the well-born, or the poor than the rich, yet they may not so much exceed in quantity as they fall short in quality; and therefore there must be a compari- 25 son of quantity and quality. Where the number of the poor is more than proportioned to the wealth of the rich, there will naturally be a democracy, varying in form with the sort of people who compose it in each case. If, for example, the husbandmen exceed in number, the first form of democracy will then arise; if the artisans and 30 labouring class, the last; and so with the intermediate forms. But where the rich and the notables exceed in quality more than they fall short in quantity, there oligarchy arises, similarly assuming various forms according to the kind of superiority possessed by the oligarchs.

35 The legislator should always include the middle class in his government; if he makes his laws oligarchical, to the middle class let him look; if he makes them democratical, he should equally by his laws try to attach this class to the state. There only can the government ever be stable where the middle class exceeds one or both of the 40 others, and in that case there will be no fear that the rich 1297ᵃ will unite with the poor against the rulers. For neither of them will ever be willing to serve the other, and if they

look for some form of government more suitable to both,
they will find none better than this, for the rich and the
poor will never consent to rule in turn, because they mis- 5
trust one another. The arbiter is always the one trusted,
and he who is in the middle is an arbiter. The more perfect the admixture of the political elements, the more
lasting will be the constitution. Many even of those who
desire to form aristocratical governments make a mistake, not only in giving too much power to the rich, but
in attempting to overreach the people. There comes a 10
time when out of a false good there arises a true evil,
since the encroachments of the rich are more destructive
to the constitution than those of the people.

**13** The devices by which oligarchies deceive the people
are five in number; they relate to (1) the assembly; (2) 15
the magistracies; (3) the courts of law; (4) the use of
arms; (5) gymnastic exercises. (1) The assemblies are
thrown open to all, but either the rich only are fined for
non-attendance, or a much larger fine is inflicted upon
them. (2) As to the magistracies, those who are qualified
by property cannot decline office upon oath, but the poor 20
may. (3) In the law-courts the rich, and the rich only,
are fined if they do not serve, the poor are let off with
impunity, or, as in the laws of Charondas, a larger fine
is inflicted on the rich, and a smaller one on the poor. In
some states all citizens who have registered themselves
are allowed to attend the assembly and to try causes; but
if after registration they do not attend either in the assembly or at the courts, heavy fines are imposed upon 25
them. The intention is that through fear of the fines they
may avoid registering themselves, and then they cannot
sit in the law-courts or in the assembly. Concerning (4)
the possession of arms, and (5) gymnastic exercises, they

30 legislate in a similar spirit. For the poor are not obliged to have arms, but the rich are fined for not having them; and in like manner no penalty is inflicted on the poor for non-attendance at the gymnasium, and consequently, having nothing to fear, they do not attend, whereas the rich are liable to a fine, and therefore they take care to attend.

35 These are the devices of oligarchical legislators, and in democracies they have counter devices. They pay the poor for attending the assemblies and the law-courts, and they inflict no penalty on the rich for non-attendance. It is obvious that he who would duly mix the two principles should combine the practice of both, and provide that the poor should be paid to attend, and the rich 40 fined if they do not attend, for then all will take part; if 1297ᵇ there is no such combination, power will be in the hands of one party only. The government should be confined to those who carry arms. As to the property qualification, no absolute rule can be laid down, but we must see what is the highest qualification sufficiently comprehensive to 5 secure that the number of those who have the rights of citizens exceeds the number of those excluded. Even if they have no share in office, the poor, provided only that they are not outraged or deprived of their property, will be quiet enough.

But to secure gentle treatment for the poor is not an 10 easy thing, since a ruling class is not always humane. And in time of war the poor are apt to hesitate unless they are fed; when fed, they are willing enough to fight. In some states the government is vested, not only in those who are actually serving, but also in those who have served; 15 among the Malians, for example, the governing body consisted of the latter, while the magistrates were chosen from those actually on service. And the earliest govern-

ment which existed among the Hellenes, after the overthrow of the kingly power, grew up out of the warrior
class, and was originally taken from the knights (for
strength and superiority in war at that time depended on
cavalry; [44] indeed, without discipline, infantry are use- 20
less, and in ancient times there was no military knowledge or tactics, and therefore the strength of armies lay
in their cavalry). But when cities increased and the
heavy-armed grew in strength, more had a share in the
government; and this is the reason why the states which
we call constitutional governments have been hitherto
called democracies. Ancient constitutions, as might be 25
expected, were oligarchical and royal; their population
being small they had no considerable middle class; the
people were weak in numbers and organization, and were
therefore more contented to be governed.

I have explained why there are various forms of government, and why there are more than is generally supposed; for democracy, as well as other constitutions, has 30
more than one form: also what their differences are, and
whence they arise, and what is the best form of government, speaking generally, and to whom the various forms
of government are best suited; all this has now been
explained.

**14** Having thus gained an appropriate basis of discus- 35
sion, we will proceed to speak of the points which follow
next in order. We will consider the subject not only in
general but with reference to particular constitutions.
All constitutions have three elements, concerning which
the good lawgiver has to regard what is expedient for
each constitution. When they are well-ordered, the constitution is well-ordered, and as they differ from one an- 40

[44] Cp. $1289^b$ 36, vi. $1321^a$ 8.

other, constitutions differ. There is (1) one element
which deliberates about public affairs; secondly (2) that
1298ᵃ concerned with the magistracies—the questions being,
what they should be, over what they should exercise
authority, and what should be the mode of electing to
them; and thirdly (3) that which has judicial power.

The deliberative element has authority in matters of
5 war and peace, in making and unmaking alliances; it
passes laws, inflicts death, exile, confiscation, elects
magistrates and audits their accounts. These powers
must be assigned either all to all the citizens or all to
some of them (for example, to one or more magistracies,
or different causes to different magistracies), or some of
them to all, and others of them only to some. That all
10 things should be decided by all is characteristic of democracy; this is the sort of equality which the people
desire. But there are various ways in which all may
share in the government; they may deliberate, not all in
one body, but by turns, as in the constitution of Telecles
the Milesian. There are other constitutions in which the
15 boards of magistrates meet and deliberate, but come into
office by turns, and are elected out of the tribes and the
very smallest divisions of the state, until every one has
obtained office in his turn. The citizens, on the other
hand, are assembled only for the purposes of legislation,
and to consult about the constitution, and to hear the
edicts of the magistrates. In another variety of democ-
20 racy the citizens form one assembly, but meet only to
elect magistrates, to pass laws, to advise about war and
peace, and to make scrutinies. Other matters are referred
severally to special magistrates, who are elected by vote
or by lot out of all the citizens. Or again, the citizens
25 meet about election to offices and about scrutinies, and
deliberate concerning war or alliances while other mat-

ters are administered by the magistrates, who, as far as is possible,[45] are elected by vote. I am speaking of those magistracies in which special knowledge is required. A fourth form of democracy is when all the citizens meet to deliberate about everything, and the magistrates de- 30 cide nothing, but only make the preliminary inquiries; and that is the way in which the last and worst form of democracy, corresponding, as we maintain,[46] to the close family oligarchy and to tyranny, is at present administered. All these modes are democratical.

On the other hand, that some should deliberate about all is oligarchical. This again is a mode which, like the 35 democratical, has many forms. When the deliberative class being elected out of those who have a moderate qualification are numerous and they respect and obey the prohibitions of the law without altering it, and any one who has the required qualification shares in the government, then, just because of this moderation, the 40 oligarchy inclines towards polity. But when only selected individuals and not the whole people share in the deliberations of the state, then, although, as in the former 1298ᵇ case, they observe the law, the government is a pure oligarchy. Or, again, when those who have the power of deliberation are self-elected, and son succeeds father, and they and not the laws are supreme—the government is of necessity oligarchical. Where, again, particu- 5 lar persons have authority in particular matters;—for example, when the whole people decide about peace and war and hold scrutinies, but the magistrates regulate everything else, and they are elected by vote—there the government is an aristocracy. And if some questions are decided by magistrates elected by vote, and others by

[45] *sc.* in an advanced democracy. Cp. vi. 1317ᵇ 21.
[46] 1292ᵃ 17–21, ᵇ7–10, 1293ᵃ 32–34.

magistrates elected by lot, either absolutely or out of
10 select candidates, or elected partly by vote, partly by
lot—these practices are partly characteristic of an aristocratical government, and partly of a pure constitutional government.

These are the various forms of the deliberative body;
they correspond to the various forms of government.
And the government of each state is administered according to one or other of the principles which have been
laid down. Now it is for the interest of democracy, according to the most prevalent notion of it (I am speaking
of that extreme form of democracy in which the people
15 are supreme even over the laws), with a view to better
deliberation to adopt the custom of oligarchies respecting courts of law. For in oligarchies the rich who are
wanted to be judges are compelled to attend under pain
of a fine, whereas in democracies the poor are paid to
attend. And this practice of oligarchies should be
adopted by democracies in their public assemblies, for
20 they will advise better if they all deliberate together—
the people with the notables and the notables with the
people. It is also a good plan that those who deliberate
should be elected by vote or by lot in equal numbers out
of the different classes; and that if the people greatly
25 exceed in number those who have political training, pay
should not be given to all, but only to as many as would
balance the number of the notables, or that the number
in excess should be eliminated by lot. But in oligarchies
either certain persons should be co-opted from the mass,
or a class of officers should be appointed such as exist
in some states, who are termed probuli and guardians of
the law; and the citizens should occupy themselves exclusively with matters on which these have previously
30 deliberated; for so the people will have a share in the

deliberations of the state, but will not be able to disturb
the principles of the constitution. Again, in oligarchies
either the people ought to accept the measures of the
government, or not to pass anything contrary to them;
or, if all are allowed to share in counsel, the decision
should rest with the magistrates. The opposite of what is
done in constitutional governments should be the rule in 35
oligarchies; the veto of the majority should be final,
their assent not final, but the proposal should be referred
back to the magistrates. Whereas in constitutional governments they take the contrary course; the few have
the negative, not the affirmative power; the affirmation 40
of everything rests with the multitude.                    1297ᵇ

These, then, are our conclusions respecting the deliberative, that is, the supreme element in states.

**15**  Next we will proceed to consider the distribution of
offices; this too, being a part of politics concerning which 5
many questions arise:—What shall their number be?
Over what shall they preside, and what shall be their
duration? Sometimes they last for six months, sometimes for less; sometimes they are annual, whilst in
other cases offices are held for still longer periods. Shall
they be for life or for a long term of years; or, if for a
short term only, shall the same persons hold them over
and over again, or once only? Also about the appoint- 10
ment to them—from whom are they to be chosen, by
whom, and how? We should first be in a position to say
what are the possible varieties of them, and then we may
proceed to determine which are suited to different forms
of government. But what are to be included under the
term 'offices'? That is a question not quite so easily answered. For a political community requires many of- 15
ficers; and not every one who is chosen by vote or by lot

is to be regarded as a ruler. In the first place there are
the priests, who must be distinguished from political
officers; masters of choruses and heralds, even ambassa-
20 dors, are elected by vote. Some duties of superintend-
ence again are political, extending either to all the
citizens in a single sphere of action, like the office of the
general who superintends them when they are in the
field, or to a section of them only, like the inspectorships
of women or of youth. Other offices are concerned with
household management, like that of the corn measurers
who exist in many states and are elected officers. There
are also menial offices which the rich have executed by
25 their slaves. Speaking generally, those are to be called
offices to which the duties are assigned of deliberating
about certain measures and of judging and commanding, especially the last; for to command is the especial
duty of a magistrate. But the question is not of any im-
portance in practice; no one has ever brought into court
30 the meaning of the word, although such problems have a
speculative interest.

What kinds of offices, and how many, are necessary to
the existence of a state, and which, if not necessary, yet
conduce to its well-being, are much more important considerations, affecting all constitutions, but more espe-
35 cially small states. For in great states it is possible, and
indeed necessary, that every office should have a special
function; where the citizens are numerous, many may
hold office. And so it happens that some offices a man
holds a second time only after a long interval, and others
he holds once only; and certainly every work is better
1299ᵇ done which receives the sole, and not the divided attention of the worker. But in small states it is necessary to
combine many offices in a few hands, since the small
number of citizens does not admit of many holding office:

—for who will there be to succeed them? And yet small
states at times require the same offices and laws as large 5
ones; the difference is that the one want them often, the
others only after long intervals. Hence there is no reason
why the care of many offices should not be imposed on
the same person, for they will not interfere with each
other. When the population is small, offices should be
like the spits which also serve to hold a lamp.[47] We must 10
first ascertain how many magistrates are necessary in
every state, and also how many are not exactly necessary, but are nevertheless useful, and then there will be
no difficulty in seeing what offices can be combined in
one. We should also know over which matters several 15
local tribunals are to have jurisdiction, and in which
authority should be centralized: for example, should one
person keep order in the market and another in some
other place, or should the same person be responsible
everywhere? Again, should offices be divided according to the subjects with which they deal, or according
to the persons with whom they deal: I mean to say,
should one person see to good order in general, or one
look after the boys, another after the women, and so on? 20
Further, under different constitutions, should the magistrates be the same or different? For example, in democracy, oligarchy, aristocracy, monarchy, should there
be the same magistrates, although they are elected, not
out of equal or similar classes of citizens, but differently
under different constitutions—in aristocracies, for example, they are chosen from the educated, in oligarchies
from the wealthy, and in democracies from the free—or 25
are there certain differences in the offices answering to
them as well, and may the same be suitable to some, but
different offices to others? For in some states it may be

[47] Cp. 1252<sup>b</sup> 2.

convenient that the same office should have a more extensive, in other states a narrower sphere. Special offices
30 are peculiar to certain forms of government:—for example that of probuli, which is not a democratic office,
although a bule or council is. There must be some body
of men whose duty is to prepare measures for the people in order that they may not be diverted from their
business; when these are few in number, the state in-
35 clines to an oligarchy: or rather the probuli must always
be few, and are therefore an oligarchical element. But
when both institutions exist in a state, the probuli are
a check on the council; for the counsellor is a democratic
element, but the probuli are oligarchical. Even the power
1300ᵃ of the council disappears when democracy has taken
that extreme form in which the people themselves are
always meeting and deliberating about everything. This
is the case when the members of the assembly receive
abundant pay; for they have nothing to do and are always
holding assemblies and deciding everything for themselves. A magistracy which controls the boys or the
5 women, or any similar office, is suited to an aristocracy
rather than to a democracy; for how can the magistrates
prevent the wives of the poor from going out of doors?
Neither is it an oligarchical office; for the wives of the
oligarchs are too fine to be controlled.

Enough of these matters. I will now inquire into ap-
10 pointments to offices. The varieties depend on three
terms, and the combinations of these give all possible
modes: first, who appoints? secondly, from whom? and
thirdly, how? Each of these three admits of three varie-
15 ties: (A) All the citizens, or (B) only some, appoint.
Either (1) the magistrates are chosen out of all or (2)
out of some who are distinguished either by a property
qualification, or by birth, or merit, or for some special

reason, as at Megara only those were eligible who had
returned from exile and fought together against the democracy. They may be appointed either (a) by vote or
(b) by lot. Again, these several varieties may be coupled, 20
I mean that (C) some officers may be elected by some,
others by all, and (3) some again out of some, and others
out of all, and (c) some by vote and others by lot. Each
variety of these terms admits of four modes.

For either (A 1 a) all may appoint from all by vote,
or (A 1 b) all from all by lot, or (A 2 a) all from some by
vote, or (A 2 b) all from some by lot (and if from all, 25
either by sections, as, for example, by tribes, and wards,
and phratries, until all the citizens have been gone
through; or the citizens may be in all cases eligible in-
discriminately); or again (A 1 c, A 2 c) to some offices
in the one way, to some in the other. Again, if it is only
some that appoint, they may do so either (B 1 a) from
all by vote, or (B 1 b) from all by lot, or (B 2 a) from
some by vote, or (B 2 b) from some by lot, or to some
offices in the one way, to others in the other, i. e. (B 1 c)
from all, to some offices by vote, to some by lot, and
(B 2 c) from some, to some offices by vote, to some by 30
lot. Thus the modes that arise, apart from two (C, 3)
out of the three couplings, number twelve. Of these systems two are popular, that all should appoint from all
(A 1 a) by vote or (A 1 b) by lot—or (A 1 c) by both.
That all should not appoint at once, but should appoint 35
from all or from some either by lot or by vote or by both,
or appoint to some offices from all and to others from
some ('by both' meaning to some offices by lot, to others
by vote), is characteristic of a polity. And (B 1 c) that
some should appoint from all, to some offices by vote, to
others by lot, is also characteristic of a polity, but more
oligarchical than the former method. And (A 3 a, b, c, 40

B 3 a, b, c) to appoint from both, to some offices from all, to others from some, is characteristic of a polity with a leaning towards aristocracy. That (B 2) some should appoint from some is oligarchical—even (B 2 b) that some should appoint from some by lot (and if this does not actually occur, it is none the less oligarchical in character), or (B 2 c) that some should appoint from some by both. (B 1 a) that some should appoint from all, and (A 2 a) that all should appoint from some, by vote, is aristocratic.

5    These are the different modes of constituting magistrates, and these correspond to different forms of government:—which are proper to which, or how they ought to be established, will be evident when we determine the nature of their powers.[48] By powers I mean such powers
10 as a magistrate exercises over the revenue or in defence of the country; for there are various kinds of power: the power of the general, for example, is not the same with that which regulates contracts in the market.


**16**  Of the three parts of government, the judicial remains to be considered, and this we shall divide on the
15 same principle. There are three points on which the varieties of law-courts depend: The persons from whom they are appointed, the matters with which they are concerned, and the manner of their appointment. I mean, (1) are the judges taken from all, or from some only? (2) how many kinds of law-courts are there? (3) are the judges chosen by vote or by lot?

First, let me determine how many kinds of law-courts
20 there are. There are eight in number: One is the court of audits or scrutinies; a second takes cognizance of ordinary offences against the state; a third is concerned

---

[48] The promise is not fulfilled in the *Politics*.

with treason against the constitution; the fourth determines disputes respecting penalties, whether raised by
magistrates or by private persons; the fifth decides the
more important civil cases; the sixth tries cases of homi- 25
cide, which are of various kinds, (*a*) premeditated, (*b*)
involuntary, (*c*) cases in which the guilt is confessed but
the justice is disputed; and there may be a fourth court
(*d*) in which murderers who have fled from justice are
tried after their return; such as the Court of Phreatto
is said to be at Athens. But cases of this sort rarely hap- 30
pen at all even in large cities. The different kinds of
homicide may be tried either by the same or by different
courts. (7) There are courts for strangers:—of these
there are two subdivisions, (*a*) for the settlement of their
disputes with one another, (*b*) for the settlement of disputes between them and the citizens. And besides all
these there must be (8) courts for small suits about sums
of a drachma up to five drachmas, or a little more, which
have to be determined, but they do not require many
judges.

Nothing more need be said of these small suits, nor of 35
the courts for homicide and for strangers:—I would
rather speak of political cases, which, when misman-
aged, create division and disturbances in constitutions.

Now if all the citizens judge, in all the different cases
which I have distinguished, they may be appointed by 40
vote or by lot, or sometimes by lot and sometimes by
vote. Or when a single class of causes are tried, the
judges who decide them may be appointed, some by
vote, and some by lot. These then are the four modes of 1301ᵃ
appointing judges from the whole people, and there will
be likewise four modes, if they are elected from a part
only; for they may be appointed from some by vote and
judge in all causes; or they may be appointed from

some by lot and judge in all causes; or they may be elected in some cases by vote, and in some cases taken by lot, or some courts, even when judging the same causes, may be composed of members some appointed by vote and some by lot. These modes, then, as was said,
5 answer to those previously mentioned.

Once more, the modes of appointment may be combined; I mean, that some may be chosen out of the whole people, others out of some, some out of both; for example, the same tribunal may be composed of some who were elected out of all, and of others who were elected out of some, either by vote or by lot or by both.

10 In how many forms law-courts can be established has now been considered. The first form, viz. that in which the judges are taken from all the citizens, and in which all causes are tried, is democratical; the second, which is composed of a few only who try all causes, oligarchical; the third, in which some courts are taken from all
15 classes, and some from certain classes only, aristocratical and constitutional.

## BOOK V

**1** The design which we proposed to ourselves is now
nearly completed.[1] Next in order follow the causes of 30
revolution in states, how many, and of what nature they
are; what modes of destruction apply to particular
states, and out of what, and into what they mostly
change; also what are the modes of preservation in
states generally, or in a particular state, and by what
means each state may be best preserved: these questions
remain to be considered.

In the first place we must assume as our starting-point 25
that in the many forms of government which have sprung
up there has always been an acknowledgement of justice
and proportionate equality, although mankind fail in attaining them, as indeed I have already explained.[2] Democracy, for example, arises out of the notion that those
who are equal in any respect are equal in all respects;
because men are equally free, they claim to be absolutely 30
equal. Oligarchy is based on the notion that those who
are unequal in one respect are in all respects unequal;
being unequal, that is, in property, they suppose themselves to be unequal absolutely. The democrats think
that as they are equal they ought to be equal in all things;
while the oligarchs, under the idea that they are un-

[1] Cp. iv. c. 2.     [2] iii. 1282ᵇ 18–30, Cp. 1280ᵃ 9 sqq.

equal, claim too much, which is one form of inequality.
35 All these forms of government have a kind of justice,
but, tried by an absolute standard, they are faulty; and,
therefore, both parties, whenever their share in the government does not accord with their preconceived ideas,
stir up revolution. Those who excel in virtue have the
40 best right of all to rebel (for they alone can with reason
1301ᵇ be deemed absolutely unequal),³ but then they are of
all men the least inclined to do so.⁴ There is also a superiority which is claimed by men of rank; for they are
thought noble because they spring from wealthy and virtuous ancestors.⁵ Here then, so to speak, are opened the
5 very springs and fountains of revolution; and hence
arise two sorts of changes in governments; the one affecting the constitution, when men seek to change from an
existing form into some other, for example, from democracy into oligarchy, and from oligarchy into democracy,
or from either of them into constitutional government
10 or aristocracy, and conversely; the other not affecting
the constitution, when, without disturbing the form of
government, whether oligarchy, or monarchy, or any
other, they try to get the administration into their own
hands.⁶ Further, there is a question of degree; an oligarchy, for example, may become more or less oligarchi-
15 cal, and a democracy more or less democratical; and in
like manner the characteristics of the other forms of government may be more or less strictly maintained. Or the
revolution may be directed against a portion of the constitution only, e. g. the establishment or overthrow of a
particular office: as at Sparta it is said that Lysander
20 attempted to overthrow the monarchy, and king Pausa-

---

³ Cp. iii. 1284ᵇ 28–34.                    ⁴ Cp. 1304ᵇ 4.
⁵ Cp. iv. 1294ᵃ 21.                         ⁶ Cp. iv. 1292ᵇ 11.

nias,[7] the ephoralty. At Epidamnus, too, the change was
partial. For instead of phylarchs or heads of tribes, a
council was appointed; but to this day the magistrates
are the only members of the ruling class who are compelled to go to the Heliaea when an election takes place, 25
and the office of the single archon [8] was another oligarchical feature. Everywhere inequality is a cause of revolution, but an inequality in which there is no proportion
—for instance, a perpetual monarchy among equals; and
always it is the desire of equality which rises in rebellion.

Now equality is of two kinds, numerical and propor-
tional; by the first I mean sameness or equality in num- 30
ber or size; by the second, equality of ratios. For example, the excess of three over two is numerically equal to
the excess of two over one; whereas four exceeds two
in the same ratio in which two exceeds one, for two is
the same part of four that one is of two, namely, the half. 35
As I was saying before,[9] men agree that justice in the
abstract is proportion, but they differ in that some think
that if they are equal in any respect they are equal absolutely, others that if they are unequal in any respect they
should be unequal in all. Hence there are two principal
forms of government, democracy and oligarchy; for good 40
birth and virtue are rare, but wealth and numbers are 1302ᵃ
more common. In what city shall we find a hundred persons of good birth and of virtue? whereas the rich everywhere abound. That a state should be ordered, simply
and wholly, according to either kind of equality, is not
a good thing; the proof is the fact that such forms of 5
government never last. They are originally based on a
mistake, and, as they begin badly, cannot fail to end
badly. The inference is that both kinds of equality should

---

[7] Cp. vii. 1333ᵇ 34.          [8] Cp. iii. 1287ᵃ 7.          [9] ᵃ26.

be employed; numerical in some cases, and proportionate in others.

Still democracy appears to be safer and less liable to
10 revolution than oligarchy.[10] For in oligarchies [11] there is
the double danger of the oligarchs falling out among
themselves and also with the people; but in democracies [12] there is only the danger of a quarrel with the oligarchs. No dissension worth mentioning arises among
the people themselves. And we may further remark that
a government which is composed of the middle class
more nearly approximates to democracy than to oli-
15 garchy, and is the safest of the imperfect forms of government.

**2** In considering how dissensions and political revolutions arise, we must first of all ascertain the beginnings
and causes of them which affect constitutions generally.
They may be said to be three in number; and we have
20 now to give an outline of each. We want to know (1)
what is the feeling? (2) what are the motives of those
who make them? (3) whence arise political disturbances
and quarrels? The universal and chief cause of this revolutionary feeling has been already mentioned; [13] viz.
25 the desire of equality, when men think that they are
equal to others who have more than themselves; or,
again, the desire of inequality and superiority, when
conceiving themselves to be superior they think that
they have not more but the same or less than their inferiors; pretensions which may and may not be just. In-
30 feriors revolt in order that they may be equal, and equals
that they may be superior. Such is the state of mind
which creates revolutions. The motives for making them

---

[10] Cp. iv. 1296ᵃ 13.　　　　　　　　　　　[11] Cp. c. 6.
[12] Cp. c. 5.　　　　　　　　　[13] 1301ᵃ 33 sqq., ᵇ35 sqq.

are the desire of gain and honour, or the fear of dishonour
and loss; the authors of them want to divert punishment
or dishonour from themselves or their friends. The
causes and reasons of revolutions, whereby men are 35
themselves affected in the way described, and about the
things which I have mentioned, viewed in one way may
be regarded as seven, and in another as more than seven.
Two of them have been already noticed; [14] but they act
in a different manner, for men are excited against one
another by the love of gain and honour—not, as in the
case which I have just supposed, in order to obtain them 40
for themselves, but at seeing others, justly or unjustly, 1302ᵇ
engrossing them. Other causes are insolence, fear, excessive predominance, contempt, disproportionate increase in some part of the state; causes of another sort
are election intrigues, carelessness, neglect about trifles,
dissimilarity of elements.

**3**  What share insolence and avarice have in creating 5
revolutions, and how they work, is plain enough. When
the magistrates are insolent and grasping they conspire
against one another and also against the constitution
from which they derive their power, making their gains
either at the expense of individuals or of the public. It is 10
evident, again, what an influence honour exerts and how
it is a cause of revolution. Men who are themselves dishonoured and who see others obtaining honours rise in
rebellion; the honour or dishonour when undeserved is
unjust; and just when awarded according to merit.
Again, superiority is a cause of revolution when one or 15
more persons have a power which is too much for the
state and the power of the government; this is a condition
of affairs out of which there arises a monarchy, or a fam-

ily oligarchy. And therefore, in some places, as at Athens and Argos, they have recourse to ostracism.[15] But how much better to provide from the first that there should 20 be no such pre-eminent individuals instead of letting them come into existence and then finding a remedy.

Another cause of revolution is fear. Either men have committed wrong, and are afraid of punishment, or they are expecting to suffer wrong and are desirous of anticipating their enemy. Thus at Rhodes the notables conspired against the people through fear of the suits that 25 were brought against them.[16] Contempt is also a cause of insurrection and revolution; for example, in oligarchies—when those who have no share in the state are the majority, they revolt, because they think that they are the stronger. Or, again, in democracies, the rich despise the disorder and anarchy of the state; at Thebes, for example, where, after the battle of Oenophyta, the bad 30 administration of the democracy led to its ruin. At Megara the fall of the democracy was due to a defeat occasioned by disorder and anarchy. And at Syracuse the democracy aroused contempt before the tyranny of Gelo arose; at Rhodes, before the insurrection.

Political revolutions also spring from a disproportion- 35 ate increase in any part of the state. For as a body is made up of many members, and every member ought to grow in proportion,[17] that symmetry may be preserved; but loses its nature if the foot be four cubits long and the rest of the body two spans; and, should the abnormal increase be one of quality as well as of quantity, 40 may even take the form of another animal: even so a state has many parts, of which some one may often grow 1303ª imperceptibly; for example, the number of poor in democracies and in constitutional states. And this dispro-

---

[15] Cp. iii. 1284ª 17.  [16] Cp. 1304ᵇ 27.  [17] Cp. iii. 1284ᵇ 8.

portion may sometimes happen by an accident, as at
Tarentum, from a defeat in which many of the notables
were slain in a battle with the Iapygians just after the
Persian War, the constitutional government in conse-  5
quence becoming a democracy; or as was the case at
Argos, where the Argives, after their army had been cut
to pieces on the seventh day of the month by Cleomenes
the Lacedaemonian, were compelled to admit to citizenship some of their perioeci; and at Athens, when, after
frequent defeats of their infantry at the time of the
Peloponnesian War, the notables were reduced in number, because the soldiers had to be taken from the roll of  10
citizens. Revolutions arise from this cause as well, in
democracies as in other forms of government, but not to
so great an extent. When the rich grow numerous or
properties increase, the form of government changes into
an oligarchy or a government of families. Forms of government also change—sometimes even without revolution, owing to election contests, as at Heraea (where,  15
instead of electing their magistrates, they took them by
lot, because the electors were in the habit of choosing
their own partisans); or owing to carelessness, when disloyal persons are allowed to find their way into the highest
offices, as at Oreum, where, upon the accession of Herac-
leodorus to office, the oligarchy was overthrown, and
changed by him into a constitutional and democratical
government.

Again, the revolution may be facilitated by the slight-  20
ness of the change; I mean that a great change may
sometimes slip into the constitution through neglect of
a small matter; at Ambracia, for instance, the qualification for office, small at first, was eventually reduced
to nothing. For the Ambraciots thought that a small
qualification was much the same as none at all.

25 Another cause of revolution is difference of races which do not at once acquire a common spirit; for a state is not the growth of a day, any more than it grows out of a multitude brought together by accident. Hence the reception of strangers in colonies, either at the time of their foundation or afterwards, has generally produced revolution; for example, the Achaeans who joined the
30 Troezenians in the foundation of Sybaris, becoming later the more numerous, expelled them; hence the curse fell upon Sybaris. At Thurii the Sybarites quarrelled with their fellow-colonists; thinking that the land belonged to them, they wanted too much of it and were driven out. At Byzantium the new colonists were detected in a conspiracy, and were expelled by force of arms; the people of Antissa, who had received the Chian
35 exiles, fought with them, and drove them out; and the Zancleans, after having received the Samians, were driven by them out of their own city. The citizens of Apollonia on the Euxine, after the introduction of a fresh body of colonists, had a revolution; the Syracusans, after
1303ᵇ the expulsion of their tyrants, having admitted strangers and mercenaries to the rights of citizenship, quarrelled and came to blows; the people Amphipolis, having received Chalcidian colonists, were nearly all expelled by them.

5 Now, in oligarchies the masses make revolution under the idea that they are unjustly treated, because, as I said before,[18] they are equals, and have not an equal share, and in democracies the notables revolt, because they are not equals, and yet have only an equal share.

Again, the situation of cities is a cause of revolution when the country is not naturally adapted to preserve the unity of the state. For example, the Chytians at Cla-

---

[18] 1301ᵃ 33.

zomenae did not agree with the people of the island; and
the people of Colophon quarrelled with the Notians; at 10
Athens too, the inhabitants of the Piraeus are more democratic than those who live in the city. For just as in
war the impediment of a ditch, though ever so small, may
break a regiment, so every cause of difference, however
slight, makes a breach in a city. The greatest opposition 15
is confessedly that of virtue and vice; next comes that of
wealth and poverty; and there are other antagonistic
elements, greater or less, of which one is this difference
of place.

**4** In revolutions the occasions may be trifling, but great
interests are at stake. Even trifles are most important
when they concern the rulers, as was the case of old at 20
Syracuse; for the Syracusan constitution was once
changed by a love-quarrel of two young men, who were
in the government. The story is that while one of them
was away from home his beloved was gained over by his
companion, and he to revenge himself seduced the other's
wife. They then drew the members of the ruling class into
their quarrel and so split all the people into portions. 25
We learn from this story that we should be on our guard
against the beginnings of such evils, and should put an
end to the quarrels of chiefs and mighty men. The mistake lies in the beginning—as the proverb says—'Well 30
begun is half done'; so an error at the beginning, though
quite small, bears the same ratio to the errors in the other
parts. In general, when the notables quarrel, the whole
city is involved, as happened in Hestiaea after the Persian War. The occasion was the division of an inheritance; one of two brothers refused to give an account of 35
their father's property and the treasure which he had
found: so the poorer of the two quarrelled with him and

enlisted in his cause the popular party, the other, who was very rich, the wealthy classes.

At Delphi, again, a quarrel about a marriage was the
**1304ᵃ** beginning of all the troubles which followed. In this case the bridegroom, fancying some occurrence to be of evil omen, came to the bride, and went away without taking her. Whereupon her relations, thinking that they were insulted by him, put some of the sacred treasure among his offerings while he was sacrificing, and then slew him, pretending that he had been robbing the temple. At Mytilene, too, a dispute about heiresses was the begin-
5 ning of many misfortunes, and led to the war with the Athenians in which Paches took their city. A wealthy citizen, named Timophanes, left two daughters; Dexander, another citizen, wanted to obtain them for his sons; but he was rejected in his suit, whereupon he stirred up a revolution, and instigated the Athenians (of whom he
10 was proxenus) to interfere. A similar quarrel about an heiress arose at Phocis between Mnaseas the father of Mnason, and Euthycrates the father of Onomarchus; this was the beginning of the Sacred War. A marriage-quarrel was also the cause of a change in the government of Epidamnus. A certain man betrothed his daughter to a
15 person whose father, having been made a magistrate, fined the father of the girl, and the latter, stung by the insult, conspired with the unenfranchised classes to overthrow the state.

Governments also change into oligarchy or into democracy or into a constitutional government because the magistrates, or some other section of the state, increase
20 in power or renown. Thus at Athens the reputation gained by the court of the Areopagus, in the Persian War, seemed to tighten the reins of government. On the

other hand, the victory of Salamis,[19] which was gained
by the common people who served in the fleet, and won
for the Athenians the empire due to command of the sea,
strengthened the democracy. At Argos, the notables, 25
having distinguished themselves against the Lacedaemonians in the battle of Mantinea, attempted to put down
the democracy. At Syracuse, the people, having been the
chief authors of the victory in the war with the Athenians, changed the constitutional government into democracy. At Chalcis, the people, uniting with the nota- 30
bles, killed Phoxus the tyrant, and then seized the government. At Ambracia,[20] the people, in like manner, having
joined with the conspirators in expelling the tyrant Periander, transferred the government to themselves. And
generally, it should be remembered that those who have
secured power to the state, whether private citizens, or 35
magistrates, or tribes, or any other part or section of the
state, are apt to cause revolutions. For either envy of
their greatness draws others into rebellion, or they themselves, in their pride of superiority, are unwilling to remain on a level with others.

Revolutions also break out when opposite parties, e. g.
the rich and the people, are equally balanced, and there 1304
is little or no middle class; for, if either party were manifestly superior, the other would not risk an attack upon
them. And, for this reason, those who are eminent in
virtue usually do not stir up insurrections, always a
minority. Such are the beginnings and causes of the dis- 5
turbances and revolutions to which every form of government is liable.

Revolutions are effected in two ways, by force and by
fraud. Force may be applied either at the time of making 10
the revolution or afterwards. Fraud, again, is of two

[19] Cp. ii. 1274[a] 12; viii. 1341[a] 29.          [20] Cp. 1311[a] 39.

kinds; for (1) sometimes the citizens are deceived into acquiescing in a change of government, and afterwards they are held in subjection against their will. This was what happened in the case of the Four Hundred, who deceived the people by telling them that the king would provide money for the war against the Lacedaemonians, and, having cheated the people, still endeavoured to retain the government. (2) In other cases the people are persuaded at first, and afterwards, by a repetition of the persuasion, their goodwill and allegiance are retained. The revolutions which effect constitutions generally spring from the above-mentioned causes.[21]

**5** And now, taking each constitution separately, we must see what follows from the principles already laid down.

Revolutions in democracies are generally caused by the intemperance of demagogues, who either in their private capacity lay information against rich men until they compel them to combine (for a common danger unites even the bitterest enemies), or coming forward in public stir up the people against them. The truth of this remark is proved by a variety of examples. At Cos the democracy was overthrown because wicked demagogues arose, and the notables combined. At Rhodes the demagogues not only provided pay for the multitude, but prevented them from making good to the trierarchs the sums which had been expended by them; and they, in consequence of the suits which were brought against them, were compelled to combine and put down the democracy.[22] The democracy at Heraclea was overthrown shortly after the foundation of the colony by the injustice of the demagogues, which drove out the notables,

[21] Cp. 1302[a] 17.     [22] Cp. 1302[b] 23.

who came back in a body and put an end to the democracy. Much in the same manner the democracy at Megara [23] was overturned; there the demagogues drove out 35
many of the notables in order that they might be able to
confiscate their property. At length the exiles, becoming
numerous, returned, and, engaging and defeating the
people, established the oligarchy. The same thing hap- 1305ᵃ
pened with the democracy of Cyme, which was overthrown by Thrasymachus. And we may observe that in
most states the changes have been of this character.
For sometimes the demagogues, in order to curry favour
with the people, wrong the notables and so force them
to combine;—either they make a division of their property, or diminish their incomes by the imposition of public services, and sometimes they bring accusations 5
against the rich that they may have their wealth to confiscate.[24]

Of old, the demagogue was also a general, and then
democracies changed into tyrannies. Most of the ancient 10
tyrants were originally demagogues.[25] They are not so
now, but they were then; and the reason is that they were
generals and not orators, for oratory had not yet come
into fashion. Whereas in our day, when the art of rhetoric
has made such progress, the orators lead the people, but
their ignorance of military matters prevents them from
usurping power; at any rate instances to the contrary
are few and slight. Tyrannies were more common for- 15
merly than now, for this reason also, that great power
was placed in the hands of individuals; thus a tyranny
arose at Miletus out of the office of the Prytanis, who had
supreme authority in many important matters.[26] Moreover, in those days, when cities were not large, the peo-

---

[23] Cp. 1302ᵇ 31, iv. 1300ᵃ 17.        [24] Cp. 1309ᵃ 14.

[25] Cp. 1310ᵇ 14; Plato, *Rep.* viii. 565 D.        [26] Cp. 1310ᵇ 20.

ple dwelt in the fields, busy at their work; and their
20 chiefs, if they possessed any military talent, seized the
opportunity, and winning the confidence of the masses
by professing their hatred of the wealthy, they succeeded
in obtaining the tyranny. Thus at Athens Peisistratus
led a faction against the men of the plain, and Theage-
nes at Megara slaughtered the cattle of the wealthy,
25 which he found by the river side, where they had put
them to graze in land not their own. Dionysius, again,
was thought worthy of the tyranny because he de-
nounced Daphnaeus and the rich; his enmity to the
notables won for him the confidence of the people.
Changes also take place from the ancient to the latest
30 form of democracy; for where there is a popular election
of the magistrates and no property qualification, the aspirants for office get hold of the people, and contrive at
last even to set them above the laws. A more or less
complete cure for this state of things is for the separate
tribes, and not the whole people, to elect the magistrates.
35 These are the principal causes of revolutions in democracies.

6 There are two patent causes of revolutions in oligarchies: (1) First, when the oligarchs oppress the
people, for then anybody is good enough to be their
champion, especially if he be himself a member of the
40 oligarchy, as Lygdamis at Naxos, who afterwards came
1305ᵇ to be tyrant. But revolutions which commence outside
the governing class may be further subdivided. Sometimes, when the government is very exclusive, the revolution is brought about by persons of the wealthy class
5 who are excluded, as happened at Massalia and Istros
and Heraclea, and other cities. Those who had no share
in the government created a disturbance, until first the

elder brothers, and then the younger, were admitted; for
in some places father and son, in others elder and
younger brothers, do not hold office together. At Mas-  10
salia the oligarchy became more like a constitutional
government, but at Istros ended in a democracy, and at
Heraclea was enlarged to 600. At Cnidos, again, the oligarchy underwent a considerable change. For the notables fell out among themselves, because only a few
shared in the government; there existed among them the
rule already mentioned, that father and son could not  15
hold office together, and, if there were several brothers,
only the eldest was admitted. The people took advantage of the quarrel, and choosing one of the notables to
be their leader, attacked and conquered the oligarchs,
who were divided, and division is always a source of
weakness. The city of Erythrae, too, in old times was
ruled, and ruled well, by the Basilidae, but the people  20
took offence at the narrowness of the oligarchy and
changed the constitution.

(2) Of internal causes of revolutions in oligarchies
one is the personal rivalry of the oligarchs, which leads
them to play the demagogue. Now, the oligarchical demagogue is of two sorts: either (*a*) he practises upon the
oligarchs themselves (for, although the oligarchy are
quite a small number, there may be a demagogue among  25
them, as at Athens Charicles' party won power by courting the Thirty, that of Phrynichus by courting the Four
Hundred); or (*b*) the oligarchs may play the demagogue with the people. This was the case at Larissa,
where the guardians of the citizens endeavoured to gain
over the people because they were elected by them; and  30
such is the fate of all oligarchies in which the magistrates
are elected, as at Abydos, not by the class to which they
belong, but by the heavy-armed or by the people, al-

though they may be required to have a high qualification, or to be members of a political club; or, again, where the law-courts are composed of persons outside the government, the oligarchs flatter the people in order to obtain 35 a decision in their own favour, and so they change the constitution; this happened at Heraclea in Pontus. Again, oligarchies change whenever any attempt is made to narrow them; for then those who desire equal rights are compelled to call in the people. Changes in the oligarchy also occur when the oligarchs waste their private 40 property by extravagant living; for then they want to 1306ª innovate, and either try to make themselves tyrants, or install some one else in the tyranny, as Hipparinus did Dionysius at Syracuse, and as at Amphipolis²⁷ a man named Cleotimus introduced Chalcidian colonists, and when they arrived, stirred them up against the rich. For a like reason in Aegina the person who carried on the 5 negotiation with Chares endeavoured to revolutionize the state. Sometimes a party among the oligarchs try directly to create a political change; sometimes they rob the treasury, and then either the thieves or, as happened at Apollonia in Pontus, those who resist them in their thieving quarrel with the rulers. But an oligarchy which 10 is at unity with itself is not easily destroyed from within; of this we may see an example at Pharsalus, for there, although the rulers are few in number, they govern a large city, because they have a good understanding among themselves.

Oligarchies, again, are overthrown when another oligarchy is created within the original one, that is to say, 15 when the whole governing body is small and yet they do not all share in the highest offices. Thus at Elis the governing body was a small senate; and very few ever

²⁷ Cp 1303ᵇ 2.

found their way into it, because the senators were only ninety in number, and were elected for life and out of certain families in a manner similar to the Lacedaemo- 20 nian elders. Oligarchy is liable to revolutions alike in war and in peace; in war because, not being able to trust the people, the oligarchs are compelled to hire mercenaries, and the general who is in command of them often ends in becoming a tyrant, as Timophanes did at Corinth; or if there are more generals than one they make 25 themselves into a company of tyrants. Sometimes the oligarchs, fearing this danger, give the people a share in the government because their services are necessary to them. And in time of peace, from mutual distrust, the two parties hand over the defence of the state to the army and to an arbiter between the two factions, who often ends the master of both. This happened at Larissa when Simos the Aleuad had the government, and at Aby- 30 dos in the days of Iphiades and the political clubs. Revolutions also arise out of marriages or lawsuits which lead to the overthrow of one party among the oligarchs by another. Of quarrels about marriages I have already mentioned[28] some instances; another occurred at Ere- 35 tria, where Diagoras overturned the oligarchy of the knights because he had been wronged about a marriage. A revolution at Heraclea, and another at Thebes, both arose out of decisions of law-courts upon a charge of adultery; in both cases the punishment was just, but executed in the spirit of party, at Heraclea upon Eury- 1306ᵇ tion, and at Thebes upon Archias; for their enemies were jealous of them and so had them pilloried in the agora. Many oligarchies have been destroyed by some members of the ruling class taking offence at their exces- 5

[28] 1303ᵇ 37–1304ᵃ 17.

sive despotism; for example, the oligarchy at Cnidus and at Chios.

Changes of constitutional governments, and also of oligarchies which limit the office of counsellor, judge, or other magistrate to persons having a certain money qualification, often occur by accident. The qualification may have been originally fixed according to the circum-
10 stances of the time, in such a manner as to include in an oligarchy a few only, or in a constitutional government the middle class. But after a time of prosperity, whether arising from peace or some other good fortune, the same property becomes many times as valuable, and then everybody participates in every office; this happens
15 sometimes gradually and insensibly, and sometimes quickly. These are the causes of changes and revolutions in oligarchies.

We must remark generally, both of democracies and oligarchies, that they sometimes change, not into the opposite forms of government, but only into another variety of the same class; I mean to say, from those forms
20 of democracy and oligarchy which are regulated by law into those which are arbitrary, and conversely.

**7** In aristocracies revolutions are stirred up when a few only share in the honours of the state; a cause which has been already shown [29] to affect oligarchies; for an aris-
25 tocracy is a sort of oligarchy, and, like an oligarchy, is the government of a few, although few not for the same reason; hence the two are often confounded. And revolutions will be most likely to happen, and must happen, when the mass of the people are of the high-spirited kind, and have a notion that they are as good as their rulers. Thus at Lacedaemon the so-called Partheniae, who were

[29] 1305$^b$ 2 sqq.

the sons [30] of the Spartan peers, attempted a revolution, 30
and, being detected, were sent away to colonize Tarentum. Again, revolutions occur when great men who are at
least of equal merit are dishonoured by those higher in
office, as Lysander was by the kings of Sparta; or, when
a brave man is excluded from the honours of the state,
like Cinadon, who conspired against the Spartans in the 35
reign of Agesilaus; or, again, when some are very poor
and others very rich, a state of society which is most
often the result of war, as at Lacedaemon in the days of
the Messenian War; this is proved from the poem of
Tyrtaeus, entitled 'Good Order'; for he speaks of cer- 1307ᴬ
tain citizens who were ruined by the war and wanted to
have a redistribution of the land. Again, revolutions
arise when an individual who is great, and might be
greater, wants to rule alone, as, at Lacedaemon, Pausanias, who was general in the Persian War, or like Hanno
at Carthage.

Constitutional governments and aristocracies are com- 5
monly overthrown owing to some deviation from justice
in the constitution itself; the cause of the downfall is,
in the former, the ill-mingling of the two elements, democracy and oligarchy; in the latter, of the three elements, democracy, oligarchy, and virtue, but especially 10
democracy and oligarchy. For to combine these is the
endeavour of constitutional governments; and most of
the so-called aristocracies have a like aim,[31] but differ
from polities in the mode of combination; hence some
of them are more and some less permanent. Those which 15
incline more to oligarchy are called aristocracies, and
those which incline to democracy constitutional governments. And therefore the latter are the safer of the two;
for the greater the number, the greater the strength, and

---

[30] i. e. the illegitimate sons.                    [31] Cp. iv. c. 7.

when men are equal they are contented. But the rich, if
20 the constitution gives them power, are apt to be insolent
and avaricious; and, in general, whichever way the constitution inclines, in that direction it changes as either
party gains strength, a constitutional government becoming a democracy, an aristocracy an oligarchy. But
the process may be reversed, and aristocracy may change
into democracy. This happens when the poor, under the
idea that they are being wronged, force the constitution to take an opposite form. In like manner constitu-
25 tional governments change into oligarchies. The only
stable principle of government is equality according to
proportion, and for every man to enjoy his own.

What I have just mentioned actually happened at
Thurii,[32] where the qualification for office, at first high,
was therefore reduced, and the magistrates increased in
number. The notables had previously acquired the whole
30 of the land contrary to law; for the government tended
to oligarchy, and they were able to encroach. . . . But
the people, who had been trained by war, soon got the
better of the guards kept by the oligarchs, until those
who had too much gave up their land.

Again, since all aristocratical governments incline to
35 oligarchy, the notables are apt to be grasping; thus at
Lacedaemon, where property tends to pass into few
hands,[33] the notables can do too much as they like, and
are allowed to marry whom they please. The city of Locri
was ruined by a marriage connexion with Dionysius, but
such a thing could never have happened in a democracy,
or in a well-balanced aristocracy.

40 I have already remarked that in all states revolutions
1307ᵇ are occasioned by trifles.[34] In aristocracies, above all,

---

[32] Cp. 1303ᵃ 31.                    [33] Cp. ii. 1270ᵃ 18.
[34] 1302ᵇ 4, 1303ᵃ 20–25, ᵇ17.

they are of a gradual and imperceptible nature. The citizens begin by giving up some part of the constitution, and so with greater ease the government change something else which is a little more important, until they have 5 undermined the whole fabric of the state. At Thurii there was a law that generals should only be re-elected after an interval of five years, and some young men who were popular with the soldiers of the guard for their military prowess, despising the magistrates and thinking that they would easily gain their purpose, wanted to abolish 10 this law and allow their generals to hold perpetual commands; for they well knew that the people would be glad enough to elect them. Whereupon the magistrates who had charge of these matters, and who are called councillors, at first determined to resist, but they afterwards consented, thinking that, if only this one law was 15 changed, no further inroad would be made on the constitution. But other changes soon followed which they in vain attempted to oppose; and the state passed into the hands of the revolutionists, who established a dynastic oligarchy.

All constitutions are overthrown either from within or from without; the latter, when there is some govern- 20 ment close at hand having an opposite interest, or at a distance, but powerful. This was exemplified in the old times of the Athenians and the Lacedaemonians; the Athenians everywhere put down the oligarchies, and the Lacedaemonians the democracies.[35]

I have now explained what are the chief causes of revolutions and dissensions in states. 25

**8**  We have next to consider what means there are of preserving constitutions in general, and in particular

[35] Cp. iv. 1296ᵃ 32.

cases. In the first place it is evident that if we know the causes which destroy constitutions, we also know the causes which preserve them; for opposites produce opposites, and destruction is the opposite of preservation.[36]

30 In all well-attempered governments there is nothing which should be more jealously maintained than the spirit of obedience to law, more especially in small matters; for transgression creeps in unperceived and at last ruins the state, just as the constant recurrence of small expenses in time eats up a fortune. The expense does not

35 take place all at once, and therefore is not observed; the mind is deceived, as in the fallacy which says that 'if each part is little, then the whole is little'. And this is true in one way, but not in another, for the whole and the all are not little, although they are made up of littles.

In the first place, then, men should guard against the

40 beginning of change, and in the second place they should not rely upon the political devices of which I have al-

1308ᵃ ready spoken[37] invented only to deceive the people, for they are proved by experience to be useless. Further, we note that oligarchies as well as aristocracies may last, not from any inherent stability in such forms of government,

5 but because the rulers are on good terms both with the unenfranchised and with the governing classes, not maltreating any who are excluded from the government, but introducing into it the leading spirits among them.[38] They should never wrong the ambitious in a matter of

10 honour, or the common people in a matter of money; and they should treat one another and their fellow-citizens in a spirit of equality. The equality which the friends of democracy seek to establish for the multitude is not only just but likewise expedient among equals. Hence, if the

---

[36] Cp. *Nic. Eth.* v. 1129ᵃ 13.    [37] Cp. iv. 1297ᵃ 13–38.
[38] Cp. vi. 1321ᵃ 26.

governing class are numerous, many democratic institu- 15
tions are useful; for example, the restriction of the tenure of offices to six months, that all those who are of
equal rank may share in them. Indeed, equals or peers
when they are numerous become a kind of democracy,
and therefore demagogues are very likely to arise among
them, as I have already remarked.[39] The short tenure of
office prevents oligarchies and aristocracies from falling
into the hands of families; it is not easy for a person to
do any great harm when his tenure of office is short, 20
whereas long possession begets tyranny in oligarchies
and democracies. For the aspirants to tyranny are either
the principal men of the state, who in democracies are
demagogues and in oligarchies members of ruling houses,
or those who hold great offices, and have a long tenure
of them.[40]

Constitutions are preserved when their destroyers are 25
at a distance, and sometimes also because they are near,
for the fear of them makes the government keep in hand
the constitution. Wherefore the ruler who has a care of
the constitution should invent terrors, and bring distant
dangers near, in order that the citizens may be on their
guard, and, like sentinels in a night-watch, never relax
their attention. He should endeavour too by help of the 30
laws to control the contentions and quarrels of the notables, and to prevent those who have not hitherto taken
part in them from catching the spirit of contention. No
ordinary man can discern the beginning of evil,[41] but
only the true statesman.

As to the change produced in oligarchies and consti- 35
tutional governments [42] by the alteration of the qualification, when this arises, not out of any variation in the

[39] 1305$^b$ 23 sqq.                    [40] Cp. 1305$^a$ 7.
[41] Cp. 1303$^b$ 17–31.                 [42] Cp. 1306$^b$ 6–16.

qualification but only out of the increase of money, it is
well to compare the general valuation of property with
40 that of past years, annually in those cities in which the
1308ᵇ census is taken annually, and in larger cities every third
or fifth year. If the whole is many times greater or many
times less than when the ratings recognized by the constitution were fixed, there should be power given by law
5 to raise or lower the qualification as the amount is greater
or less. Where this is not done a constitutional government passes into an oligarchy, and an oligarchy is
narrowed to a rule of families; or in the opposite case
constitutional government becomes democracy, and oligarchy either constitutional government or democracy.

10     It is a principle common to democracy, oligarchy, and
every other form of government not to allow the disproportionate increase of any citizen, but to give moderate
honour for a long time rather than great honour for a
short time. For men are easily spoilt; not every one can
15 bear prosperity. But if this rule is not observed, at any
rate the honours which are given all at once should be
taken away by degrees and not all at once. Especially
should the laws provide against any one having too
much power, whether derived from friends or money; if
20 he has, he should be sent clean out of the country.[43] And
since innovations creep in through the private life of
individuals also, there ought to be a magistracy which
will have an eye to those whose life is not in harmony
with the government, whether oligarchy or democracy
or any other. And for a like reason an increase of prosperity in any part of the state should be carefully
25 watched. The proper remedy for this evil is always to
give the management of affairs and offices of state to
opposite elements; such opposites are the virtuous and

[43] Cp. 1302ᵇ 18; iii. 1284ᵃ 17.

the many, or the rich and the poor. Another way is to
combine the poor and the rich in one body, or to increase the middle class: thus an end will be put to the
revolutions which arise from inequality.                    30

But above all every state should be so administered
and so regulated by law that its magistrates cannot possibly make money.[44] In oligarchies special precautions
should be used against this evil. For the people do not
take any great offence at being kept out of the government—indeed they are rather pleased than otherwise at 35
having leisure for their private business—but what irri-
tates them is to think that their rulers are stealing the
public money; then they are doubly annoyed; for they
lose both honour and profit. If office brought no profit,
then and then only could democracy and aristocracy be
combined; for both notables and people might have their 40
wishes gratified. All would be able to hold office, which 1309ᵛ
is the aim of democracy, and the notables would be magistrates, which is the aim of aristocracy. And this result
may be accomplished when there is no possibility of
making money out of the offices; for the poor will not
want to have them when there is nothing to be gained 5
from them—they would rather be attending to their own
concerns; and the rich, who do not want money from
the public treasury, will be able to take them; and so
the poor will keep to their work and grow rich, and the
notables will not be governed by the lower class. In
order to avoid peculation of the public money, the trans- 10
fer of the revenue should be made at a general assembly
of the citizens, and duplicates of the accounts deposited
with the different brotherhoods, companies, and tribes.
And honours should be given by law to magistrates who
have the reputation of being incorruptible. In democ-

[44] Cp. 1316ᵃ 39.

15 racies the rich should be spared; not only should their property not be divided, but their incomes also, which in some states are taken from them imperceptibly, should be protected. It is a good thing to prevent the wealthy citizens, even if they are willing, from undertaking expensive and useless public services, such as the giving of choruses, torch-races, and the like. In an oligarchy, 20 on the other hand, great care should be taken of the poor, and lucrative offices should go to them; if any of the wealthy classes insult them, the offender should be punished more severely than if he had wronged one of his own class. Provision should be made that estates 25 pass by inheritance and not by gift, and no person should have more than one inheritance; for in this way properties will be equalized, and more of the poor rise to competency. It is also expedient both in a democracy and in an oligarchy to assign to those who have less share in the government (i. e. to the rich in a democracy and to the 30 poor in an oligarchy) an equality or preference in all but the principal offices of state. The latter should be entrusted chiefly or only to members of the governing class.

**9**  There are three qualifications required in those who have to fill the highest offices—(1) first of all, loyalty to the established constitution; (2) the greatest admin-35 istrative capacity; (3) virtue and justice of the kind proper to each form of government; for, if what is just is not the same in all governments, the quality of justice must also differ. There may be a doubt, however, when all these qualities do not meet in the same person, how 40 the selection is to be made; suppose, for example, a good 1309ᵇ general is a bad man and not a friend to the constitution, and another man is loyal and just, which should

we choose? In making the election ought we not to consider two points? what qualities are common, and what
are rare. Thus in the choice of a general, we should regard his skill rather than his virtue; for few have mili- 5
tary skill, but many have virtue. In any office of trust
or stewardship, on the other hand, the opposite rule
should be observed; for more virtue than ordinary is
required in the holder of such an office, but the necessary
knowledge is of a sort which all men possess.

It may, however, be asked what a man wants with
virtue if he have political ability and is loyal, since these 10
two qualities alone will make him do what is for the
public interest. But may not men have both of them
and yet be deficient in self-control? If, knowing and
loving their own interests, they do not always attend to
them, may they not be equally negligent of the interests
of the public?

Speaking generally, we may say that whatever legal
enactments are held to be for the interest of various 15
constitutions, all these preserve them. And the great preserving principle is the one which has been repeatedly
mentioned [45]—to have a care that the loyal citizens
should be stronger than the disloyal. Neither should we
forget the mean, which at the present day is lost sight
of in perverted forms of government; for many practices 20
which appear to be democratical are the ruin of democracies, and many which appear to be oligarchical are
the ruin of oligarchies. Those who think that all virtue
is to be found in their own party principles push matters to extremes; they do not consider that disproportion
destroys a state. A nose which varies from the ideal of
straightness to a hook or snub may still be of good shape
and agreeable to the eye; but if the excess be very great, 25

[45] iv. 1296[b] 15, vi. 1320[a] 14, Cp. ii. 1270[b] 21 sq., iv. 1294[b] 37.

all symmetry is lost, and the nose at last ceases to be a
nose at all on account of some excess in one direction or
defect in the other; and this is true of every other part
30 of the human body. The same law of proportion equally
holds in states. Oligarchy or democracy, although a departure from the most perfect form, may yet be a good
enough government, but if any one attempts to push the
principles of either to an extreme, he will begin by spoil-
ing the government and end by having none at all.
35 Wherefore the legislator and the statesman ought to
know what democratical measures save and what destroy
a democracy, and what oligarchical measures save or
destroy an oligarchy. For neither the one nor the other
can exist or continue to exist unless both rich and poor
are included in it. If equality of property is introduced,
40 the state must of necessity take another form; for when
1310ª by laws carried to excess one or other element in the state
is ruined, the constitution is ruined.

There is an error common both to oligarchies and to
democracies:—in the latter the demagogues, when the
multitude are above the law, are always cutting the city
5 in two by quarrels with the rich, whereas they should
always profess to be maintaining their cause; just as in
oligarchies the oligarchs should profess to maintain the
cause of the people, and should take oaths the opposite
of those which they now take. For there are cities in
which they swear—'I will be an enemy to the people,
and will devise all the harm against them which I can';
10 but they ought to exhibit and to entertain the very opposite feeling; in the form of their oath there should be an
express declaration—'I will do no wrong to the people.'

But of all the things which I have mentioned that
which most contributes to the permanence of constitu-

tions is the adaptation of education to the form of government,[46] and yet in our own day this principle is universally neglected. The best laws, though sanctioned 15 by every citizen of the state, will be of no avail unless the young are trained by habit and education in the spirit of the constitution, if the laws are democratical, democratically, or oligarchically, if the laws are oligarchical. For there may be a want of self-discipline in states as well as in individuals. Now, to have been educated in the spirit of the constitution is not to perform the actions 20 in which oligarchs or democrats delight, but those by which the existence of an oligarchy or of a democracy is made possible. Whereas among ourselves the sons of the ruling class in an oligarchy live in luxury,[47] but the sons of the poor are hardened by exercise and toil, and hence they are both more inclined and better able to make a revolution.[48] And in democracies of the more 25 extreme type there has arisen a false idea of freedom which is contradictory to the true interests of the state. For two principles are characteristic of democracy, the government of the majority and freedom. Men think that what is just is equal; and that equality is the su- 30 premacy of the popular will; and that freedom means the doing what a man likes. In such democracies every one lives as he pleases, or in the words of Euripides, 'according to his fancy'. But this is all wrong; men should not think it slavery to live according to the rule 35 of the constitution; for it is their salvation.

I have now discussed generally the causes of the revolution and destruction of states, and the means of their preservation and continuance.

---

[46] Cp. viii. 1337ᵃ 14.                    [47] Cp. iv. 1295ᵇ 17.
[48] Cp. Pl. *Rep.* viii. 556 D.

**10** I have still to speak of monarchy, and the causes of
40 its destruction and preservation. What I have said al-
1310ᵇ ready respecting forms of constitutional government applies almost equally to royal and to tyrannical rule. For
royal rule is of the nature of an aristocracy, and a tyranny
is a compound of oligarchy and democracy in their most
5 extreme forms; it is therefore most injurious to its subjects, being made up of two evil forms of government,
and having the perversions and errors of both. These
two forms of monarchy are contrary in their very origin.
The appointment of a king is the resource of the better
10 classes against the people, and he is elected by them out
of their own number, because either he himself or his
family excel in virtue and virtuous actions; whereas a
tyrant is chosen from the people to be their protector
against the notables, and in order to prevent them from
being injured. History shows that almost all tyrants
have been demagogues who gained the favour of the
15 people by their accusation of the notables.⁴⁹ At any rate
this was the manner in which the tyrannies arose in the
days when cities had increased in power. Others which
were older originated in the ambition of kings wanting
to overstep the limits of their hereditary power and become despots. Others again grew out of the class which
20 were chosen to be chief magistrates; for in ancient times
the people who elected them gave the magistrates,
whether civil or religious, a long tenure. Others arose out
of the custom which oligarchies had of making some
individual supreme over the highest offices. In any of
these ways an ambitious man had no difficulty, if he de-
25 sired, in creating a tyranny, since he had the power in
his hands already, either as king or as one of the officers
of state.⁵⁰ Thus Pheidon at Argos and several others

---

⁴⁹ Cp. 1305ᵃ 8; Plato, *Rep.* viii. 565 ᴅ.          ⁵⁰ Cp. 1305ᵃ 15.

were originally kings, and ended by becoming tyrants;
Phalaris, on the other hand, and the Ionian tyrants, acquired the tyranny by holding great offices. Whereas
Panaetius at Leontini, Cypselus at Corinth, Peisistratus 30
at Athens, Dionysius at Syracuse, and several others
who afterwards became tyrants, were at first demagogues.

And so, as I was saying,[51] royalty ranks with aristocracy, for it is based upon merit, whether of the individual
or of his family, or on benefits conferred,[52] or on these
claims with power added to them. For all who have obtained this honour have benefited, or had in their power 35
to benefit, states and nations; some, like Codrus, have
prevented the state from being enslaved in war; others,
like Cyrus, have given their country freedom, or have
settled or gained a territory, like the Lacedaemonian,
Macedonian, and Molossian kings. The idea of a king 40
is to be a protector of the rich against unjust treatment, **1311ᵃ**
of the people against insult and oppression. Whereas a
tyrant, as has often been repeated,[53] has no regard to
any public interest, except as conducive to his private
ends; his aim is pleasure, the aim of a king, honour.
Wherefore also in their desires they differ; the tyrant is 5
desirous of riches, the king, of what brings honour. And
the guards of a king are citizens, but of a tyrant mercenaries.[54]

That tyranny has all the vices both of democracy and
oligarchy is evident. As of oligarchy so of tyranny, the 10
end is wealth; (for by wealth only can the tyrant maintain either his guard or his luxury). Both mistrust the
people, and therefore deprive them of their arms. Both
agree too in injuring the people and driving them out of

---

[51] l. 2 sq.                                    [52] Cp. iii. 1285ᵇ 6.
[53] iii. 1279ᵇ 6 sq., iv. 1295ᵃ 19.            [54] Cp. iii. 1285ᵃ 24.

15 the city and dispersing them. From democracy tyrants
have borrowed the art of making war upon the notables
and destroying them secretly or openly, or of exiling
them because they are rivals and stand in the way of
their power; and also because plots against them are
20 contrived by men of this class, who either want to rule
or to escape subjection. Hence Periander advised Thrasybulus [55] by cutting off the tops of the tallest ears of
corn, meaning that he must always put out of the way
the citizens who overtop the rest. And so, as I have
already intimated,[56] the beginnings of change are the
same in monarchies as in forms of constitutional gov-
25 ernment; subjects attack their sovereigns out of fear or
contempt, or because they have been unjustly treated
by them. And of injustice, the most common form is
insult, another is confiscation of property.

The ends sought by conspiracies against monarchies,
whether tyrannies or royalties, are the same as the ends
30 sought by conspiracies against other forms of government. Monarchs have great wealth and honour, which
are objects of desire to all mankind. The attacks are
made sometimes against their lives, sometimes against
the office; where the sense of insult is the motive, against
their lives. Any sort of insult (and there are many) may
stir up anger, and when men are angry, they commonly
35 act out of revenge, and not from ambition. For example,
the attempt made upon the Peisistratidae arose out of
the public dishonour offered to the sister of Harmodius
and the insult to himself. He attacked the tyrant for his
sister's sake, and Aristogeiton joined in the attack for the
sake of Harmodius. A conspiracy was also formed
40 against Periander, the tyrant of Ambracia, because,
1311ᵇ when drinking with a favourite youth, he asked him

---

[55] Cp. 1284ª 26.                         [56] 1310ª 40 sqq.

whether by this time he was not with child by him.
Philip, too, was attacked by Pausanias because he permitted him to be insulted by Attalus and his friends, and
Amyntas the little, by Derdas, because he boasted of
having enjoyed his youth. Evagoras of Cyprus, again, 5
was slain by the eunuch to revenge an insult; for his wife
had been carried off by Evagoras's son. Many conspiracies have originated in shameful attempts made by sovereigns on the persons of their subjects. Such was the
attack of Crataeas upon Archelaus; he had always hated
the connexion with him, and so, when Archelaus, having
promised him one of his two daughters in marriage, did 10
not give him either of them, but broke his word and married the elder to the king of Elymeia, when he was hard
pressed in a war against Sirrhas and Arrhabaeus, and
the younger to his own son Amyntas, under the idea that
Amyntas would then be less likely to quarrel with his
son by Cleopatra—Crataeas made this slight a pretext 13
for attacking Archelaus, though even a less reason would
have sufficed, for the real cause of the estrangement was
the disgust which he felt at his connection with the king.
And from a like motive Hellanocrates of Larissa conspired with him; for when Archelaus, who was his lover,
did not fulfil his promise of restoring him to his country,
he thought that the connection between them had originated, not in affection, but in the wantonness of power.
Pytho, too, and Heracleides of Aenos, slew Cotys in 20
order to avenge their father, and Adamas revolted from
Cotys in revenge for the wanton outrage which he had
committed in mutilating him when a child.

Many, too, irritated at blows inflicted on the person
which they deemed an insult, have either killed or at- 25
tempted to kill officers of state and royal princes by
whom they have been injured. Thus, at Mytilene, Mega-

cles and his friends attacked and slew the Penthilidae, as they were going about and striking people with clubs. At a later date Smerdis, who had been beaten and torn 30 away from his wife by Penthilus, slew him. In the conspiracy against Archelaus, Decamnichus stimulated the fury of the assassins and led the attack; he was enraged because Archelaus had delivered him to Euripides to be scourged; for the poet had been irritated at some remark made by Decamnichus on the foulness of his breath. 35 Many other examples might be cited of murders and conspiracies which have arisen from similar causes.

Fear is another motive which, as we have said,[57] has caused conspiracies as well in monarchies as in more popular forms of government. Thus Artapanes conspired against Xerxes and slew him, fearing that he would be accused of hanging Darius against his orders—he having been under the impression that Xerxes would forget what he had said in the middle of a meal, and that the offence would be forgiven.

40 Another motive is contempt, as in the case of Sar-1312ª danapalus, whom some one saw carding wool with his women, if the story-tellers say truly; and the tale may be true, if not of him, of some one else.[58] Dion attacked 5 the younger Dionysius because he despised him, and saw that he was equally despised by his own subjects, and that he was always drunk. Even the friends of a tyrant will sometimes attack him out of contempt; for the confidence which he reposes in them breeds con-10 tempt, and they think that they will not be found out. The expectation of success is likewise a sort of contempt; the assailants are ready to strike, and think nothing of the danger, because they seem to have the power in their hands. Thus generals of armies attack mon-

[57] Cp. 1302ᵇ 2, 21, 1311ª 25.     [58] Cp. i. 1259ª 7.

archs; as, for example, Cyrus attacked Astyages, despising the effeminacy of his life, and believing that his
power was worn out. Thus again, Seuthes the Thracian
conspired against Amadocus, whose general he was.

And sometimes men are actuated by more than one 15
motive, like Mithridates, who conspired against Ariobar-
zanes, partly out of contempt and partly from the love
of gain.

Bold natures, placed by their sovereigns in a high
military position, are most likely to make the attempt
in the expectation of success; for courage is emboldened 20
by power, and the union of the two inspires them with
the hope of an easy victory.

Attempts of which the motive is ambition arise in a
different way as well as in those already mentioned.
There are men who will not risk their lives in the hope of 25
gains and honours however great, but who nevertheless
regard the killing of a tyrant simply as an extraordinary
action which will make them famous and honourable in
the world; they wish to acquire, not a kingdom, but a 30
name. It is rare, however, to find such men; he who
would kill a tyrant must be prepared to lose his life if
he fail. He must have the resolution of Dion, who, when
he made war upon Dionysius, took with him very few 35
troops, saying 'that whatever measure of success he
might attain would be enough for him, even if he were
to die the moment he landed; such a death would be
welcome to him'. But this is a temper to which few can
attain.

Once more, tyrannies, like all other governments, are 40
destroyed from without by some opposite and more 1312ᵇ
powerful form of government. That such a government
will have the will to attack them is clear; for the two
are opposed in principle; and all men, if they can, do

what they will. Democracy is antagonistic to tyranny, on the principle of Hesiod, 'Potter hates Potter', because
5 they are nearly akin, for the extreme form of democracy is tyranny; and royalty and aristocracy are both alike opposed to tyranny, because they are constitutions of a different type. And therefore the Lacedaemonians put down most of the tyrannies, and so did the Syracusans during the time when they were well governed.

Again, tyrannies are destroyed from within, when the
10 reigning family are divided among themselves, as that of Gelo was, and more recently that of Dionysius; in the case of Gelo because Thrasybulus, the brother of Hiero, flattered the son of Gelo and led him into excesses in order that he might rule in his name. Whereupon the family got together a party to get rid of Thrasybulus and
15 save the tyranny; but those of the people who conspired with them seized the opportunity and drove them all out. In the case of Dionysius, Dion, his own relative, attacked and expelled him with the assistance of the people; he afterwards perished himself.

There are two chief motives which induce men to
20 attack tyrannies—hatred and contempt. Hatred of tyrants is inevitable, and contempt is also a frequent cause of their destruction. Thus we see that most of those who have acquired, have retained their power, but those who have inherited,[59] have lost it, almost at once; for, living in luxurious ease, they have become contemptible, and
25 offer many opportunities to their assailants. Anger, too, must be included under hatred, and produces the same effects. It is oftentimes even more ready to strike—the angry are more impetuous in making an attack, for they do not follow rational principle. And men are very apt to give way to their passions when they are insulted. To

[59] Cp. Plato. *Laws,* iii. 695.

this cause is to be attributed the fall of the Peisistratidae 30 and of many others. Hatred is more reasonable, for anger is accompanied by pain, which is an impediment to reason, whereas hatred is painless.[60]

In a word, all the causes which I have mentioned [61] as destroying the last and most unmixed form of oli- 35 garchy, and the extreme form of democracy, may be assumed to affect tyranny; indeed the extreme forms of both are only tyrannies distributed among several persons. Kingly rule is little affected by external causes, and is therefore lasting; it is generally destroyed from 40 within. And there are two ways in which the destruction may come about; (1) when the members of the royal 1313ᵛ family quarrel among themselves, and (2) when the kings attempt to administer the state too much after the fashion of a tyranny, and to extend their authority contrary to the law. Royalties do not now come into existence; where such forms of government arise, they are rather monarchies or tyrannies. For the rule of a king is 5 over voluntary subjects, and he is supreme in all important matters; but in our own day men are more upon an equality, and no one is so immeasurably superior to others as to represent adequately the greatness and dignity of the office. Hence mankind will not, if they can help, endure it, and any one who obtains power by force 10 or fraud is at once thought to be a tyrant. In hereditary monarchies a further cause of destruction is the fact that kings often fall into contempt, and, although possessing not tyrannical power, but only royal dignity, are apt to outrage others. Their overthrow is then readily effected; for there is an end to the king when his subjects do not 15 want to have him, but the tyrant lasts, whether they like him or not.

---

[60] Cp. *Rhetoric*, ii. 1382ᵃ 12.     [61] 1302ᵇ 25–33, 1304ᵇ 20–1306ᵇ 21.

The destruction of monarchies is to be attributed to these and the like causes.

**11** And they are preserved, to speak generally, by the opposite causes; or, if we consider them separately, (1) royalty is preserved by the limitation of its powers. The more restricted the functions of kings, the longer their power will last unimpaired; for then they are more moderate and not so despotic in their ways; and they are less envied by their subjects. This is the reason why the kingly office has lasted so long among the Molossians. And for a similar reason it has continued among the Lacedaemonians, because there it was always divided between two, and afterwards further limited by Theopompus in various respects, more particularly by the establishment of the Ephoralty. He diminished the power of the kings, but established on a more lasting basis the kingly office, which was thus made in a certain sense not less, but greater. There is a story that when his wife once asked him whether he was not ashamed to leave to his sons a royal power which was less than he had inherited from his father, 'No indeed,' he replied, 'for the power which I leave to them will be more lasting.'

As to (2) tyrannies, they are preserved in two most opposite ways. One of them is the old traditional method in which most tyrants administer their government. Of such arts Periander of Corinth is said to have been the great master, and many similar devices may be gathered from the Persians in the administration of their government. There are firstly the prescriptions mentioned some distance back,[62] for the preservation of a tyranny, in so far as this is possible; viz. that the tyrant should lop off those who are too high; he must put to death men of

---

[62] 1311ᵃ 15–22.

spirit; he must not allow common meals, clubs, educa- 1313ᵇ
tion, and the like; he must be upon his guard against
anything which is likely to inspire either courage or confidence among his subjects; he must prohibit literary
assemblies or other meetings for discussion, and he must
take every means to prevent people from knowing one
another (for acquaintance begets mutual confidence). 5
Further, he must compel all persons staying in the city to
appear in public and live at his gates; then he will know
what they are doing: if they are always kept under, they
will learn to be humble. In short, he should practise these
and the like Persian and barbaric arts, which all have
the same object. A tyrant should also endeavour to know 10
what each of his subjects says or does, and should employ
spies, like the 'female detectives' at Syracuse, and the
eavesdroppers whom Hiero was in the habit of sending to
any place of resort or meeting; for the fear of informers 15
prevents people from speaking their minds, and if they
do, they are more easily found out. Another art of the
tyrant is to sow quarrels among the citizens; friends
should be embroiled with friends, the people with the
notables, and the rich with one another. Also he should
impoverish his subjects; he thus provides against the
maintenance of a guard by the citizens, and the people, 20
having to keep hard at work, are prevented from con-
spiring. The Pyramids of Egypt afford an example of
this policy; also the offerings of the family of Cypselus,
and the building of the temple of Olympian Zeus by the
Peisistratidae, and the great Polycratean monuments at
Samos; all these works were alike intended to occupy
the people and keep them poor. Another practice of 25
tyrants is to multiply taxes, after the manner of Dionysius at Syracuse, who contrived that within five years
his subjects should bring into the treasury their whole

property. The tyrant is also fond of making war in order
that his subjects may have something to do and be always
30 in want of a leader. And whereas the power of a king is
preserved by his friends, the characteristic of a tyrant
is to distrust his friends, because he knows that all men
want to overthrow him, and they above all have the
power.

Again, the evil practices of the last and worst form
of democracy [63] are all found in tyrannies. Such are the
power given to women in their families in the hope that
they will inform against their husbands, and the licence
which is allowed to slaves in order that they may betray
35 their masters; for slaves and women do not conspire
against tyrants; and they are of course friendly to tyrannies and also to democracies, since under them they have
a good time. For the people too would fain be a monarch,
and therefore by them, as well as by the tyrant, the flat-
40 terer is held in honour; in democracies he is the demagogue; and the tyrant also has those who associate with
1314ª him in a humble spirit, which is a work of flattery.

Hence tyrants are always fond of bad men, because
they love to be flattered, but no man who has the spirit
of a freeman in him will lower himself by flattery; good
men love others, or at any rate do not flatter them. Moreover, the bad are useful for bad purposes; 'nail knocks
5 out nail', as the proverb says. It is characteristic of a
tyrant to dislike every one who has dignity or independence; he wants to be alone in his glory, but any one who
claims a like dignity or asserts his independence en-
croaches upon his prerogative, and is hated by him as
10 an enemy to his power. Another mark of a tyrant is that
he likes foreigners better than citizens, and lives with

[63] Cp. vi. 1319ᵇ 27.

them and invites them to his table; for the one are enemies, but the others enter into no rivalry with him.

Such are the notes of the tyrant and the arts by which
he preserves his power; there is no wickedness too great
for him. All that we have said may be summed up under
three heads, which answer to the three aims of the tyrant. 15
These are, (1) the humiliation of his subjects; he knows
that a mean-spirited man will not conspire against anybody: (2) the creation of mistrust among them; for a
tyrant is not overthrown until men begin to have confidence in one another; and this is the reason why tyrants
are at war with the good; they are under the idea that
their power is endangered by them, not only because 20
they will not be ruled despotically, but also because they
are loyal to one another, and to other men, and do not
inform against one another or against other men: (3) the
tyrant desires that his subjects shall be incapable of
action, for no one attempts what is impossible, and they
will not attempt to overthrow a tyranny, if they are
powerless. Under these three heads the whole policy of 25
a tyrant may be summed up, and to one or other of them
all his ideas may be referred: (1) he sows distrust among
his subjects; (2) he takes away their power; (3) he
humbles them.

This then is one of the two methods by which tyran- 30
nies are preserved; and there is another which proceeds
upon an almost opposite principle of action. The nature
of this latter method may be gathered from a comparison of the causes which destroy kingdoms, for as one
mode of destroying kingly power is to make the office of
king more tyrannical, so the salvation of a tyranny is to
make it more like the rule of a king. But of one thing 37
the tyrant must be careful; he must keep power enough
to rule over his subjects, whether they like him or not,

for if he once gives this up he gives up his tyranny. But though power must be retained as the foundation, in all
40 else the tyrant should act or appear to act in the character of a king. In the first place he should pretend a care of
1314ᵇ the public revenues, and not waste money in making presents of a sort at which the common people get excited when they see their hard-won earnings snatched from them and lavished on courtesans and strangers and
5 artists. He should give an account of what he receives and of what he spends (a practice which has been adopted by some tyrants); for then he will seem to be a steward of the public rather than a tyrant; nor need he fear that, while he is the lord of the city, he will ever be in want of money. Such a policy is at all events much more advantageous for the tyrant when he goes from
10 home, than to leave behind him a hoard, for then the garrison who remain in the city will be less likely to attack his power; and a tyrant, when he is absent from home, has more reason to fear the guardians of his treasure than the citizens, for the one accompany him, but the others remain behind. In the second place, he should
15 be seen to collect taxes and to require public services only for state purposes, and that he may form a fund in case of war, and generally he ought to make himself the guardian and treasurer of them, as if they belonged, not to him, but to the public. He should appear, not harsh, but dignified, and when men meet him they should look upon him with reverence, and not with fear. Yet it is
20 hard for him to be respected if he inspires no respect, and therefore whatever virtues he may neglect, at least he should maintain the character of a great soldier, and produce the impression that he is one. Neither he nor any of his associates should ever be guilty of the least offence against modesty towards the young of either sex

who are his subjects, and the women of his family should 25
observe a like self-control towards other women; the insolence of women has ruined many tyrannies. In the indulgence of pleasures he should be the opposite of our
modern tyrants, who not only begin at dawn and pass
whole days in sensuality, but want other men to see 30
them, that they may admire their happy and blessed
lot. In these things a tyrant should if possible be moderate, or at any rate should not parade his vices to the
world; for a drunken and drowsy tyrant is soon despised
and attacked; not so he who is temperate and wide 35
awake. His conduct should be the very reverse of nearly
everything which has been said before [64] about tyrants.
He ought to adorn and improve his city, as though he
were not a tyrant, but the guardian of the state. Also he
should appear to be particularly earnest in the service
of the Gods; for if men think that a ruler is religious and 40
has a reverence for the Gods, they are less afraid of 1315ᵇ
suffering injustice at his hands, and they are less disposed
to conspire against him, because they believe him to have
the very Gods fighting on his side. At the same time his
religion must not be thought foolish. And he should
honour men of merit, and make them think that they 5
would not be held in more honour by the citizens if they
had a free government. The honour he should distribute
himself, but the punishment should be inflicted by officers and courts of law. It is a precaution which is taken
by all monarchs not to make one person great; but if
one, then two or more should be raised, that they may
look sharply after one another. If after all some one has 10
to be made great, he should not be a man of bold spirit;
for such dispositions are ever most inclined to strike.
And if any one is to be deprived of his power, let it be

[64] 1313ᵃ 35–1314ᵃ 29.

diminished gradually, not taken from him all at once.[65]

15 The tyrant should abstain from all outrage; in particular from personal violence and from wanton conduct towards the young. He should be especially careful of his behaviour to men who are lovers of honour; for as the lovers of money are offended when their property is 20 touched, so are the lovers of honour and the virtuous when their honour is affected. Therefore a tyrant ought either not to commit such acts at all; or he should be thought only to employ fatherly correction, and not to trample upon others—and his acquaintance with youth should be supposed to arise from affection, and not from the insolence of power, and in general he should compensate the appearance of dishonour by the increase of honour.

25 Of those who attempt assassination they are the most dangerous, and require to be most carefully watched, who do not care to survive, if they effect their purpose. Therefore special precaution should be taken about any who think that either they or those for whom they care have been insulted; for when men are led away by passion to assault others they are regardless of themselves. As Heracleitus says, 'It is difficult to fight against anger; 30 for a man will buy revenge with his soul.'

And whereas states consist of two classes, of poor men and of rich, the tyrant should lead both to imagine that 35 they are preserved and prevented from harming one another by his rule, and whichever of the two is stronger he should attach to his government; for, having this advantage, he has no need either to emancipate slaves or to disarm the citizens; either party added to the force which he already has, will make him stronger than his assailants.

[65] Cp. 1308[b] 15.

But enough of these details;—what should be the 40
general policy of the tyrant is obvious. He ought to show
himself to his subjects in the light, not of a tyrant, but
of a steward and a king. He should not appropriate what 1315^b^
is theirs, but should be their guardian; he should be
moderate, not extravagant in his way of life; he should
win the notables by companionship, and the multitude
by flattery. For then his rule will of necessity be nobler
and happier, because he will rule over better men [66] whose
spirits are not crushed, over men to whom he himself is
not an object of hatred, and of whom he is not afraid.
His power too will be more lasting. His disposition will
be virtuous, or at least half virtuous; and he will not be 10
wicked, but half wicked only.

**12** Yet no forms of government are so short-lived as
oligarchy and tyranny. The tyranny which lasted longest was that of Orthagoras and his sons at Sicyon; this
continued for a hundred years. The reason was that they
treated their subjects with moderation, and to a great 15
extent observed the laws; and in various ways gained
the favour of the people by the care which they took of
them. Cleisthenes, in particular, was respected for his
military ability. If report may be believed, he crowned
the judge who decided against him in the games; and,
as some say, the sitting statue in the Agora of Sicyon is 20
the likeness of this person. (A similar story is told of
Peisistratus, who is said on one occasion to have allowed
himself to be summoned and tried before the Areopagus.)

Next in duration to the tyranny of Orthagoras was
that of the Cypselidae at Corinth, which lasted seventy-
three years and six months: Cypselus reigned thirty 25
years, Periander forty and a half, and Psammetichus the

[66] Cp. i. 1254^a^ 25.

son of Gorgus three. Their continuance was due to similar causes: Cypselus was a popular man, who during the
whole time of his rule never had a body-guard; and
Periander, although he was a tyrant, was a great soldier.
Third in duration was the rule of the Peisistratidae at
30 Athens, but it was interrupted; for Peisistratus was
twice driven out, so that during three and thirty years
he reigned only seventeen; and his sons reigned eighteen
—altogether thirty-five years. Of other tyrannies, that
of Hiero and Gelo at Syracuse was the most lasting.
35 Even this, however, was short, not more than eighteen
years in all; for Gelo continued tyrant for seven years,
and died in the eighth; Hiero reigned for ten years, and
Thrasybulus was driven out in the eleventh month. In
fact, tyrannies generally have been of quite short duration.

40　　　I have now gone through almost all the causes by
which constitutional governments and monarchies are
1316ᵃ either destroyed or preserved.

In the *Republic* of Plato,[67] Socrates treats of revolutions, but not well, for he mentions no cause of change
which peculiarly affects the first, or perfect state. He
only says that the cause is that nothing is abiding, but
5 all things change in a certain cycle; and that the origin
of the change consists in those numbers 'of which 4 and
3, married with 5, furnish two harmonies'—(he means
when the number of this figure becomes solid); he conceives that nature at certain times produces bad men
who will not submit to education; in which latter particular he may very likely be not far wrong, for there
10 may well be some men who cannot be educated and made
virtuous. But why is such a cause of change peculiar to
his ideal state, and not rather common to all states, nay,

67 This is an extract from the much fuller account in *Rep*. viii. 546 B.C.

to everything which comes into being at all? And is it by the agency of time, which, as he declares, makes all things change, that things which did not begin together, 15 change together? For example, if something has come into being the day before the completion of the cycle, will it change with things that came into being before? Further, why should the perfect state change into the Spartan? [68] For governments more often take an opposite form than one akin to them. The same remark is 20 applicable to the other changes; he says that the Spartan constitution changes into an oligarchy, and this into a democracy, and this again into a tyranny. And yet the contrary happens quite as often: for a democracy is even more likely to change into an oligarchy than into a monarchy. Further, he never says whether tyranny 25 is, or is not, liable to revolutions, and if it is, what is the cause of them, or into what form it changes. And the reason is, that he could not very well have told: for there is no rule; according to him it should revert to the first and best, and then there would be a complete cycle. But in point of fact a tyranny often changes into a tyranny, 30 as that at Sicyon changed from the tyranny of Myron into that of Cleisthenes; into oligarchy, as the tyranny of Antileon did at Chalcis; into democracy, as that of Gelo's family did at Syracuse; into aristocracy, as at Carthage, and the tyranny of Charilaus at Lacedaemon. 35 Often an oligarchy changes into a tyranny, like most of the ancient oligarchies in Sicily; for example, the oligarchy at Leontini changed into the tyranny of Panaetius; that at Gela into the tyranny of Cleander; that at Rhegium into the tyranny of Anaxilaus; the same thing has happened in many other states. And it is absurd to

[68] *Rep.* viii. 544 c.

40 suppose that the state changes into oligarchy merely be-
1316ᵇ cause the ruling class are lovers and makers of money,[69]
and not because the very rich think it unfair that the very
poor should have an equal share in the government with
themselves. Moreover, in many oligarchies there are laws
5 against making money in trade. But at Carthage, which
is a democracy, there is no such prohibition; and yet to
this day the Carthaginians have never had a revolution. It is absurd too for him to say that an oligarchy is two cities, one of the rich, and the other of the
poor.[70] Is not this just as much the case in the Spartan
constitution, or in any other in which either all do not
possess equal property, or all are not equally good men?
10 Nobody need be any poorer than he was before, and yet
the oligarchy may change all the same into a democracy,
if the poor form the majority; and a democracy may
change into an oligarchy, if the wealthy class are stronger
15 than the people, and the one are energetic, the other in-
different. Once more, although the causes of the change[71]
are very numerous, he mentions only one,[72] which is,
that the citizens become poor through dissipation and
debt, as though he thought that all, or the majority of
them, were originally rich. This is not true: though it is
true that when any of the leaders lose their property they
are ripe for revolution; but, when anybody else, it is no
20 great matter, and an oligarchy does not even then more
often pass into a democracy than into any other form
of government. Again, if men are deprived of the honours of state, and are wronged, and insulted, they make
revolutions, and change forms of government, even
although they have not wasted their substance because

---

[69] *Rep*. viii. 550 ᴇ.
[71] *sc*. from oligarchy to democracy.
[70] *Rep*. viii. 551 ᴅ.
[72] *Rep*. viii. 555 ᴅ.

they might do what they liked—of which extravagance he declares excessive freedom to be the cause.[73]

Finally, although there are many forms of oligarchies and democracies, Socrates speaks of their revolutions as though there were only one form of either of them.

[73] *Rep.* viii. 557 c, 564.

# BOOK VI

**1** We have now considered the varieties of the deliberative or supreme power in states, and the various arrangements of law-courts and state offices, and which
of them are adapted to different forms of government.[1]
We have also spoken of the destruction and preservation
35 of constitutions, how and from what causes they arise.[2]

Of democracy and all other forms of government there
are many kinds; and it will be well to assign to them
severally the modes of organization which are proper
and advantageous to each, adding what remains to be
40 said about them.[3] Moreover, we ought to consider the
1317ᵃ various combinations of these modes themselves; for
such combinations make constitutions overlap one another, so that aristocracies have an oligarchical character, and constitutional governments incline to democracies.[4]

When I speak of the combinations which remain to be
considered, and thus far have not been considered by
5 us, I mean such as these:—when the deliberative part of
the government and the election of officers is constituted
oligarchically, and the law-courts aristocratically, or
when the courts and the deliberative part of the state

[1] Bk. iv. 14–16.  [2] Bk. v.
[3] 1318ᵇ 6–1319ᵃ 6.  [4] Cp. iv. 1293ᵇ 34.

are oligarchical, and the election to offices aristocratical,
or when in any other way there is a want of harmony in
the composition of a state.[5]

I have shown already [6] what forms of democracy are 10
suited to particular cities, and what of oligarchy to particular peoples, and to whom each of the other forms of
government is suited. Further, we must not only show
which of these governments is the best for each state,
but also briefly proceed to consider [7] how these and other 15
forms of government are to be established.

First of all let us speak of democracy, which will also
bring to light the opposite form of government commonly called oligarchy. For the purposes of this inquiry
we need to ascertain all the elements and characteristics
of democracy, since from the combinations of these the 20
varieties of democratic government arise. There are
several of these differing from each other, and the difference is due to two causes. One (1) has been already
mentioned [8]—differences of population; for the popular
element may consist of husbandmen, or of mechanics, 25
or of labourers, and if the first of these be added to the
second, or the third to the two others, not only does the
democracy become better or worse, but its very nature
is changed. A second cause (2) remains to be mentioned: the various properties and characteristics of de- 30
mocracy, when variously combined, make a difference.
For one democracy will have less and another will have
more, and another will have all of these characteristics.
There is an advantage in knowing them all, whether a
man wishes to establish some new form of democracy,
or only to remodel an existing one.[9] Founders of states 35

---

[5] These questions are not actually discussed by A.          [6] iv. 12.
[7] Cp. iv. 1289[b] 20.     [8] iv. 1291[b] 17–28, 1292[b] 25 sqq., 1296[b] 26–31.
[9] Cp. iv. 1289[a] 1.

try to bring together all the elements which accord with the ideas of the several constitutions; but this is a mistake of theirs, as I have already remarked [10] when speaking of the destruction and preservation of states. We will now set forth the principles, characteristics, and aims of such states.

40 **2** The basis of a democratic state is liberty; which,
1317[b] according to the common opinion of men, can only be enjoyed in such a state;—this they affirm to be the great end of every democracy.[11] One principle of liberty is for all to rule and be ruled in turn, and indeed democratic justice is the application of numerical not proportionate
5 equality; whence it follows that the majority must be supreme, and that whatever the majority approve must be the end and the just. Every citizen, it is said, must have equality, and therefore in a democracy the poor have more power than the rich, because there are more of them, and the will of the majority is supreme. This,
10 then, is one note of liberty which all democrats affirm to be the principle of their state. Another is that a man should live as he likes.[12] This, they say, is the privilege of a freeman, since, on the other hand, not to live as a man likes is the mark of a slave. This is the second characteristic of democracy, whence has arisen the claim of
15 men to be ruled by none, if possible, or, if this is impossible, to rule and be ruled in turns; and so it contributes to the freedom based upon equality.

Such being our foundation and such the principle from which we start, the characteristics of democracy are as
20 follows:—the election of officers by all out of all; and that all should rule over each, and each in his turn over

---

[10] v. 1309[b] 18–1310[a] 36.     [11] Cp. Plato, *Rep.* viii. 557 sqq.
[12] Cp. v. 1310[a] 31.

all; that the appointment to all offices, or to all but those
which require experience and skill,[13] should be made by
lot; that no property qualification should be required for
offices, or only a very low one; that a man should not hold
the same office twice, or not often, or in the case of few except military offices: that the tenure of all offices, or of as    25
many as possible, should be brief; that all men should sit
in judgement, or that judges selected out of all should
judge, in all matters, or in most and in the greatest and
most important—such as the scrutiny of accounts, the
constitution, and private contracts; that the assembly
should be supreme over all causes, or at any rate over
the most important, and the magistrates over none or
only over a very few. Of all magistracies, a council is the    30
most democratic[14] when there is not the means of paying
all the citizens, but when they are paid even this is
robbed of its power; for the people then draw all cases
to themselves, as I said in the previous discussion.[15] The
next characteristic of democracy is payment for serv-     35
ices; assembly, law-courts, magistrates, everybody receives pay, when it is to be had; or when it is not to be
had for all, then it is given to the law-courts and to the
stated assemblies, to the council and to the magistrates,
or at least to any of them who are compelled to have
their meals together. And whereas oligarchy is characterized by birth, wealth, and education, the notes of de-    40
mocracy appear to be the opposite of these—low birth,
poverty, mean employment. Another note is that no magistracy is perpetual, but if any such have survived some   1318ᵇ
ancient change in the constitution it should be stripped
of its power, and the holders should be elected by lot and
no longer by vote. These are the points common to all
democracies; but democracy and demos in their truest

---

[13] Cp. iv. 1298ᵃ 27.     [14] Cp. iv. 1299ᵇ 32.     [15] Cp. iv. 1299ᵇ 38.

5 form are based upon the recognized principle of democratic justice, that all should count equally; for equality implies that the poor should have no more share in the government than the rich, and should not be the only rulers, but that all should rule equally according to their numbers.[16] And in this way men think that they will
10 secure equality and freedom in their state.

**3** Next comes the question, how is this equality to be obtained? Are we to assign to a thousand poor men the property qualifications of five hundred rich men? and shall we give the thousand a power equal to that of the five hundred? or, if this is not to be the mode, ought we,
15 still retaining the same ratio, to take equal numbers from each and give them the control of the elections and of the courts?—Which, according to the democratical notion, is the juster form of the constitution—this or one based on numbers only? Democrats say that justice is that to
20 which the majority agree, oligarchs that to which the wealthier class; in their opinion the decision should be given according to the amount of property. In both principles there is some inequality and injustice. For if justice is the will of the few, any one person who has more wealth than all the rest of the rich put together, ought, upon the oligarchical principle, to have the sole power—
25 but this would be tyranny; or if justice is the will of the majority, as I was before saying,[17] they will unjustly confiscate the property of the wealthy minority. To find a principle of equality in which they both agree we must inquire into their respective ideas of justice.

Now they agree in saying that whatever is decided by the majority of the citizens is to be deemed law. Granted:
30 —but not without some reserve; since there are two

---

[16] Cp. iv. 1291[b] 30.     [17] Cp. iii. 1281[a] 14.

classes out of which a state is composed—the poor and
the rich—that is to be deemed law, on which both or
the greater part of both agree; and if they disagree, that
which is approved by the greater number, and by those
who have the higher qualification. For example, suppose
that there are ten rich and twenty poor, and some measure is approved by six of the rich and is disapproved by
fifteen of the poor, and the remaining four of the rich 35
join with the party of the poor, and the remaining five of
the poor with that of the rich; in such a case the will of
those whose qualifications, when both sides are added
up, are the greatest, should prevail. If they turn out to
be equal, there is no greater difficulty than at present,
when, if the assembly or the courts are divided, recourse 40
is had to the lot, or to some similar expedient. But, al- 1318ᵇ
though it may be difficult in theory to know what is just
and equal, the practical difficulty of inducing those to
forbear who can, if they like, encroach, is far greater,
for the weaker are always asking for equality and justice, but the stronger care for none of these things.    5

**4**    Of the four kinds of democracy, as was said in the
previous discussion,[18] the best is that which comes first
in order; it is also the oldest of them all. I am speaking
of them according to the natural classification of their
inhabitants. For the best material of democracy is an
agricultural population; [19] there is no difficulty in form- 10
ing a democracy where the mass of the people live by
agriculture or tending of cattle. Being poor, they have
no leisure, and therefore do not often attend the assembly, and not having the necessaries of life they are always
at work, and do not covet the property of others. Indeed,
they find their employment pleasanter than the cares of

[18] iv. 1292ᵇ 22–1293ᵃ 10.    [19] Cp. iv. 1292ᵇ 25–33.

15 government or office where no great gains can be made
out of them, for the many are more desirous of gain than
of honour.[20] A proof is that even the ancient tyrannies
were patiently endured by them, as they still endure oligarchies, if they are allowed to work and are not de-
20 prived of their property; for some of them grow quickly
rich and the others are well enough off. Moreover, they
have the power of electing the magistrates and calling
them to account; [21] their ambition, if they have any, is
thus satisfied; and in some democracies, although they
do not all share in the appointment of offices, except
through representatives elected in turn out of the whole
25 people, as at Mantinea;—yet, if they have the power of
deliberating, the many are contented. Even this form of
government may be regarded as a democracy, and was
such at Mantinea. Hence it is both expedient and customary in the afore-mentioned [22] type of democracy that
30 all should elect to offices, and conduct scrutinies, and sit
in the law-courts, but that the great offices should be
filled up by election and from persons having a qualification; the greater requiring a greater qualification, or,
if there be no offices for which a qualification is required,
then those who are marked out by special ability should
be appointed. Under such a form of government the
citizens are sure to be governed well (for the offices will
always be held by the best persons; the people are will-
35 ing enough to elect them and are not jealous of the
good). The good and the notables will then be satisfied,
for they will not be governed by men who are their inferiors, and the persons elected will rule justly, because
others will call them to account. Every man should be
responsible to others, nor should any one be allowed to
40 do just as he pleases; for where absolute freedom is

---

[20] Cp. iv. 1297ᵇ 6.         [21] Cp. ii. 1274ᵃ 15.         [22] l. 6.

allowed there is nothing to restrain the evil which is in- 1319ᵃ
herent in every man. But the principle of responsibility
secures that which is the greatest good in states; the
right persons rule and are prevented from doing wrong,
and the people have their due. It is evident that this is
the best kind of democracy, and why? Because the 5
people are drawn from a certain class. Some of the ancient laws of most states were, all of them, useful with
a view to making the people husbandmen. They provided either that no one should possess more than a certain quantity of land, or that, if he did, the land should
not be within a certain distance from the town or the
acropolis. Formerly in many states there was a law for- 10
bidding any one to sell his original allotment of land.[23]
There is a similar law attributed to Oxylus, which is to
the effect that there should be a certain portion of every
man's land on which he could not borrow money. A useful
corrective to the evil of which I am speaking would be
the law of the Aphytaeans, who, although they are 15
numerous, and do not possess much land, are all of them
husbandmen. For their properties are reckoned in the
census; not entire, but only in such small portions that
even the poor may have more than the amount required.

Next best to an agricultural, and in many respects 20
similar, are a pastoral people, who live by their flocks;
they are the best trained of any for war, robust in body
and able to camp out. The people of whom other democracies consist are far inferior to them, for their life 25
is inferior; there is no room for moral excellence in any
of their employments, whether they be mechanics or
traders or labourers. Besides, people of this class can
readily come to the assembly, because they are contin-
ually moving about in the city and in the agora; whereas 30

[23] Cp. ii. 1266ᵇ 21.

husbandmen are scattered over the country and do not
meet, or equally feel the want of assembling together.
Where the territory also happens to extend to a distance
35 from the city, there is no difficulty in making an excellent
democracy or constitutional government; for the people
are compelled to settle in the country, and even if there
is a town population the assembly ought not to meet, in
democracies, when the country people cannot come. We
have thus explained how the first and best form of de-
40 mocracy should be constituted; it is clear that the other
or inferior sorts will deviate in a regular order, and the
1319ᵇ population which is excluded will at each stage be of a
lower kind.

The last form of democracy, that in which all share
alike, is one which cannot be borne by all states, and
will not last long unless well regulated by laws and customs. The more general causes which tend to destroy this
5 or other kinds of government have been pretty fully
considered.[24] In order to constitute such a democracy
and strengthen the people, the leaders have been in the
habit of including as many as they can, and making citizens not only of those who are legitimate, but even of
the illegitimate, and of those who have only one parent
10 a citizen, whether father or mother;[25] for nothing of
this sort comes amiss to such a democracy. This is the
way in which demagogues proceed. Whereas the right
thing would be to make no more additions when the
number of the commonalty exceeds that of the notables
and of the middle class—beyond this not to go. When in
15 excess of this point, the constitution becomes disorderly,
and the notables grow excited and impatient of the democracy, as in the insurrection at Cyrene; for no notice

[24] v. 2–7, 1311ᵃ 22–1313ᵃ 16.    [25] Cp. iii. 1278ᵃ 27.

is taken of a little evil, but when it increases it strikes the eye. Measures like those which Cleisthenes [26] passed when he wanted to increase the power of the democracy at Athens, or such as were taken by the founders of popular government at Cyrene, are useful in the extreme form of democracy. Fresh tribes and brotherhoods should be established; the private rites of families should be restricted and converted into public ones; in short, every contrivance should be adopted which will mingle the citizens with one another and get rid of old connections. Again, the measures which are taken by tyrants appear all of them to be democratic; such, for instance, as the licence permitted to slaves (which may be to a certain extent advantageous) and also that of women and children, and the allowing everybody to live as he likes.[27] Such a government will have many supporters, for most persons would rather live in a disorderly than in a sober manner.

**5**  The mere establishment of a democracy is not the only or principal business of the legislator, or of those who wish to create such a state, for any state, however badly constituted, may last one, two, or three days; a far greater difficulty is the preservation of it. The legislator should therefore endeavour to have a firm foundation according to the principles already laid down concerning the preservation and destruction of states; [28] he should guard against the destructive elements, and should make laws, whether written or unwritten, which will contain all the preservatives of states. He must not think the truly democratical or oligarchical measure to be that which will give the greatest amount of democ-

---

[26] Cp. iii. 1275[b] 35.        [27] Cp. v. 1313[b] 32.        [28] Cp. Bk. v.

racy or oligarchy, but that which will make them last longest.[29] The demagogues of our own day often get property confiscated[30] in the law-courts in order to please the people. But those who have the welfare of the state at heart should counteract them, and make a law that the property of the condemned should not be public and go into the treasury but be sacred. Thus offenders will be as much afraid, for they will be punished all the same, and the people, having nothing to gain, will not be so ready to condemn the accused. Care should also be taken that state trials are as few as possible, and heavy penalties should be inflicted on those who bring groundless accusations; for it is the practice to indict, not members of the popular party, but the notables, although the citizens ought to be all attached to the constitution as well, or at any rate should not regard their rulers as enemies.

Now, since in the last and worst form of democracy the citizens are very numerous, and can hardly be made to assemble unless they are paid, and to pay them when there are no revenues presses hardly upon the notables (for the money must be obtained by a property-tax and confiscations and corrupt practices of the courts, things which have before now overthrown many democracies); where, I say, there are no revenues, the government should hold few assemblies, and the law-courts should consist of many persons, but sit for a few days only. This system has two advantages: first, the rich do not fear the expense, even although they are unpaid themselves when the poor are paid; and secondly, causes are better tried, for wealthy persons, although they do not like to be long absent from their own affairs, do not mind going for a few days to the law-courts. Where there are

[29] Cp. v. 1313[a] 20–33.  [30] Cp. v. 1305[a] 3.

revenues the demagogues should not be allowed after
their manner to distribute the surplus; the poor are 30
always receiving and always wanting more and more, for
such help is like water poured into a leaky cask. Yet the
true friend of the people should see that they be not too
poor, for extreme poverty lowers the character of the 35
democracy; measures therefore should be taken which
will give them lasting prosperity; and as this is equally
the interest of all classes, the proceeds of the public
revenues should be accumulated and distributed among
its poor, if possible, in such quantities as may enable
them to purchase a little farm, or, at any rate, make a
beginning in trade or husbandry. And if this benevolence 1320$^b$
cannot be extended to all, money should be distributed
in turn according to tribes or other divisions, and in the
meantime the rich should pay the fee for the attendance
of the poor at the necessary assemblies; and should in
return be excused from useless public services. By ad-
ministering the state in this spirit the Carthaginians retain the affections of the people; their policy is from time 5
to time to send some of them into their dependent towns,
where they grow rich.[31] It is also worthy of a generous
and sensible nobility to divide the poor amongst them,
and give them the means of going to work. The example
of the people of Tarentum is also well deserving of imi- 10
tation, for, by sharing the use of their own property with
the poor, they gain their good will.[32] Moreover, they
divide all their offices into two classes, some of them
being elected by vote, the others by lot; the latter, that
the people may participate in them, and the former, that
the state may be better administered. A like result may
be gained by dividing the same offices, so as to have two

---

[31] Cp. ii. 1273$^b$ 18.                    [32] Cp. ii. 1263$^a$ 37.

15 classes of magistrates, one chosen by vote, the other by lot.

Enough has been said of the manner in which democracies ought to be constituted.

**6** From these considerations there will be no difficulty in seeing what should be the constitution of oligarchies. We have only to reason from opposites and compare each form of oligarchy with the corresponding form of 20 democracy.

The first and best attempered of oligarchies is akin to a constitutional government. In this there ought to be two standards of qualification; the one high, the other low—the lower qualifying for the humbler yet indispensable offices and the higher for the superior ones. He 25 who acquires the prescribed qualification should have the rights of citizenship. The number of those admitted should be such as will make the entire governing body stronger than those who are excluded, and the new citizen should be always taken out of the better class of the people. The principle, narrowed a little, gives another 30 form of oligarchy; until at length we reach the most cliquish and tyrannical of them all, answering to the extreme democracy, which, being the worst, requires vigilance in proportion to its badness. For as healthy 35 bodies and ships well provided with sailors may undergo many mishaps and survive them, whereas sickly constitutions and rotten ill-manned ships are ruined by the very least mistake, so do the worst forms of government require the greatest care. The populousness of democ-1321ᵃ racies generally preserves them (for number is to democracy in the place of justice based on proportion); whereas the preservation of an oligarchy clearly depends on an opposite principle, viz. good order.

**7**   As there are four chief divisions of the common peo- 5
ple—husbandmen, mechanics, retail traders, labourers;
so also there are four kinds of military forces—the
cavalry, the heavy infantry, the light-armed troops, the
navy.[33] When the country is adapted for cavalry, then a
strong oligarchy is likely to be established. For the se- 10
curity of the inhabitants depends upon a force of this
sort, and only rich men can afford to keep horses. The
second form of oligarchy prevails when the country is
adapted to heavy infantry; for this service is better
suited to the rich than to the poor. But the light-armed
and the naval element are wholly democratic; and now- 15
adays, where they are numerous, if the two parties quarrel, the oligarchy are often worsted by them in the
struggle. A remedy for this state of things may be found
in the practice of generals who combine a proper con-
tingent of light-armed troops with cavalry and heavy-
armed. And this is the way in which the poor get the bet- 20
ter of the rich in civil contests; being lightly armed, they
fight with advantage against cavalry and heavy infantry.
An oligarchy which raises such a force out of the lower
classes raises a power against itself. And therefore, since
the ages of the citizens vary and some are older and some
younger, the fathers should have their own sons, while
they are still young, taught the agile movements of light- 25
armed troops; and these, when they have been taken
out of the ranks of the youth, should become light-armed
warriors in reality. The oligarchy should also yield a
share in the government to the people, either, as I said
before, to those who have a property qualification,[34] or,
as in the case of Thebes,[35] to those who have abstained
for a certain number of years from mean employments, 30
or, as at Massalia, to men of merit who are selected for

---

[33] Cp. iv. 1289ᵇ 32—40.      [34] 1320ᵇ 25.      [35] Cp. iii. 1278ᵃ 25.

their worthiness, whether previously citizens or not. The
magistracies of the highest rank, which ought to be in the
hands of the governing body, should have expensive
duties attached to them, and then the people will not desire them and will take no offence at the privileges of
their rulers when they see that they pay a heavy fine for
35 their dignity. It is fitting also that the magistrates on
entering office should offer magnificent sacrifices or erect
some public edifice, and then the people who participate
in the entertainments, and see the city decorated with
votive offerings and buildings, will not desire an alteration in the government, and the notables will have
40 memorials of their munificence. This, however, is anything but the fashion of our modern oligarchs, who are as
covetous of gain as they are of honour; oligarchies like
1321ᵇ theirs may be well described as petty democracies.
Enough of the manner in which democracies and oligarchies should be organized.

**8** Next in order follows the right distribution of offices,
5 their number, their nature, their duties, of which indeed
we have already spoken.[36] No state can exist not having
the necessary offices, and no state can be well administered not having the offices which tend to preserve harmony and good order. In small states, as we have already
remarked,[37] there must not be many of them, but in
10 larger there must be a larger number, and we should
carefully consider which offices may properly be united
and which separated.

First among necessary offices is that which has the
care of the market; a magistrate should be appointed to
15 inspect contracts and to maintain order. For in every
state there must inevitably be buyers and sellers who will

supply one another's wants; this is the readiest way to
make a state self-sufficing and so fulfil the purpose for
which men come together into one state.[38] A second office
of a similar kind undertakes the supervision and embel-       20
lishment of public and private buildings, the maintaining
and repairing of houses and roads, the prevention of disputes about boundaries, and other concerns of a like
nature. This is commonly called the office of City-
warden, and has various departments, which, in more        25
populous towns, are shared among different persons, one,
for example, taking charge of the walls, another of the
fountains, a third of harbours. There is another equally
necessary office, and of a similar kind, having to do with
the same matters without the walls and in the country—
the magistrates who hold this office are called Wardens
of the country, or Inspectors of the woods. Besides these
three there is a fourth office of receivers of taxes, who     30
have under their charge the revenue which is distributed
among the various departments; these are called Receivers or Treasurers. Another officer registers all private
contracts, and decisions of the courts, all public indictments, and also all preliminary proceedings. This office     35
again is sometimes subdivided, in which case one officer is
appointed over all the rest. These officers are called Recorders or Sacred Recorders, Presidents, and the like.

Next to these comes an office of which the duties are       40
the most necessary and also the most difficult, viz. that to
which is committed the execution of punishments, or the
exaction of fines from those who are posted up according   1322*
to the registers; and also the custody of prisoners. The
difficulty of this office arises out of the odium which is
attached to it; no one will undertake it unless great
profits are to be made, and any one who does is loath to

[38] Cp. i. 1252[b] 27; *Nic. Eth.* v. 1134[a] 26; Pl. *Rep.* ii. 369.

5 execute the law. Still the office is necessary; for judicial decisions are useless if they take no effect; and if society cannot exist without them, neither can it exist without the execution of them. It is an office which, being so unpopular, should not be entrusted to one person, but divided among several taken from different courts. In like manner an effort should be made to distribute among different persons the writing up of those who are on the

10 register of public debtors. Some sentences should be executed by the magistrates also, and in particular penalties due to the outgoing magistrates should be exacted by the incoming ones; and as regards those due to magistrates already in office, when one court has given judgement, another should exact the penalty; for example, the wardens of the city should exact the fines imposed by the wardens of the agora, and others again should exact the

15 fines imposed by *them*. For penalties are more likely to be exacted when less odium attaches to the exaction of them; but a double odium is incurred when the judges who have passed also execute the sentence, and if they are always the executioners, they will be the enemies of all.

In many places, while one magistracy executes the sentence, another has the custody of the prisoners, as, for

20 example, 'the Eleven' at Athens. It is well to separate off the jailorship also, and try by some device to render the office less unpopular. For it is quite as necessary as that of the executioners; but good men do all they can to avoid it, and worthless persons cannot safely be trusted

25 with it; for they themselves require a guard, and are not fit to guard others. There ought not therefore to be a single or permanent officer set apart for this duty; but it should be entrusted to the young, wherever they are or-

ganized into a band or guard, and different magistrates
acting in turn should take charge of it.

These are the indispensable officers, and should be
ranked first;—next in order follow others, equally neces- 30
sary, but of higher rank, and requiring great experience
and fidelity. Such are the officers to which are committed
the guard of the city, and other military functions. Not
only in time of war but of peace their duty will be to de- 35
fend the walls and gates, and to muster and marshal the
citizens. In some states there are many such offices; in
others there are a few only, while small states are content
with one; these officers are called generals or command-
ers. Again, if a state has cavalry or light-armed troops or 1322ᵇ
archers or a naval force, it will sometimes happen that
each of these departments has separate officers, who are
called admirals, or generals of cavalry or of light-armed
troops. And there are subordinate officers called naval
captains, and captains of light-armed troops and of
horse; having others under them:—all these are included 5
in the department of war. Thus much of military command.

But since many, not to say all, of these offices handle
the public money, there must of necessity be another
office which examines and audits them, and has no other
functions. Such officers are called by various names— 10
Scrutineers, Auditors, Accountants, Controllers. Besides
all these offices there is another which is supreme over
them, and to this is often entrusted both the introduction and the ratification of measures, or at all events it
presides, in a democracy, over the assembly. For there
must be a body which convenes the supreme authority in 15
the state. In some places they are called 'probuli', because they hold previous deliberations, but in a democ-

racy more commonly 'councillors'.[39] These are the chief
political offices.

Another set of officers is concerned with the mainte-
20 nance of religion; priests and guardians see to the preservation and repair of the temples of the gods and to other
matters of religion. One office of this sort may be enough
in small places, but in larger ones there are a great many
besides the priesthood; for example superintendents of
25 public worship, guardians of shrines, treasurers of the
sacred revenues. Nearly connected with these there are
also the officers appointed for the performance of the
public sacrifices, except any which the law assigns to the
priests; such sacrifices derive their dignity from the public hearth of the city. They are sometimes called archons,
sometimes kings,[40] and sometimes prytanes.

30      These, then, are the necessary offices, which may be
summed up as follows: offices concerned with matters of
religion, with war, with the revenue and expenditure,
with the market, with the city, with the harbours, with
the country; also with the courts of law, with the records
35 of contracts, with execution of sentences, with custody of
prisoners, with audits and scrutinies and accounts of
magistrates; lastly, there are those which preside over
the public deliberations of the state. There are likewise
magistracies characteristic of states which are peaceful
and prosperous, and at the same time have a regard to
good order: such as the offices of guardians of women,
guardians of the laws, guardians of children, and di-
1323ª rectors of gymnastics; also superintendents of gymnastic
and Dionysiac contests, and of other similar spectacles.
Some of these are clearly not democratic offices; for ex-
5 ample, the guardianships of women and children [41]—the

---

[39] Cp. iv. 1299ᵇ 31.     [40] Cp. iii. 1285ᵇ 23.     [41] Cp. iv. 1300ª 4.

poor, not having any slaves, must employ both their women and children as servants.

Once more: there are three offices according to whose directions the highest magistrates are chosen in certain states—guardians of the law, probuli, councillors—of these, the guardians of the law are an aristocratical, the probuli an oligarchical, the council a democratical institution. Enough of the different kinds of offices.     16

## BOOK VII

**1** He who would duly inquire about the best form of a
state ought first to determine which is the most eligible
life; while this remains uncertain the best form of the
state must also be uncertain; for, in the natural order of
things, those may be expected to lead the best life who
are governed in the best manner of which their circumstances admit. We ought therefore to ascertain, first of
all, which is the most generally eligible life, and then
whether the same life is or is not best for the state and
for individuals.

Assuming that enough has been already said in discussions outside the school concerning the best life, we
will now only repeat what is contained in them. Certainly
no one will dispute the propriety of that partition of
goods which separates them into three classes,[1] viz. external goods, goods of the body, and goods of the soul, or
deny that the happy man must have all three. For no one
would maintain that he is happy who has not in him a
particle of courage or temperance or justice or prudence,
who is afraid of every insect which flutters past him, and
will commit any crime, however great, in order to gratify
his lust of meat or drink, who will sacrifice his dearest
friend for the sake of half-a-farthing, and is as feeble and

[1] Cp. Laws, iii. 697 B, v. 743 E; *N. Eth.* i. 1098$^b$ 12.

false in mind as a child or a madman. These propositions are almost universally acknowledged as soon as they are 35 uttered, but men differ about the degree or relative superiority of this or that good. Some think that a very moderate amount of virtue is enough, but set no limit to their desires of wealth, property, power, reputation, and the like. To whom we reply by an appeal to facts, which 40 easily prove that mankind do not acquire or preserve virtue by the help of external goods, but external goods by the help of virtue, and that happiness, whether con- 1323ᵇ sisting in pleasure or virtue, or both, is more often found with those who are most highly cultivated in their mind and in their character, and have only a moderate share of external goods, than among those who possess external 5 goods to a useless extent but are deficient in higher qualities; and this is not only matter of experience, but, if reflected upon, will easily appear to be in accordance with reason. For, whereas external goods have a limit, like any other instrument,[2] and all things useful are of such a nature that where there is too much of them they must either do harm, or at any rate be of no use, to their possessors, every good of the soul, the greater it is, is also of 10 greater use, if the epithet useful as well as noble is appropriate to such subjects. No proof is required to show that the best state of one thing in relation to another corresponds in degree of excellence to the interval between the 15 natures of which we say that these very states are states: so that, if the soul is more noble than our possessions or our bodies, both absolutely and in relation to us, it must be admitted that the best state of either has a similar ratio to the other. Again, it is for the sake of the soul that goods external and goods of the body are eligible at all,

[2] Cp. i. 1256ᵇ 35.

20 and all wise men ought to choose them for the sake of the soul, and not the soul for the sake of them.

Let us acknowledge then that each one has just so much of happiness as he has of virtue and wisdom, and of virtuous and wise action. God is a witness to us of this truth, for he is happy and blessed, not by reason of any external good, but in himself and by reason of his own

25 nature. And herein of necessity lies the difference between good fortune and happiness; for external goods come of themselves, and chance is the author of them, but no one is just or temperate by or through chance.[3] In like

30 manner, and by a similar train of argument, the happy state may be shown to be that which is best and which acts rightly; and rightly it cannot act without doing right actions, and neither individual nor state can do right actions without virtue and wisdom. Thus the courage,

35 justice, and wisdom of a state have the same form and nature as the qualities which give the individual who possesses them the name of just, wise, or temperate.

Thus much may suffice by way of preface: for I could not avoid touching upon these questions, neither could I go through all the arguments affecting them; these are the business of another science.

40 Let us assume then that the best life, both for individ-
1324ª uals and states, is the life of virtue, when virtue has external goods enough for the performance of good actions. If there are any who controvert our assertion, we will in this treatise pass them over, and consider their objections hereafter.

5 **2** There remains to be discussed the question, Whether the happiness of the individual is the same as that of the state, or different? Here again there can be no doubt—no

---

[3] *Nic. Eth.* i. 1099ᵇ 2.

one denies that they are the same. For those who hold
that the well-being of the individual consists in his
wealth, also think that riches make the happiness of the
whole state, and those who value most highly the life of a 10
tyrant deem that city the happiest which rules over the
greatest number; while they who approve an individual
for his virtue say that the more virtuous a city is, the happier it is. Two points here present themselves for consideration: first (1), which is the more eligible life, that 15
of a citizen who is a member of a state, or that of an alien
who has no political ties; and again (2), which is the best
form of constitution or the best condition of a state,
either on the supposition that political privileges are desirable for all, or for a majority only? Since the good of
the state and not of the individual is the proper subject 20
of political thought and speculation, and we are engaged
in a political discussion, while the first of these two points
has a secondary interest for us, the latter will be the main
subject of our inquiry.

Now it is evident that the form of government is best
in which every man, whoever he is, can act best and live 25
happily. But even those who agree in thinking that the
life of virtue is the most eligible raise a question, whether
the life of business and politics is or is not more eligible
than one which is wholly independent of external goods,
I mean than a contemplative life, which by some is maintained to be the only one worthy of a philosopher. For
these two lives—the life of the philosopher and the life of
the statesman—appear to have been preferred by those 30
who have been most keen in the pursuit of virtue, both in
our own and in other ages. Which is the better is a question of no small moment; for the wise man, like the wise
state, will necessarily regulate his life according to the
best end. There are some who think that while a despotic 35

rule over others is the greatest injustice, to exercise a constitutional rule over them, even though not unjust, is a great impediment to a man's individual well-being. Others take an opposite view; they maintain that the true 40 life of man is the practical and political, and that every 1324ᵇ virtue admits of being practised, quite as much by statesmen and rulers as by private individuals. Others, again, are of opinion that arbitrary and tyrannical rule alone consists with happiness; indeed, in some states the entire aim both of the laws and of the constitution is to give men 5 despotic power over their neighbours. And, therefore, although in most cities the laws may be said generally to be in a chaotic state, still, if they aim at anything, they aim at the maintenance of power: thus in Lacedaemon and Crete the system of education and the greater part of the laws are framed with a view to war.⁴ And in all nations 10 which are able to gratify their ambition military power is held in esteem, for example among the Scythians and Persians and Thracians and Celts. In some nations there are even laws tending to stimulate the warlike virtues, as at Carthage, where we are told that men obtain the 15 honour of wearing as many armlets as they have served campaigns. There was once a law in Macedonia that he who had not killed an enemy should wear a halter, and among the Scythians no one who had not slain his man was allowed to drink out of the cup which was handed round at a certain feast. Among the Iberians, a warlike nation, the number of enemies whom a man has slain is 20 indicated by the number of obelisks which are fixed in the earth round his tomb; and there are numerous practices among other nations of a like kind, some of them established by law and others by custom. Yet to a reflecting mind it must appear very strange that the statesman

⁴ Cp. Plato, *Laws,* i. 633 ff.

should be always considering how he can dominate and 25
tyrannize over others, whether they will or not. How can
that which is not even lawful be the business of the statesman or the legislator? Unlawful it certainly is to rule
without regard to justice, for there may be might where
there is no right. The other arts and sciences offer no
parallel; a physician is not expected to persuade or co- 30
erce his patients, nor a pilot the passengers in his ship.
Yet most men appear to think that the art of despotic
government is statesmanship, and what men affirm to be
unjust and inexpedient in their own case they are not
ashamed of practising towards others; they demand 35
just rule for themselves, but where other men are concerned they care nothing about it. Such behaviour is
irrational; unless the one party is, and the other is not,
born to serve, in which case men have a right to command, not indeed all their fellows, but only those who
are intended to be subjects; just as we ought not to hunt
mankind, whether for food or sacrifice, but only the animals which may be hunted for food or sacrifice, this is to 40
say, such wild animals as are eatable. And surely there
may be a city happy in isolation, which we will assume to 1325ᵃ
be well-governed (for it is quite possible that a city thus
isolated might be well-administered and have good
laws); but such a city would not be constituted with any
view to war or the conquest of enemies—all that sort of
thing must be excluded. Hence we see very plainly that 5
warlike pursuits, although generally to be deemed honourable, are not the supreme end of all things, but only
means. And the good lawgiver should inquire how states
and races of men and communities may participate in a
good life, and in the happiness which is attainable by
them. His enactments will not be always the same; and 10

where there are neighbours [5] he will have to see what sort
of studies should be practised in relation to their several
characters, or how the measures appropriate in relation
to each are to be adopted. The end at which the best form
of government should aim may be properly made a mat-
15 ter of future consideration.[6]

3 Let us now address those who, while they agree that
the life of virtue is the most eligible, differ about the man-
20 ner of practising it. For some renounce political power,
and think that the life of the freeman is different from
the life of the statesman and the best of all; but others
think the life of the statesman best. The argument of the
latter is that he who does nothing cannot do well, and
that virtuous activity is identical with happiness. To both
we say: 'you are partly right and partly wrong.' The first
25 class are right in affirming that the life of the freeman is
better than the life of the despot; for there is nothing
grand or noble in having the use of a slave, in so far as he
is a slave; or in issuing commands about necessary
things. But it is an error to suppose that every sort of rule
is despotic like that of a master over slaves, for there is
as great a difference between the rule over freemen and
the rule over slaves as there is between slavery by nature
30 and freedom by nature, about which I have said enough
at the commencement of this treatise.[7] And it is equally
a mistake to place inactivity above action, for happiness
is activity, and the actions of the just and wise are the
realization of much that is noble.

But perhaps some one, accepting these premises, may
still maintain that supreme power is the best of all things,
35 because the possessors of it are able to perform the greatest number of noble actions. If so, the man who is able to

[5] Cp. ii. 1265ᵃ 20, 1267ᵃ 19.        [6] 1333ᵃ 11 sqq.        [7] i 4–7.

rule, instead of giving up anything to his neighbour, ought rather to take away his power; and the father should make no account of his son, nor the son of his father, nor friend of friend; they should not bestow a thought on one another in comparison with this higher object, for the best is the most eligible and 'doing well' is 40 the best. There might be some truth in such a view if we 1325ᵇ assume that robbers and plunderers attain the chief good. But this can never be; their hypothesis is false. For the actions of a ruler cannot really be honourable, unless he is as much superior to other men as a husband is to a wife, or a father to his children, or a master to his slaves. And 5 therefore he who violates the law can never recover by any success, however great, what he has already lost in departing from virtue. For equals the honourable and the just consist in sharing alike, as is just and equal. But that the unequal should be given to equals, and the unlike to those who are like, is contrary to nature, and nothing which is contrary to nature is good. If therefore, there is 10 any one [8] superior in virtue and in the power of performing the best actions, him we ought to follow and obey, but he must have the capacity for action as well as virtue.

If we are right in our view, and happiness is assumed to be virtuous activity, the active life will be the best, 15 both for every city collectively, and for individuals. Not that a life of action must necessarily have relation to others, as some persons think, nor are those ideas only to be regarded as practical which are pursued for the sake of practical results, but much more the thoughts and contemplations which are independent and complete in 20 themselves; since virtuous activity, and therefore a certain kind of action, is an end, and even in the case of external actions the directing mind is most truly said to act.

[8] Cp. iii. 1284ᵇ 32 and 1288ᵃ 28.

Neither, again, is it necessary that states which are cut
off from others and choose to live alone should be in-
25 active; for activity, as well as other things, may take
place by sections; there are many ways in which the sections of a state act upon one another. The same thing is
equally true of every individual. If this were otherwise,
God and the universe, who have no external actions over
30 and above their own energies, would be far enough from
perfection. Hence it is evident that the same life is best
for each individual, and for states and for mankind collectively.

**4**   Thus far by way of introduction. In what has pre-
35 ceded [9] I have discussed other forms of government; in
what remains the first point to be considered is what
should be the conditions of the ideal or perfect state; for
the perfect state cannot exist without a due supply of the
means of life. And therefore we must pre-suppose many
purely imaginary conditions,[10] but nothing impossible.
40 There will be a certain number of citizens, a country in
which to place them, and the like. As the weaver or ship-
builder or any other artisan must have the material
1326ᵃ proper for his work (and in proportion as this is better
prepared, so will the result of his art be nobler), so the
statesman or legislator must also have the materials
suited to him.

5   First among the materials required by the statesman
is population: he will consider what should be the number and character of the citizens, and then what should
be the size and character of the country. Most persons
think that a state in order to be happy ought to be large;
but even if they are right, they have no idea what is a
10 large and what a small state. For they judge of the size

---

⁹ Bk. ii.                              ¹⁰ Cp. ii. 1265ᵃ 17.

of the city by the number of the inhabitants; whereas
they ought to regard, not their number, but their power.
A city too, like an individual, has a work to do; and that
city which is best adapted to the fulfilment of its work is
to be deemed greatest, in the same sense of the word great 15
in which Hippocrates might be called greater, not as a
man, but as a physician, than some one else who was
taller. And even if we reckon greatness by numbers, we
ought not to include everybody, for there must always be
in cities a multitude of slaves and sojourners and foreign- 20
ers; but we should include those only who are members
of the state, and who form an essential part of it. The
number of the latter is a proof of the greatness of a city;
but a city which produces numerous artisans and com-
paratively few soldiers cannot be great, for a great city is
not to be confounded with a populous one. Moreover, experience shows that a very populous city can rarely, if 25
ever, be well governed; since all cities which have a reputation for good government have a limit of population.
We may argue on grounds of reason, and the same result
will follow. For law is order, and good law is good order;
but a very great multitude cannot be orderly: to intro- 30
duce order into the unlimited is the work of a divine
power—of such a power as holds together the universe.
Beauty is realized in number and magnitude,[11] and the
state which combines magnitude with good order must
necessarily be the most beautiful. To the size of states 35
there is a limit, as there is to other things, plants, animals,
implements; for none of these retain their natural power
when they are too large or too small, but they either
wholly lose their nature, or are spoiled. For example,[12] a 40
ship which is only a span long will not be a ship at all, nor
a ship a quarter of a mile long; yet there may be a ship

[11] Cp. *Poet.* 1450b 36.                    [12] Cp. v. 1309b 23.

1326ᵇ of a certain size, either too large or too small, which will
still be a ship, but bad for sailing. In like manner a state
when composed of too few is not, as a state ought to be,
self-sufficing; when of too many, though self-sufficing in
all mere necessaries, as a nation may be, it is not a state,
5 being almost incapable of constitutional government.
For who can be the general of such a vast multitude, or
who the herald, unless he have the voice of a Stentor?

A state, then, only begins to exist when it has attained
a population sufficient for a good life in the political com-
10 munity: it may indeed, if it somewhat exceed this number, be a greater state. But, as I was saying, there must
be a limit. What should be the limit will be easily ascer-
tained by experience. For both governors and governed
have duties to perform; the special functions of a gov-
15 ernor are to command and to judge. But if the citizens of
a state are to judge and to distribute offices according to
merit, then they must know each other's characters;
where they do not possess this knowledge, both the election to offices and the decision of lawsuits will go wrong.
When the population is very large they are manifestly
20 settled at haphazard, which clearly ought not to be. Besides, in an over-populous state foreigners and metics
will readily acquire the rights of citizens, for who will
find them out? Clearly then the best limit of the population of a state is the largest number which suffices for the
25 purposes of life, and can be taken in at a single view.
Enough concerning the size of a state.

**5**    Much the same principle will apply to the territory of
the state: every one would agree in praising the territory
which is most entirely self-sufficing; and that must be the
territory which is all-producing, for to have all things and
30 to want nothing is sufficiency. In size and extent it should

be such as may enable the inhabitants to live at once temperately and liberally in the enjoyment of leisure.[13]
Whether we are right or wrong in laying down this limit
we will inquire more precisely hereafter,[14] when we have
occasion to consider what is the right use of property and 35
wealth: a matter which is much disputed, because men
are inclined to rush into one of two extremes, some into
meanness, others into luxury.

It is not difficult to determine the general character of
the territory which is required (there are, however, some
points on which military authorities should be heard); it 40
should be difficult of access to the enemy, and easy of
egress to the inhabitants. Further, we require that the 1327ᵃ
land as well as the inhabitants of whom we were just now
speaking [15] should be taken in at a single view, for a country which is easily seen can be easily protected. As to the
position of the city, if we could have what we wish, it
should be well situated in regard both to sea and land. 5
This then is one principle, that it should be a convenient
centre for the protection of the whole country: the other
is, that it should be suitable for receiving the fruits of the
soil, and also for the bringing in of timber and any other 10
products that are easily transported.

**6**  Whether a communication with the sea is beneficial
to a well-ordered state or not is a question which has
often been asked. It is argued that the introduction of
strangers brought up under other laws, and the increase
of population, will be adverse to good order; the increase 15
arises from their using the sea and having a crowd of
merchants coming and going, and is inimical to good government.[16] Apart from these considerations, it would be

[13] Cp. ii. 1265ᵃ 32.                    [14] This promise is not fulfilled.
[15] 1326ᵇ 22–24.                         [16] Cp. Plato, *Laws*, iv. 704 D–705 B.

20 undoubtedly better, both with a view to safety and to the provision of necessaries, that the city and territory should be connected with the sea; the defenders of a country, if they are to maintain themselves against an enemy, should be easily relieved both by land and by sea; and even if they are not able to attack by sea and land at once, they will have less difficulty in doing mischief to their assailants on one element, if they themselves can 25 use both. Moreover, it is necessary that they should import from abroad what is not found in their own country, and that they should export what they have in excess; for a city ought to be a market, not indeed for others, but for herself.

Those who make themselves a market for the world 30 only do so for the sake of revenue, and if a state ought not to desire profit of this kind it ought not to have such an emporium. Nowadays we often see in countries and cities dockyards and harbours very conveniently placed outside the city, but not too far off; and they are kept in de- 35 pendence by walls and similar fortifications. Cities thus situated manifestly reap the benefit of intercourse with their ports; and any harm which is likely to accrue may be easily guarded against by the laws, which will pronounce and determine who may hold communication with one another, and who may not.

40 There can be no doubt that the possession of a mod-
1327ᵇ erate naval force is advantageous to a city; the city should be formidable not only to its own citizens but to some of its neighbours,[17] or, if necessary, able to assist them by sea as well as by land. The proper number or magnitude of this naval force is relative to the character of the state; for if her function is to take a leading part in 5 politics, her naval power should be commensurate with

[17] Cp. ii. 1265ᵃ 20.

the scale of her enterprises. The population of the state
need not be much increased, since there is no necessity
that the sailors should be citizens: the marines who have
the control and command will be freemen, and belong
also to the infantry; and wherever there is a dense popu- 10
lation of Perioeci and husbandmen, there will always be
sailors more than enough. Of this we see instances at the
present day. The city of Heraclea, for example, although
small in comparison with many others, can man a con- 15
siderable fleet. Such are our conclusions respecting the
territory of the state, its harbours, its towns, its relations
to the sea, and its maritime power.

7    Having spoken of the number of the citizens,[18] we
will proceed to speak of what should be their character. 20
This is a subject which can be easily understood by any
one who casts his eye on the more celebrated states of
Hellas, and generally on the distribution of races in the
habitable world. Those who live in a cold climate and in
Europe are full of spirit, but wanting in intelligence and 25
skill; and therefore they retain comparative freedom,
but have no political organization, and are incapable of
ruling over others. Whereas the natives of Asia are intelligent and inventive, but they are wanting in spirit, and
therefore they are always in a state of subjection and
slavery. But the Hellenic race, which is situated between
them, is likewise intermediate in character, being high- 30
spirited and also intelligent.[19] Hence it continues free,
and is the best-governed of any nation, and, if it could be
formed into one state, would be able to rule the world.
There are also similar differences in the different tribes of
Hellas; for some of them are of a one-sided nature, and
are intelligent or courageous only, while in others there is 35

---

[18] 1326ᵃ 9–ᵇ24.                    [19] Cp. Plato, *Rep.* iv. 435 ᴇ, 436 ᴀ.

a happy combination of both qualities. And clearly those whom the legislator will most easily lead to virtue may be expected to be both intelligent and courageous. Some [20] say that the guardians should be friendly towards those 40 whom they know, fierce towards those whom they do not 1328ᵃ know. Now, passion is the quality of the soul which begets friendship and enables us to love; notably the spirit within us is more stirred against our friends and acquaintances than against those who are unknown to us, when we think that we are despised by them; for which reason Archilochus, complaining of his friends, very naturally addresses his soul in these words,

5 'For surely thou art plagued on account of friends.'

The power of command and the love of freedom are in all men based upon this quality, for passion is commanding and invincible. Nor is it right to say that the guardians should be fierce towards those whom they do not know, for we ought not to be out of temper with any one; and a lofty spirit is not fierce by nature, but only when 10 excited against evil-doers. And this, as I was saying before, is a feeling which men show most strongly towards their friends if they think they have received a wrong at their hands: as indeed is reasonable; for, besides the actual injury, they seem to be deprived of a benefit by those who owe them one. Hence the saying,

15 'Cruel is the strife of brethren,'

and again,

'They who love in excess also hate in excess.'

Thus we have nearly determined the number and character of the citizens of our state, and also the size and

[20] *Rep.* ii. 375 c.

nature of their territory. I say 'nearly', for we ought not 20
to require the same minuteness in theory as in the facts
given by perception.[21]

**8**  As in other natural compounds the conditions of a
composite whole are not necessarily organic parts of it, so
in a state or in any other combination forming a unity not
everything is a part, which is a necessary condition.[22]
The members of an association have necessarily some
one thing the same and common to all, in which they 25
share equally or unequally; for example, food or land or
any other thing. But where there are two things of which
one is a means and the other an end, they have nothing in
common except that the one receives what the other produces. Such, for example, is the relation in which work- 30
men and tools stand to their work; the house and the
builder have nothing in common, but the art of the
builder is for the sake of the house. And so states require 35
property, but property, even though living beings are included in it,[23] is no part of a state; for a state is not a
community of living beings only, but a community of
equals, aiming at the best life possible. Now, whereas
happiness is the highest good, being a realization and
perfect practice of virtue, which some can attain, while
others have little or none of it, the various qualities of
men are clearly the reason why there are various kinds 40
of states and many forms of government; for different
men seek after happiness in different ways and by differ- 1328ᵛ
ent means, and so make for themselves different modes of
life and forms of government. We must see also how
many things are indispensable to the existence of a state,
for what we call the parts of a state will be found among

21 Cp. 1331ᵇ 18.       22 Cp. iii. 1278ᵃ 2.       23 Cp. i. 1253ᵇ 32.

the indispensables. Let us then enumerate the functions
5 of a state, and we shall easily elicit what we want:

First, there must be food; secondly, arts, for life requires many instruments; thirdly, there must be arms,
for the members of a community have need of them, and
in their own hands, too, in order to maintain authority
10 both against disobedient subjects and against external
assailants; fourthly, there must be a certain amount of
revenue, both for internal needs, and for the purposes of
war; fifthly, or rather first, there must be a care of religion, which is commonly called worship; sixthly, and
most necessary of all, there must be a power of deciding
what is for the public interest, and what is just in men's
dealings with one another.

15    These are the services which every state may be said
to need. For a state is not a mere aggregate of persons,
but a union of them sufficing for the purposes of life; and
if any of these things be wanting, it is as we maintain [24]
impossible that the community can be absolutely self-
sufficing. A state then should be framed with a view to
the fulfilment of these functions. There must be husband-
20 men to procure food, and artisans, and a warlike and a
wealthy class, and priests, and judges to decide what is
necessary and expedient.


9    Having determined these points, we have in the next
place to consider whether all ought to share in every sort
25 of occupation. Shall every man be at once husbandman,
artisan, councillor, judge, or shall we suppose the several
occupations just mentioned assigned to different persons? or, thirdly, shall some employments be assigned to
individuals and others common to all? The same ar-
30 rangement, however, does not occur in every constitu-

[24] Cp. ii. 1261$^b$ 12, iii. 1275$^b$ 20, v. 1303$^a$ 26.

tion; as we were saying, all may be shared by all, or not all by all, but only by some; and hence arise the differences of constitutions, for in democracies all share in all, in oligarchies the opposite practice prevails. Now, since we are here speaking of the best form of government, i. e. that under which the state will be most happy (and happiness, as has been already said, cannot exist without virtue [25]), it clearly follows that in the state which is best governed and possesses men who are just absolutely, and not merely relatively to the principle of the constitution, the citizens must not lead the life of mechanics or tradesmen, for such a life is ignoble, and inimical to virtue.[26] Neither must they be husbandmen, since leisure is necessary both for the development of virtue and the performance of political duties.

Again, there is in a state a class of warriors, and another of councillors, who advise about the expedient and determine matters of law, and these seem in an especial manner parts of a state. Now, should these two classes be distinguished, or are both functions to be assigned to the same persons? Here again there is no difficulty in seeing that both functions will in one way belong to the same, in another, to different persons. To different persons in so far as these employments are suited to different primes of life,[27] for the one requires wisdom and the other strength. But on the other hand, since it is an impossible thing that those who are able to use or to resist force should be willing to remain always in subjection, from this point of view the persons are the same; for those who carry arms can always determine the fate of the constitution. It remains therefore that both functions should be entrusted

[25] Cp. 1323ᵃ 21–1324ᵃ 4, 1328ᵃ 37 sq.
[26] Cp. Plato, *Laws,* xi. 919 c–e.
[27] i. e. the physical and the mental.

by the ideal constitution to the same persons, not, however, at the same time, but in the order prescribed by
15 nature, who has given to young men strength and to
older men wisdom. Such a distribution of duties will be
expedient and also just, and is founded upon a principle
of conformity to merit. Besides, the ruling class should
be the owners of property, for they are citizens, and the
20 citizens of a state should be in good circumstances;
whereas mechanics or any other class which is not a pro-
ducer of virtue have no share in the state. This follows
from our first principle,[28] for happiness cannot exist without virtue, and a city is not to be termed happy in regard
to a portion of the citizens, but in regard to them all.[29]
25 And clearly property should be in their hands, since the
husbandmen will of necessity be slaves or barbarian
Perioeci.[30]

Of the classes enumerated there remain only the
priests, and the manner in which their office is to be regulated is obvious. No husbandman or mechanic should be
appointed to it; for the Gods should receive honour from
30 the citizens only. Now since the body of the citizens is
divided into two classes, the warriors and the councillors,
and it is beseeming that the worship of the Gods should
be duly performed, and also a rest provided in their service for those who from age have given up active life, to
the old men of these two classes should be assigned the
duties of the priesthood.

We have shown what are the necessary conditions, and
35 what the parts of a state: husbandmen, craftsmen, and
labourers of all kinds are necessary to the existence of
states, but the parts of the state are the warriors and
councillors. And these are distinguished severally from

[28] Cp. 1328[b] 35.

[29] Cp. ii. 1264[b] 17–24.

[30] Cp. *infra*, 1330[a] 25–31.

one another, the distinction being in some cases permanent, in others not.

10    It is not a new or recent discovery of political philosophers that the state ought to be divided into classes, and that the warriors should be separated from the husbandmen. The system has continued in Egypt and in Crete to this day, and was established, as tradition says, by a law of Sesostris in Egypt and of Minos in Crete. The institution of common tables also appears to be of ancient date, being in Crete as old as the reign of Minos, and in Italy far older. The Italian historians say that there was a certain Italus king of Oenotria, from whom the Oenotrians were called Italians, and who gave the name of Italy to the promontory of Europe lying within the Scylletic and Lametic Gulfs,[31] which are distant from one another only half a day's journey. They say that this Italus converted the Oenotrians from shepherds into husbandmen, and besides other laws which he gave them, was the founder of their common meals; even in our day some who are derived from him retain this institution and certain other laws of his. On the side of Italy towards Tyrrhenia dwelt the Opici, who are now, as of old, called Ausones; and on the side towards Iapygia and the Ionian Gulf, in the district called Siritis, the Chones, who are likewise of Oenotrian race. From this part of the world originally came the institution of common tables; the separation into castes from Egypt, for the reign of Sesostris is of far greater antiquity than that of Minos. It is true indeed that these and many other things have been invented several times over [32] in the course of ages, or rather times without number; for necessity may be

---

[31] i. e. between these gulfs and the Strait of Messina.

[32] Cp. Plato, *Laws*, iii. 676; Aristotle, *Metaph.* xii. 1074[b] 10; and *Pol.* ii. 1264[a] 3.

supposed to have taught men the inventions which were
absolutely required, and when these were provided, it
was natural that other things which would adorn and en-
30 rich life should grow up by degrees. And we may infer
that in political institutions the same rule holds. Egypt [33]
witnesses to the antiquity of all these things, for the
Egyptians appear to be of all people the most ancient;
and they have laws and a regular constitution existing
from time immemorial. We should therefore make the
35 best use of what has been already discovered, and try to
supply defects.

I have already remarked that the land ought to belong
to those who possess arms and have a share in the government,[34] and that the husbandmen ought to be a class distinct from them; and I have determined what should be
the extent and nature of the territory. Let me proceed to
discuss the distribution of the land, and the character of
40 the agricultural class; for I do not think that property
1330ᵃ ought to be common, as some maintain,[35] but only that by
friendly consent there should be a common use of it; and
that no citizen should be in want of subsistence.

As to common meals, there is a general agreement that
a well-ordered city should have them; and we will hereafter explain what are our own reasons for taking this
5 view.[36] They ought, however, to be open to all the citizens.[37] And yet it is not easy for the poor to contribute the
requisite sum out of their private means, and to provide
also for their household. The expense of religious worship
10 should likewise be a public charge. The land must there-

[33] Cp. *Metaph*. i. 981ᵇ 23; *Meteor*. i. 14. 352ᵇ 19; Plato, *Timaeus*, 22
ʙ; *Laws*, ii. 656, 657.
[34] 1328ᵇ 33–1329ᵃ 2, 1329ᵃ 17–26, 1326ᵇ 26–32.
[35] Cp. ii. 5, *Rep*. iii. 416 ᴅ.
[36] Aristotle does not give any explanation in the *Politics*.
[37] Cp. ii. 1271ᵃ 28.

fore be divided into two parts, one public and the other private, and each part should be subdivided, part of the public land being appropriated to the service of the Gods, and the other part used to defray the cost of the common meals; while of the private land, part should be near the 15 border, and the other near the city, so that, each citizen having two lots, they may all of them have land in both places; there is justice and fairness in such a division, and it tends to inspire unanimity among the people in their border wars. Where there is not this arrangement, some of them are too ready to come to blows with their neighbours, while others are so cautious that they quite 20 lose the sense of honour. Wherefore there is a law in some places which forbids those who dwell near the border to take part in public deliberations about wars with neighbours, on the ground that their interests will pervert their judgment. For the reasons already mentioned, then, the land should be divided in the manner described. The very 25 best thing of all would be that the husbandmen should be slaves taken from among men who are not all of the same race [38] and not spirited, for if they have no spirit they will be better suited for their work, and there will be no danger of their making a revolution. The next best thing would be that they should be Perioeci of foreign race,[39] 30 and of a like inferior nature; some of them should be the slaves of individuals, and employed in the private estates of men of property, the remainder should be the property of the state and employed on the common land.[40] I will hereafter explain[41] what is the proper treatment of slaves, and why it is expedient that liberty should be always held out to them as the reward of their services.

[38] Cp. Plato, *Laws*, vi. 777 c, d.          [39] Cp. 1329ᵃ 26.
[40] Cp. ii. 1267ᵇ 16.
[41] A. does not do so in the *Politics*, but Cp. *Oec.* 1344ᵇ 15.

**11** We have already said that the city should be open
35 to the land and to the sea,[42] and to the whole country as
far as possible. In respect of the place itself our wish
would be that its situation should be fortunate in four
things. The first, health—this is a necessity: cities which
lie towards the east, and are blown upon by winds com-
40 ing from the east, are the healthiest; next in healthful-
ness are those which are sheltered from the north wind,
for they have a milder winter. The site of the city should
1330ᵇ likewise be convenient both for political administration
and for war. With a view to the latter it should afford
easy egress to the citizens, and at the same time be inac-
cessible and difficult of capture to enemies.[43] There
should be a natural abundance of springs and fountains
5 in the town, or, if there is a deficiency of them, great
reservoirs may be established for the collection of rain-
water, such as will not fail when the inhabitants are cut
off from the country by war. Special care should be taken
of the health of the inhabitants, which will depend chiefly
on the healthiness of the locality and of the quarter to
10 which they are exposed, and secondly, on the use of pure
water; this latter point is by no means a secondary consideration. For the elements which we use most and
oftenest for the support of the body contribute most to
health, and among these are water and air. Wherefore, in
15 all wise states, if there is a want of pure water, and the
supply is not all equally good, the drinking water ought to
be separated from that which is used for other purposes.

As to strongholds, what is suitable to different forms of
20 government varies: thus an acropolis is suited to an oligarchy or a monarchy, but a plain to a democracy;
neither to an aristocracy, but rather a number of strong
places. The arrangement of private houses is considered

---

[42] 1327ᵃ 4–40.    [43] Repetition of 1326ᵇ 40.

to be more agreeable and generally more convenient, if the streets are regularly laid out after the modern fashion which Hippodamus [44] introduced, but for security in war the antiquated mode of building, which made it difficult for strangers to get out of a town and for assailants to find their way in, is preferable. A city should therefore adopt both plans of building: it is possible to arrange the houses irregularly, as husbandmen plant their vines in what are called 'clumps'. The whole town should not be laid out in straight lines, but only certain quarters and regions; thus security and beauty will be combined.

As to walls, those who say [45] that cities making any pretension to military virtue should not have them, are quite out of date in their notions; and they may see the cities which prided themselves on this fancy confuted by facts. True, there is little courage shown in seeking for safety behind a rampart when an enemy is similar in character and not much superior in number; but the superiority of the besiegers may be and often is too much both for ordinary human valour and for that which is found only in a few; and if they are to be saved and to escape defeat and outrage, the strongest wall will be the truest soldierly precaution, more especially now that missiles and siege engines have been brought to such perfection. To have no walls would be as foolish as to choose a site for a town in an exposed country, and to level the heights; or as if an individual were to leave his house unwalled, lest the inmates should become cowards. Nor must we forget that those who have their cities surrounded by walls may either take advantage of them or not, but cities which are unwalled have no choice.

If our conclusions are just, not only should cities have

[44] Cp. ii. 1267ᵇ 22.          [45] Cp. Plato, *Laws*, vi. 778 ᴅ.

walls, but care should be taken to make them orna-
mental, as well as useful for warlike purposes, and
adapted to resist modern inventions. For as the assail-
15 ants of a city do all they can to gain an advantage, so
the defenders should make use of any means of defence
which have been already discovered, and should devise
and invent others, for when men are well prepared no
enemy even thinks of attacking them.

**12**  As the walls are to be divided by guard-houses and
20 towers built at suitable intervals, and the body of citizens must be distributed at common tables,[46] the idea
will naturally occur that we should establish some of the
common tables in the guard-houses. These might be arranged as has been suggested; while the principal com-
25 mon tables of the magistrates will occupy a suitable
place, and there also will be the buildings appropriated
to religious worship except in the case of those rites
which the law or the Pythian oracle has restricted to a
special locality.[47] The site should be a spot seen far and
30 wide, which gives due elevation to virtue and towers over
the neighbourhood. Below this spot should be established
an agora, such as that which the Thessalians call the
'freemen's agora'; from this all trade should be excluded,
and no mechanic, husbandman, or any such person al-
35 lowed to enter, unless he be summoned by the magistrates. It would be a charming use of the place, if the
gymnastic exercises of the elder men were performed
there. For in this noble practice different ages should be
separated, and some of the magistrates should stay with
40 the boys, while the grown-up men remain with the magistrates; for the presence of the magistrates is the best

---

[46] Cp. 1330ᵃ 3.
[47] Cp. Plato, *Laws*, v. 738 b–d, vi. 759 c, 778 c, viii. 848 d–e.

mode of inspiring true modesty and ingenuous fear.
There should also be a traders' agora, distinct and apart **1331ᵇ**
from the other, in a situation which is convenient for the
reception of goods both by sea and land.

But in speaking of the magistrates we must not forget another section of the citizens, viz. the priests, for 5
whom public tables should likewise be provided in their
proper place near the temples. The magistrates who deal
with contracts, indictments, summonses, and the like,
and those who have the care of the agora and of the city
respectively, ought to be established near an agora and 10
some public place of meeting; the neighbourhood of the
traders' agora will be a suitable spot; the upper agora
we devote to the life of leisure, the other is intended for
the necessities of trade.

The same order should prevail in the country, for
there too the magistrates, called by some 'Inspectors of 15
Forests' and by others 'Wardens of the Country', must
have guard-houses and common tables while they are on
duty; temples should also be scattered throughout the
country, dedicated, some to Gods, and some to heroes.

But it would be a waste of time for us to linger over
details like these. The difficulty is not in imagining but
in carrying them out. We may talk about them as much 20
as we like, but the execution of them will depend upon
fortune. Wherefore let us say no more about these matters for the present.

**13**   Returning to the constitution itself, let us seek to
determine out of what and what sort of elements the 25
state which is to be happy and well-governed should be
composed. There are two things in which all well-being
consists: one of them is the choice of a right end and aim
of action, and the other the discovery of the actions

30 which are means towards it; for the means and the end
may agree or disagree. Sometimes the right end is set
before men, but in practice they fail to attain it; in
other cases they are successful in all the means, but they
propose to themselves a bad end; and sometimes they
fail in both. Take, for example, the art of medicine;
physicians do not always understand the nature of
35 health, and also the means which they use may not effect the desired end. In all arts and sciences both the
end and the means should be equally within our control.

The happiness and well-being which all men mani-
40 festly desire, some have the power of attaining, but to
others, from some accident or defect of nature, the at-
tainment of them is not granted; for a good life requires
1332ª a supply of external goods, in a less degree when men
are in a good state, in a greater degree when they are in
a lower state. Others again, who possess the conditions
of happiness, go utterly wrong from the first in the pursuit of it. But since our object is to discover the best form
5 of government, that, namely, under which a city will be
best governed, and since the city is best governed which
has the greatest opportunity of obtaining happiness, it is
evident that we must clearly ascertain the nature of
happiness.

We maintain, and have said in the *Ethics*,[48] if the arguments there adduced are of any value, that happiness is
the realization and perfect exercise of virtue, and this
10 not conditional, but absolute. And I used the term 'conditional' to express that which is indispensable, and 'absolute' to express that which is good in itself. Take the
case of just actions; just punishments and chastisements
do indeed spring from a good principle, but they are
good only because we cannot do without them—it would

[48] *Nic. Eth.* i. 1098ª 16, x. 1176ᵇ 4; and Cp. 1328ª 37.

be better that neither individuals nor states should need anything of the sort—but actions which aim at honour 15 and advantage are absolutely the best. The conditional action is only the choice of a lesser evil; whereas these are the foundation and creation of good. A good man may make the best even of poverty and disease, and the other ills of life; but he can only attain happiness under 20 the opposite conditions [49] (for this also has been determined in accordance with ethical arguments,[50] that the good man is he for whom, because he is virtuous, the things that are absolutely good are good; it is also plain that his use of these goods must be virtuous and in the 25 absolute sense good). This makes men fancy that external goods are the cause of happiness, yet we might as well say that a brilliant performance on the lyre was to be attributed to the instrument and not to the skill of the performer.

It follows then from what has been said that some things the legislator must find ready to his hand in a state, others he must provide. And therefore we can only say: May our state be constituted in such a manner as to be blessed with the goods of which fortune disposes (for we acknowledge her power): whereas virtue and 30 goodness in the state are not a matter of chance but the result of knowledge and purpose. A city can be virtuous only when the citizens who have a share in the government are virtuous, and in our state all the citizens share in the government; let us then inquire how a man be- 35 comes virtuous. For even if we could suppose the citizen body to be virtuous, without each of them being so, yet the latter would be better, for in the virtue of each the virtue of all is involved.

[49] *Nic. Eth.* i. 1100[b] 22, 1101[a] 13.
[50] *Nic. Eth.* iii. 1113[a] 22–[b]1; *E. E.* vii. 1248[b] 26; *M. M.* ii. 1207[b] 31.

There are three things which make men good and vir-
40 tuous; these are nature, habit, rational principle.[51] In
the first place, every one must be born a man and not
some other animal; so, too, he must have a certain character, both of body and soul. But some qualities there is
1332ᵇ no use in having at birth, for they are altered by habit,
and there are some gifts which by nature are made to be
turned by habit to good or bad. Animals lead for the most
part a life of nature, although in lesser particulars some
are influenced by habit as well. Man has rational prin-
5 ciple, in addition, and man only. Wherefore nature,
habit, rational principle must be in harmony with one
another; for they do not always agree; men do many
things against habit and nature, if rational principle
persuades them that they ought. We have already determined what natures are likely to be most easily moulded
by the hands of the legislator.[52] All else is the work of
10 education; we learn some things by habit and some by
instruction.

**14** Since every political society is composed of rulers
and subjects let us consider whether the relations of one
15 to the other should interchange or be permanent.[53] For
the education of the citizens will necessarily vary with
the answer given to this question. Now, if some men ex-
celled others in the same degree in which gods and
heroes are supposed to excel mankind in general (having
20 in the first place a great advantage even in their bodies,
and secondly in their minds), so that the superiority of
the governors was undisputed and patent to their subjects, it would clearly be better that once for all the one
class should rule and the others serve.[54] But since this

---

[51] Cp. *Nic. Eth.* x. 1179ᵇ 20.                [52] 1327ᵇ 36.
[53] Cp. iii. 1279ᵃ 8.                        [54] Cp. i. 1254ᵇ 16, 1284ᵃ 3.

is unattainable, and kings have no marked superiority over their subjects, such as Scylax affirms to be found among the Indians, it is obviously necessary on many 25 grounds that all the citizens alike should take their turn of governing and being governed. Equality consists in the same treatment of similar persons, and no government can stand which is not founded upon justice. For if the government be unjust every one in the country unites with the governed in the desire to have a revolution, and it is an impossibility that the members of the 30 government can be so numerous as to be stronger than all their enemies put together. Yet that governors should excel their subjects is undeniable. How all this is to be effected, and in what way they will respectively share in the government, the legislator has to consider. The 35 subject has been already mentioned.[55] Nature herself has provided the distinction when she made a difference between old and young within the same species, of whom she fitted the one to govern and the other to be governed. No one takes offence at being governed when he is young, nor does he think himself better than his governors, es- 40 pecially if he will enjoy the same privilege when he reaches the required age.

We conclude that from one point of view governors and governed are identical, and from another different. And therefore their education must be the same and also 1333ᵃ different. For he who would learn to command well must, as men say, first of all learn to obey.[56] As I observed in the first part of this treatise, there is one rule which is for the sake of the rulers and another rule which is for the sake of the ruled; [57] the former is a despotic, the latter a 5 free government. Some commands differ not in the thing

[55] 1329ᵃ 2–17.                                    [56] Cp. iii. 1277ᵇ 9.
[57] iii. 1278ᵇ 32–1279ᵃ 8, Cp. 1277ᵃ 33–ᵇ 30.

commanded, but in the intention with which they are
imposed. Wherefore, many apparently menial offices are
an honour to the free youth by whom they are per-
10 formed; for actions do not differ as honourable or dis-
honourable in themselves so much as in the end and
intention of them. But since we say [58] that the virtue of
the citizen and ruler is the same as that of the good man,
and that the same person must first be a subject and
15 then a ruler, the legislator has to see that they become
good men, and by what means this may be accomplished,
and what is the end of the perfect life.

Now the soul of man is divided into two parts, one of
which has a rational principle in itself, and the other,
not having a rational principle in itself, is able to obey
such a principle.[59] And we call a man in any way good
because he has the virtues of these two parts. In which
20 of them the end is more likely to be found is no matter
of doubt to those who adopt our division; for in the
world both of nature and of art the inferior always exists
for the sake of the better or superior, and the better or
superior is that which has a rational principle. This principle, too, in our ordinary way of speaking, is divided into
25 two kinds, for there is a practical and a speculative principle.[60] This part, then, must evidently be similarly divided. And there must be a corresponding division of
actions; the actions of the naturally better part are to be
preferred by those who have it in their power to attain
to two out of the three or to all, for that is always to
every one the most eligible which is the highest attain-
30 able by him. The whole of life is further divided into
two parts, business and leisure,[61] war and peace, and of
actions some aim at what is necessary and useful, and

[58] Cp. iii. 4, 5.                                    [59] Cp. *Nic. Eth.* i. 1102$^b$ 28.
[60] Cp *Nic. Eth.* vi. 1139$^a$ 6.            [61] *Nic. Eth.* x. 1177$^b$ 4.

some at what is honourable. And the preference given to
one or the other class of actions must necessarily be like
the preference given to one or other part of the soul and 35
its actions over the other; there must be war for the sake
of peace, business for the sake of leisure, things useful
and necessary for the sake of things honourable. All
these points the statesman should keep in view when he
frames his laws; he should consider the parts of the soul
and their functions, and above all the better and the end; 40
he should also remember the diversities of human lives
and actions. For men must be able to engage in business
and go to war, but leisure and peace are better; they must 1333ᵇ
do what is necessary and indeed what is useful, but what
is honourable is better. On such principles children and
persons of every age which requires education should be 5
trained. Whereas even the Hellenes of the present day
who are reputed to be best governed, and the legislators
who gave them their constitutions, do not appear to have
framed their governments with a regard to the best end,
or to have given them laws and education with a view to
all the virtues, but in a vulgar spirit have fallen back on
those which promised to be more useful and profitable.
Many modern writers have taken a similar view: they 10
commend the Lacedaemonian constitution, and praise
the legislator for making conquest and war his sole
aim,[62] a doctrine which may be refuted by argument and 15
has long ago been refuted by facts. For most men desire
empire in the hope of accumulating the goods of fortune;
and on this ground Thibron and all those who have written about the Lacedaemonian constitution have praised
their legislator, because the Lacedaemonians, by being 20
trained to meet dangers, gained great power. But surely
they are not a happy people now that their empire has

[62] Cp. Plato, *Laws,* i. 628, 638.

passed away, nor was their legislator right. How ridiculous is the result, if, while they are continuing in the ob-
servance of his laws and no one interferes with them, they
25 have lost the better part of life! These writers further
err about the sort of government which the legislator
should approve, for the government of freemen is nobler
and implies more virtue than despotic government.[63]
Neither is a city to be deemed happy or a legislator to be
30 praised because he trains his citizens to conquer and obtain dominion over their neighbours, for there is great
evil in this. On a similar principle any citizen who could,
should obviously try to obtain the power in his own state
—the crime which the Lacedaemonians accuse king Pausanias of attempting,[64] although he had so great honour
35 already. No such principle and no law having this object
is either statesmanlike or useful or right. For the same
things are best both for individuals and for states, and
these are the things which the legislator ought to im-
plant in the minds of his citizens. Neither should men
study war with a view to the enslavement of those who
40 do not deserve to be enslaved; but first of all they should
provide against their own enslavement, and in the second place obtain empire for the good of the governed,
1334ᵃ and not for the sake of exercising a general despotism,
and in the third place they should seek to be masters
only over those who deserve to be slaves. Facts, as well
5 as arguments, prove that the legislator should direct all
his military and other measures to the provision of leisure and the establishment of peace. For most of these
military states are safe only while they are at war,[65] but
fall when they have acquired their empire; like unused
10 iron they lose their temper in time of peace. And for this

63 Cp. i. 1254ᵃ 25.          64 Cp. v. 1301ᵇ 20, 1307ᵃ 3.
65 Cp. ii 1271ᵇ 3.

the legislator is to blame, he never having taught them
how to lead the life of peace.

**15**  Since the end of individuals and of states is the
same, the end of the best man and of the best constitution must also be the same; it is therefore evident that
there ought to exist in both of them the virtues of leisure;
for peace, as has been often repeated,[66] is the end of war, 15
and leisure of toil. But leisure and cultivation may be
promoted, not only by those virtues which are practised
in leisure, but also by some of those which are useful
to business.[67] For many necessaries of life have to be
supplied before we can have leisure. Therefore a city
must be temperate and brave, and able to endure: for 20
truly, as the proverb says, 'There is no leisure for slaves,'
and those who cannot face danger like men are the slaves
of any invader. Courage and endurance are required for
business and philosophy for leisure, temperance and justice for both, and more especially in times of peace and 25
leisure, for war compels men to be just and temperate,
whereas the enjoyment of good fortune and the leisure
which comes with peace tend to make them insolent.
Those then who seem to be the best-off and to be in the
possession of every good, have special need of justice and
temperance—for example, those (if such there be, as the 30
poets say) who dwell in the Islands of the Blest; they
above all will need philosophy and temperance and justice, and all the more the more leisure they have, living
in the midst of abundance. There is no difficulty in seeing why the state that would be happy and good ought 35
to have these virtues. If it be disgraceful in men not to

[66] 1333ᵃ 35, 1334ᵃ 2.
[67] i. e. 'not only by some of the speculative but also by some of the
practical virtues'.

be able to use the goods of life, it is peculiarly disgraceful not to be able to use them in time of leisure—to show
excellent qualities in action and war, and when they
have peace and leisure to be no better than slaves.
40 Wherefore we should not practise virtue after the manner of the Lacedaemonians.[68] For they, while agreeing
with other men in their conception of the highest goods,
**1334<sup>b</sup>** differ from the rest of mankind in thinking that they are
to be obtained by the practice of a single virtue. And
since [they think] these goods and the enjoyment of
5 them greater than the enjoyment derived from the virtues . . . and that [it should be practised] for its own
sake, is evident from what has been said; we must now
consider how and by what means it is to be attained.

We have already determined that nature and habit
and rational principle are required,[69] and, of these, the
proper *nature* of the citizens has also been defined by
us.[70] But we have still to consider whether the training
of early life is to be that of rational principle or habit,
for these two must accord, and when in accord they will
10 then form the best of harmonies. The rational principle
may be mistaken and fail in attaining the highest ideal
of life, and there may be a like evil influence of habit.
Thus much is clear in the first place, that, as in all other
things, birth implies an antecedent beginning,[71] and that
there are beginnings whose end is relative to a further
end. Now, in men rational principle and mind are the
end towards which nature strives,[72] so that the birth and
15 moral discipline of the citizens ought to be ordered with
a view to them. In the second place, as the soul and body

---

[68] Cp. ii. 1271<sup>a</sup> 41.　　　　　　　　　　[69] 1332<sup>a</sup> 39 sqq.
[70] c. 7.　　　　　　　　　　[71] i. e. the union of the parents.
[72] i. e. the birth of the offspring, which is the end of the union of the
parents, points to a further end, the development of mind.

are two, we see also that there are two parts of the soul, the rational and the irrational, and two corresponding states—reason and appetite. And as the body is prior 20 in order of generation to the soul, so the irrational is prior to the rational. The proof is that anger and wishing and desire are implanted in children from their very birth, but reason and understanding are developed as they grow older. Wherefore, the care of the body ought to 25 precede that of the soul, and the training of the appetitive part should follow: none the less our care of it must be for the sake of the reason, and our care of the body for the sake of the soul.

**16**    Since the legislator should begin by considering how the frames of the children whom he is rearing may be as 30 good as possible, his first care will be about marriage—at what age should his citizens marry, and who are fit to marry? In legislating on this subject he ought to consider the persons and the length of their life, that their pro-creative life may terminate at the same period, and that 35 they may not differ in their bodily powers, as will be the case if the man is still able to beget children while the woman is unable to bear them, or the woman able to bear while the man is unable to beget, for from these causes arise quarrels and differences between married persons. Secondly, he must consider the time at which the chil-dren will succeed to their parents; there ought not to be 40 too great an interval of age, for then the parents will be too old to derive any pleasure from their affection, or to be of any use to them. Nor ought they to be too nearly 1335$^a$ of an age; to youthful marriages there are many objec-tions—the children will be wanting in respect to the par-ents, who will seem to be their contemporaries, and disputes will arise in the management of the household.

Thirdly, and this is the point from which we digressed,[73]
the legislator must mould to his will the frames of newly-
born children. Almost all these objects may be secured
by attention to one point. Since the time of generation is
commonly limited within the age of seventy years in the
case of a man, and of fifty in the case of a woman, the
commencement of the union should conform to these
periods. The union of male and female when too young
is bad for the procreation of children; in all other animals the offspring of the young are small and ill-devel-
oped, and with a tendency to produce female children,
and therefore also in man, as is proved by the fact that
in those cities in which men and women are accustomed
to marry young, the people are small and weak; in child-
birth also younger women suffer more, and more of them
die; some persons say that this was the meaning of the
response once given to the Troezenians[74]—the oracle
really meant that many died because they married too
young; it had nothing to do with the ingathering of the
harvest. It also conduces to temperance not to marry
too soon; for women who marry early are apt to be
wanton; and in men too the bodily frame is stunted if
they marry while the seed is growing (for there is a time
when the growth of the seed, also, ceases, or continues
to but a slight extent). Women should marry when they
are about eighteen years of age, and men at seven and
thirty; then they are in the prime of life, and the decline
in the powers of both will coincide. Further, the children,
if their birth takes place soon, as may reasonably be
expected, will succeed in the beginning of their prime,
when the fathers are already in the decline of life, and
have nearly reached their term of three-score years and
ten.

[73] 1334ᵇ 29 sqq.    [74] 'Plough not the young field'.

Thus much of the age proper for marriage: the season of the year should also be considered; according to our present custom, people generally limit marriage to the season of winter, and they are right. The precepts of physicians and natural philosophers about generation 40 should also be studied by the parents themselves; the physicians give good advice about the favourable conditions of the body, and the natural philosophers about 1335ᵇ the winds; of which they prefer the north to the south.

What constitution in the parent is most advantageous to the offspring is a subject which we will consider more carefully [75] when we speak of the education of children, and we will only make a few general remarks at present. The constitution of an athlete is not suited to the life 5 of a citizen, or to health, or to the procreation of children, any more than the valetudinarian or exhausted constitution, but one which is in a mean between them. A man's constitution should be inured to labour, but not to labour which is excessive or of one sort only, such as is practised by athletes; he should be capable of all the actions 10 of a freeman. These remarks apply equally to both parents.

Women who are with child should be careful of themselves; they should take exercise and have a nourishing diet. The first of these prescriptions the legislator will 15 easily carry into effect by requiring that they shall take a walk daily to some temple, where they can worship the gods who preside over birth.[76] Their minds, however, unlike their bodies, they ought to keep quiet, for the offspring derive their natures from their mothers as plants do from the earth.

As to the exposure and rearing of children, let there be 20 a law that no *deformed* child shall live, but that on the

[75] A. does not actually do so.          [76] Cp. Plato, *Laws*, vii. 789 ᴇ.

ground of an *excess* in the number of children, if the
established customs of the state forbid this (for in our
state population has a limit), no child is to be exposed,
but when couples have children in excess, let abortion
25 be procured before sense and life have begun; what may
or may not be lawfully done in these cases depends on the
question of life and sensation.

And now, having determined at what ages men and
women are to begin their union, let us also determine
how long they shall continue to beget and bear offspring
for the state; men who are too old, like men who are too
30 young, produce children who are defective in body and
mind; the children of very old men are weakly. The limit,
then, should be the age which is the prime of their intelligence, and this in most persons, according to the notion
of some poets who measure life by periods of seven years,
35 is about fifty; at four or five years later, they should
cease from having families; and from that time forward
only cohabit with one another for the sake of health; or
for some similar reason.

As to adultery, let it be held disgraceful, in general,
40 for any man or woman to be found in any way unfaithful
when they are married, and called husband and wife.
1336ᵃ If during the time of bearing children anything of the
sort occur, let the guilty person be punished with a loss
of privileges in proportion to the offence.⁷⁷

**17** After the children have been born, the manner of
5 rearing them may be supposed to have a great effect on
their bodily strength. It would appear from the example
of animals, and of those nations who desire to create the
military habit, that the food which has most milk in it
is best suited to human beings; but the less wine the

⁷⁷ Cp. *Laws,* viii. 841 D, E.

better, if they would escape diseases. Also all the motions to which children can be subjected at their early age are very useful. But in order to preserve their tender limbs from distortion, some nations have had recourse to mechanical appliances which straighten their bodies. To accustom children to the cold from their earliest years is also an excellent practice, which greatly conduces to health, and hardens them for military service. Hence many barbarians have a custom of plunging their children at birth into a cold stream; others, like the Celts, clothe them in a light wrapper only. For human nature should be early habituated to endure all which by habit it can be made to endure; but the process must be gradual. And children, from their natural warmth, may be easily trained to bear cold. Such care should attend them in the first stage of life.

The next period lasts to the age of five: during this no demand should be made upon the child for study or labour, lest its growth be impeded; and there should be sufficient motion to prevent the limbs from being inactive. This can be secured, among other ways, by amusement, but the amusement should not be vulgar or tiring or effeminate. The Directors of Education, as they are termed, should be careful what tales or stories the children hear,[78] for all such things are designed to prepare the way for the business of later life, and should be for the most part imitations of the occupations which they will hereafter pursue in earnest.[79] Those are wrong who in their laws attempt to check the loud crying and screaming of children, for these contribute towards their growth, and, in a manner, exercise their bodies.[80] Straining the voice has a strengthening effect similar to that pro-

[78] Plato, *Rep.* ii. 377 ff.      [79] Plato, *Laws*, i. 643.
[80] Plato, *Laws*, vii. 792 A.

40 duced by the retention of the breath in violent exertions.
The Directors of Education should have an eye to their
bringing up, and in particular should take care that they
are left as little as possible with slaves. For until they are
1336ᵇ seven years old they must live at home; and therefore,
even at this early age, it is to be expected that they should
acquire a taint of meanness from what they hear and see.
Indeed, there is nothing which the legislator should be
5 more careful to drive away than indecency of speech;
for the light utterance of shameful words leads soon to
shameful actions. The young especially should never be
allowed to repeat or hear anything of the sort. A freeman who is found saying or doing what is forbidden, if
10 he be too young as yet to have the privilege of reclining
at the public tables, should be disgraced and beaten, and
an elder person degraded as his slavish conduct deserves.
And since we do not allow improper language, clearly we
should also banish pictures or speeches from the stage
15 which are indecent. Let the rulers take care that there
be no image or picture representing unseemly actions,
except in the temples of those Gods at whose festivals
the law permits even ribaldry, and whom the law also
permits to be worshipped by persons of mature age on
behalf of themselves, their children, and their wives.
But the legislator should not allow youth to be specta-
20 tors of iambi or of comedy until they are of an age to
sit at the public tables and to drink strong wine; by that
time education will have armed them against the evil
influences of such representations.

We have made these remarks in a cursory manner—
25 they are enough for the present occasion; but hereafter [81] we will return to the subject and after a fuller
discussion determine whether such liberty should or

[81] An unfulfilled promise.

should not be granted, and in what way granted, if at all. Theodorus, the tragic actor, was quite right in saying that he would not allow any other actor, not even if he 30 were quite second-rate, to enter before himself, because the spectators grew fond of the voices which they first heard. And the same principle applies universally to association with things as well as with persons, for we always like best whatever comes first. And therefore youth should be kept strangers to all that is bad, and especially 35 to things which suggest vice or hate. When the five years have passed away, during the two following years they must look on at the pursuits which they are hereafter to learn. There are two periods of life with reference to which education has to be divided, from seven to the age of puberty, and onwards to the age of one and twenty. The poets who divide ages by sevens [82] are in the main 40 right: but we should observe the divisions actually made 1337ᵃ by nature; for the deficiencies of nature are what art and education seek to fill up.

Let us then first inquire if any regulations are to be laid down about children, and secondly, whether the care of them should be the concern of the state or of private 5 individuals, which latter is in our own day the common custom, and in the third place, what these regulations should be.

[82] Cp. 1335ᵇ 33.

## BOOK VIII

**1** No one will doubt that the legislator should direct his attention above all to the education of youth; for the neglect of education does harm to the constitution. The citizen should be moulded to suit the form of government under which he lives.[1] For each government has
15 a peculiar character which originally formed and which continues to preserve it. The character of democracy creates democracy, and the character of oligarchy creates oligarchy; and always the better the character, the better the government.

Again, for the exercise of any faculty or art a previous
20 training and habituation are required; clearly therefore for the practice of virtue. And since the whole city has one end, it is manifest that education should be one and the same for all, and that it should be public, and not private—not as at present, when every one looks
25 after his own children separately, and gives them separate instruction of the sort which he thinks best; the training in things which are of common interest should be the same for all. Neither must we suppose that any one of the citizens belongs to himself, for they all belong to the state, and are each of them a part of the state, and
30 the care of each part is inseparable from the care of the

[1] Cp. v. 1310ᵃ 12–36.

320

whole. In this particular as in some others the Lacedaemonians are to be praised, for they take the greatest
pains about their children, and make education the business of the state.[2]

**2**   That education should be regulated by law and
should be an affair of state is not to be denied, but what
should be the character of this public education, and how
young persons should be educated, are questions which
remain to be considered. As things are, there is disagree-
ment about the subjects. For mankind are by no means 35
agreed about the things to be taught, whether we look to
virtue or the best life. Neither is it clear whether education is more concerned with intellectual or with moral
virtue. The existing practice is perplexing; no one knows
on what principle we should proceed—should the useful 40
in life, or should virtue, or should the higher knowledge,
be the aim of our training; all three opinions have been 1337
entertained. Again, about the means there is no agreement; for different persons, starting with different ideas
about the nature of virtue, naturally disagree about the
practice of it. There can be no doubt that children should
be taught those useful things which are really necessary,
but not all useful things; for occupations are divided into 5
liberal and illiberal; and to young children should be
imparted only such kinds of knowledge as will be useful
to them without vulgarizing them. And any occupation,
art, or science, which makes the body or soul or mind of 10
the freeman less fit for the practice or exercise of virtue,
is vulgar; wherefore we call those arts vulgar which tend
to deform the body, and likewise all paid employments,
for they absorb and degrade the mind. There are also
some liberal arts quite proper for a freeman to acquire, 15

[2] Cp. *Nic. Eth.* x. 1180ᵃ 24.

but only in a certain degree, and if he attend to them too
closely, in order to attain perfection in them, the same
evil effects will follow. The object also which a man sets
before him makes a great difference; if he does or learns
anything for his own sake [3] or for the sake of his friends,
or with a view to excellence, the action will not appear
20 illiberal; but if done for the sake of others, the very same
action will be thought menial and servile. The received
subjects of instruction, as I have already remarked,[4] are
partly of a liberal and partly of an illiberal character.

**3**  The customary branches of education are in number
four; they are—(1) reading and writing, (2) gymnastic
25 exercises, (3) music, to which is sometimes added (4)
drawing. Of these, reading and writing and drawing are
regarded as useful for the purposes of life in a variety
of ways, and gymnastic exercises are thought to infuse
courage. Concerning music a doubt may be raised—in
our own day most men cultivate it for the sake of pleasure, but originally it was included in education, because
30 nature herself, as has been often said,[5] requires that we
should be able, not only to work well, but to use leisure
well; for, as I must repeat once again, the first principle
of all action is leisure. Both are required, but leisure is
better than occupation and is its end; and therefore the
question must be asked, what ought we to do when at
35 leisure? Clearly we ought not to be amusing ourselves,
for then amusement would be the end of life. But if this
is inconceivable, and amusement is needed more amid
serious occupations than at other times (for he who is
hard at work has need of relaxation, and amusement
gives relaxation, whereas occupation is always accom-

---

³ Cp. iii. 1277ᵇ 3.                                    ⁴ a39–ᵇ3.
⁵ ii. 1271ᵃ 41 sqq., vii. 1333ᵃ 16–1334ᵇ 3; *Nic. Eth.* x. 6.

panied with exertion and effort, we should introduce 40
amusements only at suitable times, and they should be
ɔur medicines, for the emotion which they create in the
soul is a relaxation, and from the pleasure we obtain
rest. But leisure of itself gives pleasure and happiness 1338ᵃ
and enjoyment of life, which are experienced, not by the
busy man, but by those who have leisure. For he who
is occupied has in view some end which he has not at- 5
tained; but happiness is an end, since all men deem it
to be accompanied with pleasure and not with pain. This
pleasure, however, is regarded differently by different
persons, and varies according to the habit of individuals;
the pleasure of the best man is the best, and springs
from the noblest sources. It is clear then that there are
branches of learning and education which we must study 10
merely with a view to leisure spent in intellectual activity,
and these are to be valued for their own sake; whereas
those kinds of knowledge which are useful in business
are to be deemed necessary, and exist for the sake of
other things. And therefore our fathers admitted music
into education, not on the ground either of its necessity
or utility, for it is not necessary, nor indeed useful in the 15
same manner as reading and writing, which are useful
in money-making, in the management of a household,
in the acquisition of knowledge and in political life,
nor like drawing, useful for a more correct judgement of
the works of artists, nor again like gymnastic, which 20
gives health and strength; for neither of these is to be
gained from music. There remains, then, the use of
music for intellectual enjoyment in leisure; which is in
fact evidently the reason of its introduction, this being
one of the ways in which it is thought that a freeman
should pass his leisure; as Homer says—

25    'But he who alone should be called [6] to the pleasant feast',

and afterwards he speaks of others whom he describes as
inviting

'The bard who would delight them all'.[7]

And in another place Odysseus says there is no better
way of passing life than when men's hearts are merry and

'The banqueters in the hall, sitting in order, hear the voice
of the minstrel'.[8]

30    It is evident, then, that there is a sort of education in
which parents should train their sons, not as being useful
or necessary, but because it is liberal or noble. Whether
this is of one kind only, or of more than one, and if so,
what they are, and how they are to be imparted, must
hereafter be determined.[9] Thus much we are now in a
35 position to say, that the ancients witness to us; for their
opinion may be gathered from the fact that music is one
of the received and traditional branches of education.
Further, it is clear that children should be instructed in
some useful things—for example, in reading and writing
—not only for their usefulness, but also because many
40 other sorts of knowledge are acquired through them.
With a like view they may be taught drawing, not to
prevent their making mistakes in their own purchases,
or in order that they may not be imposed upon in the
1338ᵇ buying or selling of articles, but perhaps rather because
it makes them judges of the beauty of the human form.
To be always seeking after the useful does not become
free and exalted souls.[10] Now it is clear that in education
5 practice must be used before theory, and the body be

---

[6] The line does not occur in our text of Homer, but in Aristotle's text
it probably came instead of, or after, *Od.* xvii. 383.

[7] *Od.* xvii. 385.                                                                [8] *Od.* ix. 7

[9] An unfulfilled promise.                    [10] Cp. Plato, *Rep.* vii. 525 ff.

trained before the mind; and therefore boys should be handed over to the trainer, who creates in them the proper habit of body, and to the wrestling-master, who teaches them their exercises.

**4** Of those states which in our own day seem to take the greatest care of children, some aim at producing in them an athletic habit, but they only injure their forms 10 and stunt their growth. Although the Lacedaemonians have not fallen into this mistake, yet they brutalize their children by laborious exercises which they think will make them courageous. But in truth, as we have often repeated,[11] education should not be exclusively, or prin- 15 cipally, directed to this end. And even if we suppose the Lacedaemonians to be right in their end, they do not attain it. For among barbarians and among animals courage is found associated, not with the greatest ferocity, but with a gentle and lion-like temper. There are many 20 races who are ready enough to kill and eat men, such as the Achaeans and Heniochi, who both live about the Black Sea; [12] and there are other mainland tribes, as bad or worse, who all live by plunder, but have no courage. It is notorious that the Lacedaemonians themselves, 25 while they alone were assiduous in their laborious drill, were superior to others, but now they are beaten both in war and gymnastic exercises. For their ancient superiority did not depend on their mode of training their youth, but only on the circumstance that they trained them when their only rivals did not. Hence we may infer that what is noble, not what is brutal, should have the first place; no wolf or other wild animal will face a really 30 noble danger; such dangers are for the brave man.[13] And

---

[11] ii. 1271ᵃ 41–ᵇ10, vii. 1333ᵇ 5 sqq., 1334ᵃ 40 sqq.
[12] Cp. *Nic. Eth.* vii, 1148ᵇ 21.        [13] Cp. *Nic. Eth.* iii. 1115ᵃ 29.

parents who devote their children to gymnastics while
they neglect their necessary education, in reality vul-
garize them; for they make them useful to the art of
35 statesmanship in one quality only, and even in this the
argument proves them to be inferior to others. We should
judge the Lacedaemonians not from what they have
been, but from what they are; for now they have rivals
who compete with their education; formerly they had
none.

It is an admitted principle, that gymnastic exercises
40 should be employed in education, and that for children
they should be of a lighter kind, avoiding severe diet or
painful toil, lest the growth of the body be impaired. The
evil of excessive training in early years is strikingly
1339ᵃ proved by the example of the Olympic victors; for not
more than two or three of them have gained a prize both
as boys and as men; their early training and severe
gymnastic exercises exhausted their constitutions. When
boyhood is over, three years should be spent in other
5 studies; the period of life which follows may then be
devoted to hard exercise and strict diet. Men ought not
to labour at the same time with their minds and with
their bodies; [14] for the two kinds of labour are opposed
to one another; the labour of the body impedes the mind,
10 and the labour of the mind the body.

5 Concerning music there are some questions which
we have already raised; [15] these we may now resume and
carry further; and our remarks will serve as a prelude
to this or any other discussion of the subject. It is not
15 easy to determine the nature of music, or why any one
should have a knowledge of it. Shall we say, for the sake
of amusement and relaxation, like sleep or drinking,

[14] Cp. Plato, *Rep.* vii. 537 B.    [15] 1337ᵇ 27–1338ᵃ 30.

which are not good in themselves, but are pleasant, and
at the same time 'make care to cease', as Euripides says?
And for this end men also appoint music, and make use
of all three alike—sleep, drinking, music—to which some 20
add dancing. Or shall we argue that music conduces to
virtue, on the ground that it can form our minds and
habituate us to true pleasures as our bodies are made by
gymnastic to be of a certain character? Or shall we say 25
that it contributes to the enjoyment of leisure and mental
cultivation, which is a third alternative? Now obviously
youths are not to be instructed with a view to their
amusement, for learning is no amusement, but is accompanied with pain. Neither is intellectual enjoyment suit- 30
able to boys of that age, for it is the end, and that which
is imperfect cannot attain the perfect or end. But perhaps it may be said that boys learn music for the sake
of the amusement which they will have when they are
grown up. If so, why should they learn themselves, and
not, like the Persian and Median kings, enjoy the pleas- 35
ure and instruction which is derived from hearing others?
(for surely persons who have made music the business
and profession of their lives will be better performers
than those who practise only long enough to learn). If
they must learn music, on the same principle they should 40
learn cookery, which is absurd. And even granting that
music may form the character, the objection still holds:
why should we learn ourselves? Why cannot we attain
true pleasure and form a correct judgement from hear- 1339ᵇ
ing others, like the Lacedaemonians?—for they, without
learning music, nevertheless can correctly judge, as they
say, of good and bad melodies. Or again, if music should
be used to promote cheerfulness and refined intellectual
enjoyment, the objection still remains—why should we 5
learn ourselves instead of enjoying the performances of

others? We may illustrate what we are saying by our conception of the Gods; for in the poets Zeus does not himself sing or play on the lyre. Nay, we call professional performers vulgar; no freeman would play or sing unless he were intoxicated or in jest. But these matters

10 may be left for the present.[16]

The first question is whether music is or is not to be a part of education. Of the three things mentioned in our discussion, which does it produce?—education or amusement or intellectual enjoyment, for it may be reckoned under all three, and seems to share in the nature of all

15 of them. Amusement is for the sake of relaxation, and relaxation is of necessity sweet, for it is the remedy of pain caused by toil; and intellectual enjoyment is universally acknowledged to contain an element not only of the noble but of the pleasant, for happiness is made up

20 of both. All men agree that music is one of the pleasantest things, whether with or without song; as Musaeus says,

'Song is to mortals of all things the sweetest.'

Hence and with good reason it is introduced into social gatherings and entertainments, because it makes the

25 hearts of men glad: so that on this ground alone we may assume that the young ought to be trained in it. For innocent pleasures are not only in harmony with the perfect end of life, but they also provide relaxation. And whereas men rarely attain the end, but often rest by the way and amuse themselves, not only with a view to a

30 further end, but also for the pleasure's sake, it may be well at times to let them find a refreshment in music. It sometimes happens that men make amusement the end, for the end probably contains some element of pleas-

[16] Cp. c. 6.

ure, though not any ordinary or lower pleasure; but they mistake the lower for the higher, and in seeking for the one find the other, since every pleasure has a likeness to the end of action.[17] For the end is not eligible for the 35 sake of any future good, nor do the pleasures which we have described exist for the sake of any future good but of the past, that is to say, they are the alleviation of past toils and pains. And we may infer this to be the reason why men seek happiness from these pleasures.     40

But music is pursued, not only as an alleviation of past toil, but also as providing recreation. And who can say whether, having this use, it may not also have a nobler one? In addition to this common pleasure, felt 1340ᵃ and shared in by all (for the pleasure given by music is natural, and therefore adapted to all ages and charac- 5 ters), may it not have also some influence over the character and the soul? It must have such an influence if characters are affected by it. And that they are so affected is proved in many ways, and not least by the power which the songs of Olympus exercise; for beyond question they 10 inspire enthusiasm, and enthusiasm is an emotion of the ethical part of the soul. Besides, when men hear imitations, even apart from the rhythms and tunes them- 15 selves, their feelings move in sympathy. Since then music is a pleasure, and virtue consists in rejoicing and loving and hating aright, there is clearly nothing which we are so much concerned to acquire and to cultivate as the power of forming right judgements, and of taking delight in good dispositions and noble actions.[18] Rhythm and melody supply imitations of anger and gentleness, and also of courage and temperance, and of all the quali- 20 ties contrary to these, and of the other qualities of char-

---

[17] Cp. *Nic. Eth.* vii. 1153ᵇ 33.
[18] Cp. Plato, *Rep.* iii. 401, 402; *Laws,* ii. 659 c–e.

acter, which hardly fall short of the actual affections, as
we know from our own experience, for in listening to such
strains our souls undergo a change. The habit of feeling
pleasure or pain at mere representations is not far removed from the same feeling about realities; [19] for ex-
25 ample, if any one delights in the sight of a statue for its
beauty only, it necessarily follows that the sight of the
original will be pleasant to him. The objects of no other
sense, such as taste or touch, have any resemblance to
30 moral qualities; in visible objects there is only a little,
for there are figures which are of a moral character, but
only to a slight extent, and all do not participate in the
feeling about them. Again, figures and colours are not
imitations, but signs, of moral habits, indications which
the body gives of states of feeling. The connection of
35 them with morals is slight, but in so far as there is any,
young men should be taught to look, not at the works of
Pauson, but at those of Polygnotus,[20] or any other
painter or sculptor who expresses moral ideas. On the
other hand, even in mere melodies there is an imitation
40 of character, for the musical modes differ essentially
from one another, and those who hear them are differ-
1340[b] ently affected by each. Some of them make men sad and
grave, like the so-called Mixolydian, others enfeeble the
mind, like the relaxed modes, another, again, produces
a moderate and settled temper, which appears to be the
peculiar effect of the Dorian; the Phrygian inspires en-
5 thusiasm. The whole subject has been well treated by
philosophical writers [21] on this branch of education, and
they confirm their arguments by facts. The same principles apply to rhythms; [22] some have a character of
rest, others of motion, and of these latter again, some

19 Cp. Plato, *Rep*. iii. 395.              20 Cp. *Poet*. 1448[a] 5, 1450[a] 26.
21 Cp. *Rep*. 398 E sqq.                    22 *Rep*. iii. 399 E, 400.

have a more vulgar, others a nobler movement. Enough 10
has been said to show that music has a power of forming
the character, and should therefore be introduced into
the education of the young. The study is suited to the
stage of youth, for young persons will not, if they can 15
help, endure anything which is not sweetened by pleasure, and music has a natural sweetness. There seems to
be in us a sort of affinity to musical modes and rhythms,
which makes some philosophers say that the soul is a
tuning, others, that it possesses tuning.

**6**   And now we have to determine the question which 20
has been already raised,[23] whether children should be
themselves taught to sing and play or not. Clearly there
is a considerable difference made in the character by the
actual practice of the art. It is difficult, if not impossible,
for those who do not perform to be good judges of the
performance of others.[24] Besides, children should have 25
something to do, and the rattle of Archytas, which people
give to their children in order to amuse them and prevent
them from breaking anything in the house, was a capital
invention, for a young thing cannot be quiet. The rattle
is a toy suited to the infant mind, and education is a 30
rattle or toy for children of a larger growth. We conclude then that they should be taught music in such a
way as to become not only critics but performers.

The question what is or is not suitable for different
ages may be easily answered; nor is there any difficulty
in meeting the objection of those who say that the study
of music is vulgar.[25] We reply (1) in the first place, that 35
they who are to be judges must also be performers, and
that they should begin to practise early, although when
they are older they may be spared the execution; they

[23] 1339ᵃ 33—ᵇ10.     [24] Cp. 1339ᵃ 42.     [25] Cp. 1339ᵇ 8, 1341ᵇ 14.

must have learned to appreciate what is good and to delight in it, thanks to the knowledge which they ac-
40 quired in their youth. As to (2) the vulgarizing effect which music is supposed to exercise, this is a question which we shall have no difficulty in determining, when we have considered to what extent freemen who are
1341ᵃ being trained to political virtue should pursue the art, what melodies and what rhythms they should be allowed to use, and what instruments should be employed in teaching them to play; for even the instrument makes a difference. The answer to the objection turns upon these distinctions; for it is quite possible that certain methods of teaching and learning music do really have a degrad-
5 ing effect. It is evident then that the learning of music ought not to impede the business of riper years, or to degrade the body or render it unfit for civil or military training, whether for bodily exercises at the time or for later studies.

10 The right measure will be attained if students of music stop short of the arts which are practised in professional contests, and do not seek to acquire those fantastic marvels of execution which are now the fashion in such contests, and from these have passed into education. Let the young practise even such music as we have prescribed, only until they are able to feel delight in noble melodies
15 and rhythms, and not merely in that common part of music in which every slave or child and even some animals find pleasure.

From these principles we may also infer what instruments should be used. The flute, or any other instrument which requires great skill, as for example the harp, ought not to be admitted into education, but only such as will
20 make intelligent students of music or of the other parts of education. Besides, the flute is not an instrument

which is expressive of moral character; it is too exciting.
The proper time for using it is when the performance
aims not at instruction, but at the relief of the passions.[26]
And there is a further objection; the impediment which
the flute presents to the use of the voice detracts from
its educational value. The ancients therefore were right 25
in forbidding the flute to youths and freemen, although
they had once allowed it. For when their wealth gave
them a greater inclination to leisure, and they had loftier
notions of excellence, being also elated with their success,
both before and after the Persian War, with more zeal 30
than discernment they pursued every kind of knowledge,
and so they introduced the flute into education. At
Lacedaemon there was a choragus who led the chorus
with a flute, and at Athens the instrument became so
popular that most freemen could play upon it. The popularity is shown by the tablet which Thrasippus dedicated when he furnished the chorus to Ecphantides. 35
Later experience enabled men to judge what was or was
not really conducive to virtue, and they rejected both the
flute and several other old-fashioned instruments, such
as the Lydian harp, the many-stringed lyre, the 'hepta- 40
gon', 'triangle', 'sambuca', and the like—which are intended only to give pleasure to the hearer, and require 1341ᵇ
extraordinary skill of hand.[27] There is a meaning also in
the myth of the ancients, which tells how Athene invented the flute and then threw it away. It was not a bad
idea of theirs, that the Goddess disliked the instrument 5
because it made the face ugly; but with still more reason
may we say that she rejected it because the acquirement
of flute-playing contributes nothing to the mind, since
to Athene we ascribe both knowledge and art.

Thus then we reject the professional instruments and

[26] Cp. 1341ᵇ 38.                     [27] Cp. Plato. *Rep*. iii. 399 c, d.

also the professional mode of education in music (and
10 by professional we mean that which is adopted in contests), for in this the performer practises the art, not for
the sake of his own improvement, but in order to give
pleasure, and that of a vulgar sort, to his hearers. For
this reason the execution of such music is not the part
of a freeman but of a paid performer, and the result is
15 that the performers are vulgarized, for the end at which
they aim is bad.[28] The vulgarity of the spectator tends
to lower the character of the music and therefore of the
performers; they look to him—he makes them what they
are, and fashions even their bodies by the movements
which he expects them to exhibit.

**7**   We have also to consider rhythms and modes, and
20 their use in education. Shall we use them all or make a
distinction? and shall the same distinction be made for
those who practise music with a view to education, or
shall it be some other? Now we see that music is produced by melody and rhythm, and we ought to know
25 what influence these have respectively on education, and
whether we should prefer excellence in melody or excellence in rhythm. But as the subject has been very well
treated by many musicians of the present day, and also
by philosophers [29] who have had considerable experience
30 of musical education, to these we would refer the more
exact student of the subject; we shall only speak of it
now after the manner of the legislator, stating the general principles.

We accept the division of melodies proposed by certain philosophers into ethical melodies, melodies of action, and passionate or inspiring melodies, each having,
as they say, a mode corresponding to it. But we main-

[28] Cp. Plato, *Laws,* iii. 700.    [29] Cp. *Rep.* iii. 398 d sqq.

tain further that music should be studied, not for the sake 35
of one, but of many benefits, that is to say, with a view
to (1) education, (2) purgation (the word 'purgation'
we use at present without explanation, but when hereafter we speak of poetry,[30] we will treat the subject with
more precision); music may also serve (3) for intellectual enjoyment, for relaxation and for recreation after 40
exertion. It is clear, therefore, that all the modes must 1342ª
be employed by us, but not all of them in the same manner. In education the most ethical modes are to be preferred, but in listening to the performances of others we
may admit the modes of action and passion also. For 5
feelings such as pity and fear, or, again, enthusiasm,
exist very strongly in some souls, and have more or less
influence over all. Some persons fall into a religious
frenzy, whom we see as a result of the sacred melodies—
when they have used the melodies that excite the soul to 10
mystic frenzy—restored as though they had found healing and purgation. Those who are influenced by pity or
fear, and every emotional nature, must have a like experience, and others in so far as each is susceptible to 15
such emotions, and all are in a manner purged and their
souls lightened and delighted. The purgative melodies
likewise give an innocent pleasure to mankind. Such are
the modes and the melodies in which those who perform
music at the theatre should be invited to compete. But
since the spectators are of two kinds—the one free and
educated, and the other a vulgar crowd composed of
mechanics, labourers, and the like—there ought to be 20
contests and exhibitions instituted for the relaxation of
the second class also. And the music will correspond to
their minds; for as their minds are perverted from the

[30] Cp. *Poet.* 1449ᵇ 27, though the promise is really unfulfilled. The
reference is probably to a lost part of the *Poetics*.

natural state, so there are perverted modes and highly
strung and unnaturally coloured melodies. A man re-
25 ceives pleasure from what is natural to him, and therefore professional musicians may be allowed to practise
this lower sort of music before an audience of a lower
type. But, for the purposes of education, as I have
already said,[31] those modes and melodies should be employed which are ethical, such as the Dorian, as we said
30 before; [32] though we may include any others which are
approved by philosophers who have had a musical education. The Socrates of the *Republic*[33] is wrong in re-
1342ᵇ taining only the Phrygian mode along with the Dorian,
and the more so because he rejects the flute; for the
Phrygian is to the modes what the flute is to musical
instruments—both of them are exciting and emotional.
5 Poetry proves this, for Bacchic frenzy and all similar
emotions are most suitably expressed by the flute, and
are better set to the Phrygian than to any other mode.
The dithyramb, for example, is acknowledged to be
Phrygian, a fact of which the connoisseurs of music offer
many proofs, saying, among other things, that Phi-
10 loxenus, having attempted to compose his *Mysians* as a
dithyramb in the Dorian mode, found it impossible, and
fell back by the very nature of things into the more
appropriate Phrygian. All men agree that the Dorian
music is the gravest and manliest. And whereas we say
15 that the extremes should be avoided and the mean followed, and whereas the Dorian is a mean between the
other modes,[34] it is evident that our youth should be
taught the Dorian music.

Two principles have to be kept in view, what is possible, what is becoming: at these every man ought to

---

31 1342ᵃ 2.                              32 1340ᵇ 3 sq.
33 Plato, *Rep.* iii. 399 A.               34 Cp. 1340ᵃ 42.

aim. But even these are relative to age; the old, who
have lost their powers, cannot very well sing the high-
strung modes, and nature herself seems to suggest that
their songs should be of the more relaxed kind. Wherefore the musicians likewise blame Socrates,[35] and with
justice, for rejecting the relaxed modes in education under the idea that they are intoxicating, not in the ordinary sense of intoxication (for wine rather tends to excite men), but because they have no strength in them.
And so, with a view also to the time of life when men
begin to grow old, they ought to practise the gentler
modes and melodies as well as the others, and, further,
any mode, such as the Lydian above all others appears
to be, which is suited to children of tender age, and possesses the elements both of order and of education. Thus
it is clear that education should be based upon three
principles—the mean, the possible, the becoming, these
three.

[35] *Rep.* iii. 398 e sqq.

# The Best of the World's Best Books

## COMPLETE LIST OF TITLES IN

# THE MODERN LIBRARY

### For convenience in ordering use number at right of title

## MISCELLANEOUS